# The Progressive Architecture of Frederick G. Scheibler, Jr.

Fig. 1. Frederick G. Scheibler, Jr., portrait, ca. 1898

The Progressive Architecture of
Frederick G. Scheibler, Jr.

Martin Aurand

University of Pittsburgh Press

Pittsburgh and London

Published by the University of Pittsburgh Press,
Pittsburgh, PA 15260

Copyright © 1994, University of Pittsburgh Press

All rights reserved

Printed on acid free paper in the United States of America

This paperback edition, 2015

ISBN 13: 978-0-8229-6330-1
ISBN 10: 0-8229-6330-2

ILLUSTRATION CREDITS:

American Architect and Building News 91:1619 (january 5, 1907), figs. 22, 23; *Architectural Record* 106 (july 1949), fig. 61; *Architektur von Olbrich* (Berlin: Ernst Wasmuth, 1901-1908), figs. 24, 25, 26, 28, 83; *Ausgefürte Bauten und Entwürfte von Frank Lloyd Wright* (Berlin: Ernst Wasmuth, 1910), figs. 51, 74; Fred Bruckman, fig. 52; Carnegie Mellon University Architecture Archives, Pittsburgh, Pa., figs. I, 8, 10, 11, 12, 13, 14, 15, 16, 20, 27, 32, 34, 35, 41, 43, 44, 45, 46, 53, 54, 55, 59, 60, 63, 64, 65, 66, 67, 68, 77, 84, 85, 86, 87, 88, 93, 94, 101, 103, 104, 105, 106, 108, 110, 112, 113, 114, 115, 116, 118, 119, 123, 124; *Charette* 42:10 (October 1962), fig. 117; Chicago Historical Society, Chicago, Ill., fig. 18; Gary Cirrincione, fig. 19; *Dekorative Kunst*, March 1902, figs. 37, 42, 92; *Dekorative Kunst*, July 1905, fig. 69; Graphischen Sammlung Albertina, Vienna, Austria © 1992 ARS, New York/VBK, Vienna, fig. 38; Historisches Museen der Stadt Wien, Vienna, Austria, figs. 2, 40; Lockwood Hoehl, figs. 4, 70, 7 l, 78; Charles Holme, *Modern British Domestic Architecture and Decoration* (London: The Studio, 1901), fig. 95; *Inland Architect and News Record* 50:1 (july 1907), fig. 73; Mildred Kilham, figs. 5, 6; Library of Congress, Washington, D.C., fig. 29; Helen Livingston-Broome, fig. 107; Hermann Muthesius, *Das Moderne Landhaus und seine innere Ausstattung*, 2d ed. (Munich: A. Bruckman, 1905), fig. 97; Phil Phillips and Katherine West, fig. 76; Pittsburgh Architectural Club, *Catalogue of the Third Exhibition* (Pittsburgh: 1905), fig. 3; Pittsburgh Architectural Club, *Catalogue of the Fifth Exhibition* (Pittsburgh: 1910), figs. 31, 99; Pittsburgh Architectural Club, *Catalogue of the Ninth Exhibition* (Pittsburgh: 1914), fig. 72; Pittsburgh Architectural Club, *Catalogue of the Tenth Exhibition* (Pittsburgh: 1915), fig. 75; Pittsburgh History and Landmarks Foundation, Pittsburgh, Pa., figs. 2 I, 36, 39, 48, 49, 50, 56, 96, 100, 122; *Pittsburgh Post-Gazette*, fig. 125; Harvey Rice and Lorraine Rice, fig. 120; M. H. Baillie Scott, *Hauser und Garten* (Berlin: E. Wasmuth, 1906), figs. 79, 81, 82; Ruth Young Silverman, figs. 109, I II; *Souvenir Book: Silver Anniversary 1887-1912* (Wilkinsburg, Pa.: 1912), fig. 17; *Studio* 61 (March 1914), fig. 58; Thomas Sutton, fig. 9; University of California Art Gallery, Santa Barbara, Calif., fig. 62.

Contents

List of Illustrations   vii
Preface   xi

Introduction   3

1. Man and Architect   9
2. Half and Half   18
3. Old Heidelberg   28
4. The New Manner   39
5. Group Cottages   54
6. Highland Towers   70
7. The Artistic House   83
8. Charmed Territory   105
9. Up-to-Date and Familiar   122
10. A Place Among Progressives   132

Appendix 1   Catalogue of the Works of Frederick G. Scheibler, Jr.   139
Appendix 2   Scheibler's Library   153
Notes   155
Selected Bibliography   167
Index   169

List of Illustrations

1. Fredeick G. Scheibler, Jr., portrait, ca. 1898.
2. Joseph Maria Olbrich, Secession Building, 1898.
3. Titus de Bobula, design for a parochial school, ca. 1904, perspective rendering.
4. McNall house, ca. 1909, art glass and I-beam.
5. Scheibler cottage, 1898, perspective rendering.
6. Carl Building, postcard, ca. 1907.
7. White house, ca. 1914?, detail.
8. Frederick G. Scheibler, Jr., portrait, 1919.
9. Scheibler sketches, 1915.
10. Scheibler lettered signature, ca. 1922.
11. Kitzmiller house, 1901, front elevation.
12. Steel house, ca. 1901.
13. Matthews house, 1901, first floor plan.
14. Steel house, ca. 1901, dining room.
15. Hawkins School, 1904, perspective rendering.
16. Matthews store building, 1902.
17. Hamnett store building, ca. 1903.
18. Louis Sullivan, Gage Building facade, 1898–1899.
19. Syria, Kismet, Nelda apartment buildings, 1904, first floor plan (measured drawing).
20. Syria, Kismet, Nelda apartment buildings, 1904.
21. Arden apartment building, 1904.
22. Old Heidelberg apartment building, 1905.
23. Old Heidelberg apartment building, 1905, first floor plan.
24. Joseph Maria Olbrich, Christiansen house, 1901, perspective rendering.
25. Joseph Maria Olbrich, Blaue house, 1903–1904.
26. Joseph Maria Olbrich, Stade double house, ca. 1902.
27. Old Heidelberg apartment building, 1905, interior elevations.
28. Joseph Maria Olbrich, Kuntze house, 1902–1903, hall, perspective rendering.
29. Old Heidelberg apartment building, 1905, a dining room.
30. Old Heidelberg apartment building, 1905, schematic plan.
31. Old Heidelberg apartment building, cottage additions, and Hoffman house, 1905–1909.
32. Old Heidelberg apartment building, cottage additions, and Hoffman house, 1905–1909, postcard.
33. Whitehall apartment building, 1906.
34. Linwood apartment building, 1906.
35. Coleman apartment building, 1906, front elevation.
36. Coleman apartment building, 1906.
37. Charles Rennie Mackintosh, design for an artist's country cottage and studio, 1901, elevations.
38. Adolph Loos, Steiner house, 1910.
39. Minnetonka Building, 1908.
40. Otto Wagner, Linke Wienzeile 38 apartment building, 1898–1899.
41. Minnetonka Building, 1908, detail.

42. Charles Rennie Mackintosh, Windyhill, 1901, rose motif.
43. Minnetonka Building, 1908, stair sections.
44. Minnetonka Building, 1908, second floor plan.
45. Wilkins School, 1907, postcard.
46. Wilkinsburg Natatorium, 1907, front elevation.
47. Titus de Bobula, row houses, 1905.
48. Inglenook Place row houses, 1907.
49. Bennett Street row houses, 1909.
50. Aurelia Street row houses, 1909.
51. Frank Lloyd Wright, Larkin Company workmen's houses, 1904, perspective rendering and plans.
52. Hamilton Cottages, 1910–1911, perspective rendering.
53. Hamilton Cottages, 1910–1911.
54. Hamilton Cottages, 1910–1911.
55. Willo'mound, 1911, perspective rendering.
56. Meado'cots, 1912.
57. Meado'cots, schematic plan.
58. M. H. Baillie Scott, workmen's houses, ca. 1908–1910, perspective rendering.
59. Dillinger double house, 1914.
60. Vilsack Row, 1913.
61. Vilsack Row, 1913, front and rear elavations, plans (measured drawing).
62. Irving Gill, Lewis Courts, ca. 1910.
63. Highland Towers apartment building, 1913–1914, sketch.
64. Highland Towers apartment building, 1913–1914.
65. Highland Towers apartment building, 1913–1914, perspective rendering.
66. Highland Towers apartment building, 1913–1914, first floor plan.
67. Text of Highland Towers advertising brochure.
68. Highland Towers apartment building, 1913–1914.
69. Peter Behrens, fabric design, ca. 1905.
70. Highland Towers apartment building, 1913–1914, a living room and solarium.
71. Highland Towers apartment building, 1913–1914, detail of a living room.
72. Highland Towers apartment building, 1913–1914, art glass.
73. Frank Lloyd Wright, Larkin Building, 1904.
74. Frank Lloyd Wright, McArthur apartment building, 1906, perspective rendering and plans.
75. Kiehnel and Elliott, Stengel house, ca. 1915, exterior and living room.
76. Miller house, 1905.
77. Ebberts house, 1910, front elevation.
78. Ament house, 1907.
79. M. H. Baillie Scott, Springcot, 1903, perspective rendering.
80. Ament house, schematic plan.
81. M. H. Baillie Scott, Springcot, 1903, house and garden plan.
82. M. H. Baillie Scott, A house and garden in Switzerland, ca. 1903–1904, elevations.
83. Joseph Maria Olbrich, Silber house, 1906–1907, elevations.
84. Baird house, 1909.
85. Baird house, 1909.
86. Baird house, 1909, dining room.
87. Baird house, 1909, music room.
88. Baird house, 1909, living room.
89. Scott house, ca. 1910.
90. Rockledge, 1910.

91. Rockledge, 1910.
92. Charles Rennie Mackintosh, Windyhill, 1900.
93. Rockledge, 1910, first floor plan.
94. Wesley Jones house, 1915, front elevation.
95. C. F. A. Voysey, the Orchard, 1899, garden elevation.
96. Hellmund house, 1915.
97. C. F. A. Voysey, House and studio for A. Sutro, 1896, front elevation.
98. Hellmund house, 1915, first floor plan.
99. George W. Maher, Schultz house, 1907.
100. McLaughlin house, 1915.
101. Nolan house, 1919, elevations and plans.
102. Wach house, ca. 1920.
103. Pyle house, 1919.
104. Johnston house, ca. 1920, sketches.
105. Johnston house, 1921–1922, front elevation.
106. Johnston house, 1921–1922, first floor plan.
107. Harter house (Ventnor City, N.J.), ca. 1929.
108. Harter house (Pittsburgh), 1922–1924.
109. Harter house (Pittsburgh), 1922–1924.
110. Harter house (Pittsburgh), 1922–1924, first floor plan.
111. Harter house (Pittsburgh), 1922–1924, living room.
112. Klages house, 1922–1923, front elevation.
113. Klages house, 1922–1923, detail.
114. Klages house, 1922–1923, interior elevations.
115. Klages house, 1922–1923, living room.
116. Parkstone Dwellings, 1922.
117. Parkstone Dwellings, 1922, fireplace detail.
118. The Woodlands, 1925, front elevations.
119. Starr houses, ca. 1927, side elevation.
120. Frease house, 1928.
121. Rubins houses, ca. 1929.
122. Rubins store and apartment building, ca. 1935?
123. Unidentified store and office building, ca. 1939?, front elevation.
124. Democrat Messenger newspaper plant and office building, 1939.
125. Daily Republican Model Home, 1939.

Preface

I FIRST ENCOUNTERED the buildings of Frederick G. Scheibler, Jr., when visiting my future wife in Pittsburgh. She took me to see two buildings near her apartment that had caught her eye: two stucco apartment buildings decorated with birds and mushrooms. Since that time we have been eleven years together, living among Scheibler's buildings. They are good and captivating neighbors.

This study of architect Frederick G. Scheibler, Jr., is addressed to the academic and the enthusiast, the architect and the student, the preservationist and the property owner—all those who, like us, have been drawn to Scheibler's buildings. The work expands significantly upon previous efforts to address this subject. A critical essay with illustrations, few of which have been previously published, addresses the career, work, and significance of the architect, placing him for the first time within the larger context of the architects and architecture of his times. A catalogue of works is the most complete attempt thus far at compiling a catalogue raisonné; it expands and corrects previous efforts and includes a list of common misattributions. The first substantial Scheibler bibliography also appears here. This book is monographic in its scope; but it still leaves ample room for additional scholarship in the interpretation of the work and in the likely discovery of additional commissions for the catalog. I hope that it will inspire such investigations.

In this study I have not questioned the normative presumption of the turn-of-the-century progressive architectural movements, that is that they were in fact *progressive*. Though the International Style modernism that ultimately resulted from their progress has been partly discredited in recent years, the progressive impetus need not be discredited on account of its offspring. In fact, ironically, these turn-of-the-century progressive movements have recently garnered extraordinary attention and acclaim, even as modernism has been decried. Modernism was a natural outgrowth of these movements and, I believe, a noble and necessary experiment; and I am not at all abashed to say that Scheibler's Vilsack Row was his most progressive—as it was his most modern—design, though other Scheibler projects may more fully represent the values of our current postmodern times.

One such value is a respectful historicism that results in a preservationist ethic. Scheibler himself provided the lesson for why we must always build anew; but simple cultural respect requires us to value the progressives of each age. Thus far Scheibler's known buildings have suffered primarily from a nonlethal but regrettable combination of neglect and artistic compromise, committed under the twin guises of ignorance and improvement. Soon, no doubt, a key work by Scheibler will face total destruction. I hope that this book may serve to encourage the owners of

Scheibler properties to value what they have and to choose maintenance and restoration over decay and compromise. It may also serve to apprise the community at large of one man's invaluable bequest to its streets and neighborhoods. Thus we may all assure a sufficient inheritance for the future.

I am grateful to the staffs of many repositories including the Archives of Industrial Society of the University of Pittsburgh Libraries, the Carnegie Library of Pittsburgh, the Historical Society of Western Pennsylvania, the Pittsburgh Builders Exchange, the Pittsburgh History and Landmarks Foundation, the Spruance Library of the Mercer Museum, the Wilkinsburg-Penn Joint Water Authority, and public libraries and courthouses and other government repositories throughout Pennsylvania and neighboring states. Many people tolerated my persistent presence and fielded my inquiries into Scheibler minutiae. I am also grateful to my own repository and employer, the Carnegie Mellon University Architecture Archives and Carnegie Mellon University Libraries, for necessary support and encouragement. And I am grateful to property owners, residents, and other informants, who welcomed me in from their doorsteps or responded to my mail or telephone inquiries.

My thanks to Scheibler family members Mildred Kilham, and Milton and Diane Zimmer and family, whose enthusiasm for this work was a great encouragement. Thanks also to Fred Bruckman, Gary Cirrincione, Kasey Connors, Michael Eversmeyer, Jane Flanders, David Golden, Lockwood Hoehl, Andrew Jamrom, Marianne Kolson, Terry Necciai, Ann Paul, Henry Pisciotta, Richard Schoenwald, Thomas Sutton, Gary Thomas, James D. Van Trump, Franklin West, and David Wilkins for various and key contributions to the cause.

Special thanks to Gillian H. Belnap, whose own study of Scheibler's multifamily projects provided the impetus for a full-length study, who inadvertently bluffed me into doing that study, and who roundly and rightly critiqued my initial manuscript and spurred it along to better shape and intelligence.

And to Joann (lower-case *a*, no *e*), who lured me to Pittsburgh, introduced me to Scheibler's buildings, and shared my subsequent fixation with sufficient patience and enthusiasm to see us through.

The Progressive Architecture of Frederick G. Scheibler, Jr.

# Introduction

THE WORK AND SIGNIFICANCE of architect Frederick G. Scheibler, Jr., were first noted in print in an article by reporter Penelope Redd published in the *Pittsburgh Sunday Sun-Telegraph* in 1934. She wrote: "The younger generation of American museum officials have spent much time and effort in tracing back the beginnings of contemporary art in the United States. A major share of the research has centered upon architecture. The name of Frank Lloyd Wright is pre-eminent since his work is regarded as being directly responsible for the 'International Style of Architecture.' Few persons, other than architects, know that Pittsburgh also has a forerunner in contemporary architecture in the person of Frederick Scheibler." These comments were made in reference to *Modern Architecture: International Exhibition*, the famous Museum of Modern Art exhibit of two years before.[1] Having placed Scheibler among pretty lofty company, Redd ended her short discussion by saying, "In Frederick Scheibler, one finds an architect who tempered his intuitive intelligence for absolute functionalism with a concept of romantic beauty in detail. In any study of the sources of contemporary American architecture, Frederick Scheibler merits a monograph."[2]

In about 1948, John Knox Shear and Robert W. Schmertz, architecture professors at Carnegie Institute of Technology, visited and interviewed Scheibler and purposefully publicized his work. In an article published in *Charette*, the magazine of the Pittsburgh Architectural Club, they gave special praise to Scheibler's so-called group cottages, and singled out his Vilsack Row noting: "That the Vilsack Row was constructed in 1912 is difficult to believe. The alternation of blank wall and great glass areas, the simple slab-form roofs, the slight canopy supports, and the clean lines of the well-proportioned forms are far in advance of their time. . . . When compared with its neighbors it is impossible to escape the conclusion that this man was alone here in his time." They remarked upon the architects "whose work in a time of general dissimulation, disguise, complexity and artificiality, stood out boldly contrasted in its frankness, simplicity and inventiveness," and asserted that Scheibler "must be nominated to the peerage of creative pioneers."[3]

The *Charette* article caught the attention of two important figures on the architectural scene: Peter Blake, then curator of the Department of Architecture and Design at the Museum of Modern Art, and Kenneth Stowell, editor of *Architectural Record*. Blake expressed an interest in collecting photographs of Scheibler's works for exhibition in New York, perhaps at MOMA itself, though this idea was apparently not pursued to fruition. Stowell requested permission to reprint the *Charette* article in *Architect-*

ural Record, where it appeared in 1949 in an edited and annotated version under the title "Pittsburgh Rediscovers an Architect Pioneer."⁴ The editorial voice, perhaps Stowell's, remarked that Scheibler's Highland Towers apartment building was "quite an astonishing creation for the year 1913 . . . an orderly and strongly plastic structure," and that "the whole is more convincing today than many an 'advanced' building of the intervening years." Regarding Vilsack Row, he agreed with Shear and Schmertz that the exterior elements were "far in advance of their time" and added that they "escape their time altogether as good architecture regardless of date. Such treatment would come as a fresh innovation again today."⁵

After Scheibler's death in 1958, a photographic exhibition of Scheibler's work was held at the Carnegie Institute in Pittsburgh. James D. Van Trump curated the exhibition and published his own article on Scheibler in *Charette*. Van Trump stated that Scheibler "was undoubtedly the most important 'original' architect that Pittsburgh has produced, as well as a distinguished and unique pioneer of the modern architectural movement in Pennsylvania," and went on to assert that Scheibler's "best work can compare favorably with any thing of the same sort being produced in America at the time" and "should assure him a minor and not unmemorable place in the whole chronicle of American architecture."⁶

Frederick G. Scheibler, Jr. (1872–1958), never attained the heights of his profession. The big names in Pittsburgh architecture in the early twentieth century were Frederick J. Osterling, Alden and Harlow, Henry Hornbostel, and Benno Janssen. It was these architects that rode the architectural wave of regional industrialization and received the major commissions from Pittsburgh's leading institutions and nouveau riche industrialists. It was these architects who largely established the masculine and conservative norms of Pittsburgh architecture. It was these architects that received the few out-of-town commissions that were entrusted to Pittsburgh architects. And it was these architects who were featured in the special Pittsburgh issue of *Architectural Record* in September 1911—not Scheibler.⁷

Scheibler's commissions relegated him to an arena of lesser architects and builders. A rough breakdown of his work shows that fully half of his commissions were for single-family houses; another third were for small apartment buildings or other types of multifamily housing; and small commercial buildings, schools, and miscellany comprised the remainder. Scheibler received none of the prominent commissions of his time and built no landmarks in the conventional sense.

Scheibler was also a parochial architect. Nearly eight out of every ten Scheibler commissions were for locations in Pittsburgh's East End neighborhoods and eastern suburbs, and most of the remainder were for sites elsewhere in Pittsburgh and Western Pennsylvania. Only five documented projects were located in other portions of Pennsylvania and points beyond. These occasional commissions in Philadelphia (Wynnewood), Maryland, New Jersey, and California were all for clients with Pittsburgh connections.

On its surface, his was not a career to be remembered and chronicled.

But Scheibler was different. Diverging from the

norms of his time and place, Scheibler found his peers at the periphery of the national and international scene and produced a distinctive and progressive architecture. This architecture transcends any question of prominence and demands consideration on its own terms.

The so-called progressive artistic movements appeared at the turn of the century in reaction against the prevailing revival styles of the nineteenth century and in quest of contemporary artistic expression. Such movements were fueled by a change in attitude toward historical styles, whereby styles were treated not so much as mutually exclusive vocabularies but as a sourcebook from which elements might be chosen at will and reinterpreted by the architect. This attitude led to rampant eclecticism; but it also offered the opportunity—seized by a few—to develop free and ahistorical approaches to design. What was commonly disciplined by cultural associations and stylistic canons could become more neutral in content and more freely composed. As Joseph Maria Olbrich stated it:

> From day to day the rift grows greater between the Artist-Architect with his creative genius, with his abundance of purpose-expressing forms, and the architect with the library of clumsy forms which he eagerly copies with tracing-paper and carefully pieces together. On one side the young creative artistic talent, on the other side the motif-copiers and tradition-idolisers![8]

The progressive movements found further inspiration in the principles of Englishman William Morris who affirmed the average man and his aesthetic sensibilities in the face of a traditional aristocracy and the powerful new forces of industrial society. Morris maintained that handcraft was the fundamental basis of all art, and his followers found inspiration in the naive but authentic vocabulary of vernacular building. In this way the progressives maintained a traditional grounding for their work and, consequently, were sometimes called the New Traditionalists.

Many of the progressives also insisted on rational building, based on functional considerations and human scale, and their work developed a tendency toward geometric simplification. This rationalism also extended, in part, to an acceptance of the new materials and devices of modern technology. Some of the progressives adopted up-to-date construction methods and used modern materials such as iron and steel unconcealed and without apology. In this, they were heirs to a line of rationalist thinking dating back to Viollet-le-Duc in the mid-nineteenth century.

Equally important was the appeal of the organic forms of nature, derived in large part from the new influence in Europe of Japanese art. The progressives explored the forces of growth of tendril, vine, and bud; they adopted flower motifs such as the lily and the iris.[9] The Japanese color woodblock print, in particular, was highly influential, with its absence of central perspective in favor of broad receding planes, its use of line in establishing rhythm, its use of color for a flat pattern effect instead of illusionistic modeling, and its simplification of natural forms.[10] These characteristics provided for a simple transition from woodblock and paper to architectural materials like art glass and tile.

The progressives perceived each building as an individual work of art. Their quest for architectural unity led to the integration of exterior and interior spaces and the integration of architecture and ornamentation, with the full inclusion of landscaping and furnishings in the architectural concept. The irony was that artistic movements that issued from ideals of artistic freedom and democracy resulted in a scenario whereby the architect had total control.

These ideas held broad, if limited, appeal. They appeared more or less simultaneously in various locations and were subsequently spread by way of publications, exhibitions, and personal visits between architects. Many a progressive architect was influenced by another. Architects regularly appropriate entire architectural vocabularies called *styles;* but those with experimental tendencies observe new developments closely and often borrow from each other with self-awareness and the desire to work creatively with provocative ideas. Progressive work acted as a shared context, like a style, but one that was used as a starting point for personal expression.

When focused on a key figure or two, progressive art and architecture coalesced as a *progressive movement.* Such turn-of-the-century movements included the English Arts and Crafts Movement and the Glasgow Secession in the British Isles; Art Nouveau, the Viennese Secession, Jugendstil, and the Floreale on the Continent; and the Shingle Style, the Chicago School, and the Prairie School in the United States. In 1898 the Secessionists in Vienna attempted to establish an institutional presence for themselves and other progressives by building a headquarters and gallery building (fig. 2), designed by the outspoken Olbrich, and hosting international exhibitions of progressive art. They attained a degree of success and notoriety, as did most of the progressive movements; but all remained apart from the academies and out of the architectural mainstream and were ultimately short-lived. Nevertheless, the impact on the contemporary art world was extraordinary. By challenging the establishment and unleashing pent-up creativity, the progressives set the stage for the more radical modernism that followed.

Scheibler's opportunities for direct contact with the progressive movements were severely limited, but he did have access to publications. The proliferation of books and periodicals about art and architecture was of key importance to the development of the progressive movements. The Viennese Seccessionists issued a periodical as one of their first acts. Everyone read the the *Studio,* an English periodical that covered developments in Britain and throughout Europe after 1893. The continental progressives learned about English developments in Hermann Muthesius's landmark study *Das Englische Haus* (1904), which was specifically commissioned for this purpose by the German government. And so forth.

Publications were *the* key for Scheibler. He likely came across issues of the *Studio,* or new and different architectural books, at Pittsburgh's Carnegie Library. Soon he was consulting such sources regularly, acquiring them for his personal library, and learning and applying their lessons. Younger than most of the progressives, and late to begin independent practice, he was in an excellent position to benefit from the leading figures of the day. It was crucial that Scheibler should master some of the progressive ideas of others in order to tap into an architectural expression beyond what he could learn in Pittsburgh. These ideas gave Scheibler the courage to be different.

Although Scheibler left no acknowledgment of

Fig. 2. Joseph Maria Olbrich, Secession Building, 1898.

his sources, many can be identified by comparing his work with illustrations in the publications of the period. Scheibler sometimes copied decorative details literally. But otherwise, to his credit, his borrowing was superficial: he always made extensive adaptations to suit new requirements. His reliance on the work of any one architect was brief, and he managed to avoid some of the excesses of those whose work inspired him. Ideas, once borrowed, were refined and personalized to become Scheibler's own.

Scheibler might also have had contact with Titus de Bobula (1878–1961), a Pittsburgh architect and Hungarian immigrant whose work reflected both his eastern European heritage and the influence of the Viennese Secession.[11] De Bobula exhibited a group of extraordinary drawings at the Pittsburgh Architectural Club exhibition in 1905, a display reviewed with some skepticism by the club president and master ecclesiastical architect, John T. Comes:

Pittsburgh has among its architects one who is devoted to the propagation of the style of Art Nouveau, of the secessionist style, as it is known in Vienna and Austria. Mr. Titus de Bobula has outgrown the traditions and styles of former periods and is industriously endeavoring to develop a new style which he thinks is more American and reasonable than the copying of historic styles.[12]

De Bobula built a few local buildings, including a parochial school in Braddock, Pennsylvania (fig. 3) that was based in part on Olbrich's Secession Build-

Introduction 7

Fig. 3. Titus de Bobula, design for a parochial school, ca. 1904, perspective rendering.

Fig. 4. McNall house, ca. 1909, art glass and I-beam.

ing.[13] Most of his visionary schemes went unbuilt, however, and he was but a fleeting figure on the Pittsburgh architectural scene.

Scheibler, on the other hand, persevered against the odds. Once under the sway of progressive art, he ran with it. He adopted ahistorical architectural language. He mastered the craft aesthetic. He developed principles of rational building to a virtually unprecedented degree. And he embraced the seeming dichotomy of nature vis-à-vis technology, as revealed by his art-glass irises and I-beam lintels (see fig. 4).

Scheibler's career earned him a unique and respected position in the history of Pittsburgh architecture. Today, architects and aficionados cultivate an interest in Scheibler's work. Walking tours of Scheibler's buildings draw hundreds, and Scheibler's name is a recognized asset in the real estate market. Gillian H. Belnap has written an important dissertation treating Scheibler's apartment buildings.[14] But Scheibler has never received the monograph that Penelope Redd called for in 1934 to demonstrate his place in the larger community of progressives.[15] Thus this book.

1 🌸 Man and Architect

FREDERICK GUSTAVUS SCHEIBLER, JR., was born on May 12, 1872, the son of William Augustus and Eleanor Seidel Scheibler.[1] Although his father's name was William, Frederick was a junior because he was named for his uncle Frederick. William Scheibler was variously a clerk, a bookkeeper, a salesman, and a partner in McAllister and Scheibler, wholesale grocers. The Scheiblers resided on Bouquet Street near Craft Avenue in Pittsburgh's South Oakland district. Frederick was the second child—he had an older sister, Eleanor. They were later joined by younger siblings Anna and William.

Little is known of the maternal side of the family, save that a great-grandfather raised horses in Sewickley, a pastoral community northwest of Pittsburgh. Clearly there were close ties to the other side of the family, since Scheibler's paternal grandparents, Gustavus and Eliza Scheibler and his aunts Amelia and Julia lived next door. Gustavus Scheibler had emigrated from Dusseldorf, and the family identification with its German heritage appears to have been strong.

There was an artistic side to the Scheibler family. Gustavus Scheibler, a bookbinder by trade, likely produced fine bindings as part of his handicraft, and family lore holds that his portrait was painted by Pittsburgh artist George Hetzel, who had been trained in Dusseldorf. It was also a musical family. A relative of Frederick's mother was reportedly a founder of the famous Bethlehem (Pennsylvania) Bach Choir, and Aunt Julia was a music teacher. According to his brother, Will, Frederick was much given to drawing as a child. He also played the violin as a youth and would later play occasionally for his wife and children. Years later Scheibler recalled in an interview that he loved both the violin and architecture when very young, but decided that he could not give himself to both and do them justice. Architecture won out.[2]

Frederick Scheibler attended the Bellefield Grammar School and then enrolled in an academic curriculum at Pittsburgh's Central High School. At the age of sixteen he left school to become an apprentice in an architectural office. This decision may have been influenced by the erection of a new house for his family, a short distance west of the former homestead, in 1887–1888. The house was designed by Bartberger and Dietrich, architects with good German credentials.[3]

Scheibler's initial apprenticeship to the highly respected architect Henry Moser (or Möser) may have been arranged through such contacts in the German community. For approximately ten years, from 1888 to 1898, Scheibler learned his trade in the offices of Moser, V. Wyse Thalman, and Longfellow, Alden and

Harlow.⁴ An extended period of apprenticeship was a common means of architectural training at this time. There was no school of architecture in Pittsburgh—the school of architecture at Carnegie Tech, now Carnegie Mellon University, was not established until 1905—and an architectural degree was the exception rather than the rule among local architects.

How good was Scheibler's training? What did he learn as an apprentice? We have no first-hand reports. Moser's schools and public buildings were generally designed within the quasi-Romanesque parameters of the Rundbogenstil (round-arched style) that he must have learned in his native Germany. Scheibler may have picked up an affinity for picturesque but controlled design and Germanic sources from Moser. Thalman claimed to have received diplomas in Stuttgart, Paris, and Zurich, though little is known of his work nor of what Scheibler stood to gain from him.⁵

Longfellow, Alden and Harlow, with offices in both Boston and Pittsburgh, was among the most prominent of local firms. Longfellow and Alden had filled key roles in the office of Henry Hobson Richardson, while Harlow came to the firm from McKim, Mead and White. Longfellow, Alden and Harlow used the revived classical vocabulary of the Renaissance for many important turn-of-the-century commissions. Scheibler would have learned the intricacies of the classical orders and the basics of classical organization from Longfellow, Alden and Harlow, if he hadn't learned them previously.⁶ But Frank Alden, head of the Pittsburgh office, had a particular sympathy for his mentor Richardson, and he perpetuated a sort of American Arts and Crafts manner that was characteristic of much of Richardson's work. Most important for Scheibler, this entailed the design of total environments.

Scheibler's connection to Richardson, through Alden, was a distant brush with genius. Richardson (1838–1886) laid the groundwork for the American progressive movements that followed. Scheibler's training was fortunate in some respects; but it did not dictate the parameters of his future practice. It did get him off and running in the profession.

In 1898, at the age of twenty-six, Scheibler married Antonia Oehmler of Pittsburgh. Antonia was also from a musically talented family and had a somewhat tenuous artistic credential: she was the niece of the well-known Pittsburgh painter Emil Foerster. Prior to the wedding, Scheibler drew up plans for a "honeymoon cottage" (fig. 5), the first known building of his design. The house was accordingly built, and the Scheiblers took up housekeeping in Swissvale, a town adjacent to Pittsburgh's eastern edge. Thus began Scheibler's personal and professional focus on Pittsburgh's East End and eastern suburbs.

In short order, Scheibler entered private practice and established a partnership with Louis A. Raisig in Wilkinsburg, a community adjoining both Pittsburgh and Swissvale.⁷ The firm of Raisig and Scheibler is known to have undertaken only two projects. Scheibler probably obtained both clients and finished the second project in his name only, which suggests that he quickly deemed the partnership to be unnecessary. In fact, Raisig was a builder, not an architect, and it is hard to figure what he brought to the short-lived partnership other than an initial sense of security for a young architect.⁸

Fig. 5. Scheibler cottage, 1898, perspective rendering.

By 1901 Scheibler had established himself in independent practice. Wilkinsburg lay at the center of a large geographic area that held great promise for development, and Scheibler stayed here for about twelve years, making his living largely with local projects. The area was good to him, as he was to it, though his suburban location set him a bit apart from professional opportunities in Pittsburgh. Nevertheless, Scheibler participated in professional activities during these years as a member of the Pittsburgh Architectural Club, the Pittsburgh Chapter of the American Institute of Architects, and the Pittsburgh Board of Trade. In 1905 he was elected vice-president of the Pittsburgh Architectural Club.[9] In the same year he exhibited in the club's exhibition for the first time, and ultimately exhibited thirteen projects at four Pittsburgh Architectural Club Exhibitions between 1905 and 1912.[10]

Back in Swissvale, Scheibler belonged to the Knights of Malta and the Swissvale Presbyterian Church. He demonstrated an interest in horses, inherited from his great-grandfather perhaps, and kept a horse named Richard and a sulky at his disposal. Scheibler was quick to jump on the automobile bandwagon, however: he was very proud of his first Pope-Hartford automobile and joined an automobile club (see fig. 6). His interest in his private transportation did not translate into wanderlust, however. Scheibler

Man and Architect 11

Fig. 6. Carl Building, postcard, ca. 1907. Scheibler's office was located here ca. 1907–1912. The automobile is Scheibler's.

may have visited the Louisiana Purchase International Exposition in St. Louis, Missouri, in 1904.[11] And he may have visited the sites of architectural projects in New Jersey, Maryland, and other parts of Pennsylvania. Otherwise, he rarely ventured outside of southwestern Pennsylvania.

The Scheiblers had three children during their years in Swissvale: a son Harold (born 1899), and two daughters, Mildred (born 1901) and Dorothea (born 1909). Mildred Scheibler Kilham reports that the older children often accompanied their father on inspections of his buildings and that he playfully dedicated the mushroom reliefs on his Old Heidelberg apartment building to her. In 1911, however, the family scene fell apart when Harold, age twelve, died of scarlet fever. Antonia Scheibler became ill as well, and soon left with her daughters for her mother's home, then in Pasadena, California. They did not return.

These crises caused abrupt changes in Scheibler's affairs at a time when he was doing his best work. Around 1912 he moved his office to Pittsburgh's East Liberty section, marking the beginning of ten years of personal and professional focus on East Liberty and its vicinity.[12] He dropped his professional memberships in the Pittsburgh Architectural Club and the A.I.A. chapter. He was divorced from Antonia Oehmler Scheibler and left the honeymoon cottage in Swissvale. His place of residence did not appear in city directories for a few years; reportedly he stayed for awhile with Frank and Eva Harter.[13] Frank Harter was a kindred spirit and close personal friend; Eva Harter kept Scheibler's financial books for many years. They later became important clients as well.

According to his brother, Will, Scheibler's life was

disrupted again during World War I when he worked in Fairfield, Alabama, for the Tennessee Coal and Iron Company, a U.S. Steel subsidiary. The exact timing of his absence from Pittsburgh and his practice is unclear, however. When Scheibler reappeared in the city directories in 1918, his address was that of a house in Highland Park, just north of East Liberty, which he extensively remodeled for its owner, Caroline A. White (fig. 7). Some years earlier, White, a music teacher, had rented a room in the Carl Building in Wilkinsburg, one story below Scheibler's office. Years later, she was calling herself Claire VonScheibler, C. A. VonScheibler, and C. A. Scheibler, and claimed to be Scheibler's wife.[14] There is no marriage record in Allegheny County, and White's claim is doubtful; but she may have been the so-called other woman rumored to be a cause of the demise of Scheibler's first marriage.[15]

In 1923, at age fifty-one, Scheibler married Blanche Clawson of Indiana, Pennsylvania, and moved to Glenshaw, a few miles north of Pittsburgh. There are rumors of illness in the 1920s, and the 1928 city directory lists Scheibler at Will's Sewickley residence. In 1930, Frederick and Blanche Scheibler relocated to Talley Cavey Road, another five miles north of the city, at first renting and then purchasing a small house from a client.[16] The house was a 1923 Potomac model marketed by the Alladin Company of Bay City, Michigan. It was most ironic that a man and architect who devoted himself to the careful custom design of his buildings should end his career and his life in a mail-order house. (A family photograph from the 1950s suggests that he couldn't resist making a few modest improvements.) A few years later Scheibler moved his office out to his home and,

Fig. 7. White house, ca. 1914?, detail.

though his practice was in decline, shifted his professional focus one last time to outlying locations, including new opportunities in the Monongahela Valley, south of Pittsburgh.

These years were highlighted by a measure of public attention. The first article on Scheibler's work was published in the *Pittsburgh Sunday Sun-Telegraph* in 1934. In 1939 he was invited to design a model home as a local housing promotion. And in 1948 he was interviewed for articles that appeared in *Charette*, the magazine of the Pittsburgh Architectural Club, and *Architectural Record*. On the whole, however, Scheibler's final years were years of inactivity and solitude. He lived and worked at a truly remote location and had long since cut himself off from professional circles in Pittsburgh. For at least the last ten years of his life he experienced progressive blindness. Scheibler received his last known commission in 1948 and died

Fig. 8. Frederick G. Scheibler, Jr., portrait, 1919. The framed photograph on the rear wall is Highland Towers. A photograph of Vilsack Row is inside the cabinet.

ten years later on June 15, 1958, at the age of eighty-six.

A portrait photograph shows Scheibler as a young man, dapper in dress if a bit serious in demeanor, with soft but penetrating eyes (frontispiece). A photograph taken twenty years later shows Scheibler as a slight man posed at studied ease before his desk in a three-piece suit (fig. 8). This is Scheibler the working professional; in the background are display photographs of his Highland Towers and Vilsack Row projects and numerous rolls of drawings.

He was apparently the sort of man who acquired nicknames: some called him Fritz, and others called him Freddie. Will Scheibler described his brother as "very likable," a man of happy disposition. Blanche Scheibler, his wife of thirty-five years, said that he was a "wonderful man [and] husband . . . kind and considerate." To the young Mary Pyle, the daughter of a client, he was a "small man, very quiet and unassuming but absolutely devoted to his profession and a really artistic soul." On the other hand, George Bailey, the son of Scheibler's favorite plumbing supplier, found Scheibler eccentric, difficult, and impatient in their professional contacts late in the architect's career. Earl Harter, son of Frank and Eva Harter, says Scheibler was a true artist, but imperious and temperamental—not the perfect house guest.

In Wilkinsburg, Scheibler represented an undermanned profession in a town still small enough to encourage personal contact. A bit of a dandy, it seems he cut a not unattractive figure. Most of his commissions were obtained by personal acquaintance and word of mouth. Many clients can be traced one to another through family connections, places of residence, and so forth. Others may have been drawn by ethnic proclivity. In fifty years of professional practice, Scheibler received approximately 150 known commissions. The average of three commissions per year is misleading, however, for there were many busy years at the beginning and many fallow ones toward the end. All in all, he was not particularly prolific.

Approximately one-third of Scheibler's clients were professionals or business proprietors; one-third were in real estate; one-quarter were lower-level white-collar workers (clerks, bookkeepers, etcetera); and the remainder were blue-collar workers and miscellaneous others. These clients were predominantly self-made people of modest social and economic status. There were many repeat clients. One, Fred Bruckman, favorably regarded Scheibler's buildings as

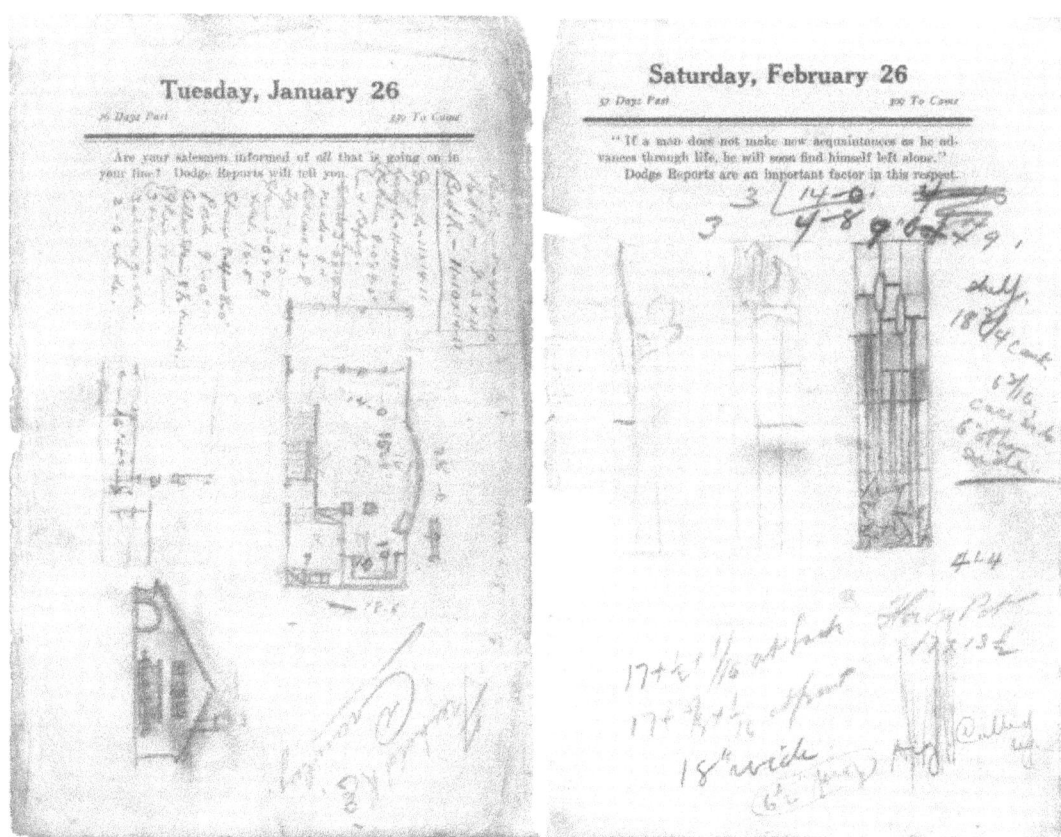

Fig. 9. Scheibler sketches, 1915.

"modern."[17] But most of his clients probably chose him for nonideological reasons. Scheibler was the local man. That he was a man with new and different ideas would have appealed to some but would have needed to be sold to others.[18]

Scheibler explored his ideas in sketches on scrap paper (fig. 9) or large sheets of heavy drawing paper and finalized his designs in inked working drawings on drawing linen. He apparently did all the necessary drafting himself—his drawings all appear to be in the same hand. Even working drawings show evidence of ongoing revisions. Early in his career, Scheibler prepared different sheets of working drawings for each elevation and plan. Later he tended to crowd as much onto a sheet as possible, and some fairly complicated houses are represented by only a single sheet of working drawings incorporating plans, elevations, a structural section, and interior details. He never used a title block, but signed his drawings from the start and later lettered a stylized form of his name as well (fig. 10).[19]

In most cases, Scheibler apparently used sketches or incomplete working drawings to present his ideas to clients. Only five rendered images are known, all watercolors, and even these may not have been executed by Scheibler himself—one is clearly signed by another artist—and may not have been prepared primarily for presentation purposes. One depicts Scheibler's own house, three were probably displayed at the Pittsburgh Architectural Club exhibitions, and two were probably commissioned by the client specifically for marketing purposes: one of these features the names of both the owner and the rental agents, and the other appears prominently in a marketing brochure.[20]

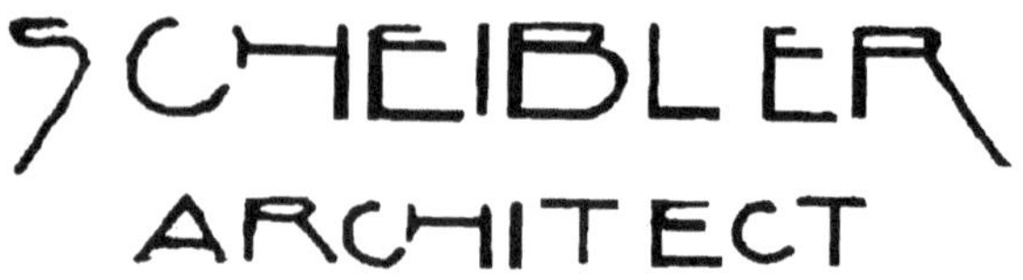

SCHEIBLER ARCHITECT

Fig. 10. Scheibler lettered signature, ca. 1922.

Scheibler incorporated furnishings and ornamentation in each design. He prepared large shop drawings for built-in cabinetwork and other woodworking detail, and he designed and ordered custom light fixtures. He also custom designed numerous art-glass windows, preparing full-size watercolor cartoons that were then fabricated by the Rudy Brothers Company of Pittsburgh. He did not design his own tile, but ordered it from the catalogs of the Rookwood Pottery in Cincinnati and Henry Mercer's Moravian Pottery and Tile Works in Doylestown, Pennsylvania, America's premier Arts and Crafts potteries.[21]

Most of the stories that are told about Scheibler involve incidents that arose while he was supervising the construction of his buildings. He himself said in an interview that he had trouble with his contractors. As reported by Shear and Schmertz, who interviewed Scheibler in 1948:

"I got hell," [Scheibler] admits, "More from the workmen than from anyone else." They said they couldn't do it. They said they wouldn't do it. They walked off the job. He advertised in the papers for day laborers and more than once went to work with an unskilled crew to put something together.[22]

At the Old Heidelberg apartment building, two short lengths of scalloped ornament almost stopped the job. Scheibler insisted on having them, the owner liked them, the contractor said they couldn't be made. Impasse. Time elapsed. Then it appeared that the contractor could make them—or have them made—but for a price. The price was outrageous. The owner didn't like them that much. Scheibler still liked them but agreed that he did not want to be a party to the daylight robbery of his client. However he knew of a man who would do them for one hundred dollars if that was agreeable to the owner and the contractor. It was. "So I took off my coat," says Scheibler, "Climbed on the scaffold and in two hours made one hundred dollars and didn't even get my hands dirty."[23]

And at the Pyle House (as recalled by the daughter of the house):

Mr. Scheibler was constantly on the job to see that the contractor carried out his specifications. In our case this was a battle as the house was very expensive and they attempted to chisel. I remember the cement fireplace fell apart almost immediately and had to be done over. The roof slate was of poor quality and Mr. Scheibler made the roofer take it back and buy the required quality. For a long time the house was covered only by tar paper much to my Mother's distress. He constantly had to tell the workmen how to carry out the specifications.[24]

At Highland Towers, Scheibler reportedly forced bricklayers to remove several courses of brick because it was not precisely the right color. At the Harter house, the floors were replaced because the wrong type of mahogany had been ordered. At the Parkstone Dwellings, Scheibler reportedly got down on his hands and knees and laid out the decorative tile spandrels himself after workmen refused to make the attempt.

Perhaps Scheibler was hard to work for, and perhaps he was lax in supervision. But difficulties arose in part because he was asking workmen for types of work that were out of the ordinary. C.F.A. Voysey, the English Arts and Crafts architect, reportedly made drawings—as many as eighteen for one house— showing workman what to *omit* in the way of routine details that they would have added because they always did it that way.[25] Scheibler would have understood the problem.

Scheibler's contacts with manufacturers and supliers were happier. As reported by Shear and Schmertz, Scheibler always found them helpful: "Mills, ironworkers, brick manufacturers, fixture houses, and many others aided him understandingly when he was trying to explore their fields for simpler and better ways of doing things."[26]

The unconventional nature of Scheibler's work and his artistic temperament both restricted the possibilities for cooperation with others. He had no partners after Raisig, and his only other professional collaboration was a curious liaison with Kantero Kato (1889–1926), a Japanese theatrical designer who contributed to some of Scheibler's later decorative schemes.[27] Frank Harter may have exerted important influence on Scheibler's work as both friend and client. But Scheibler succeeded and failed as a solitary figure.

2 Half and Half

SCHEIBLER DID NOT IMMEDIATELY take up the progressive banner. Like many a young architect, his first independent efforts as a designer were constrained by his training and the need to find commissions. From the start he demonstrated fluency with a neoclassical vocabulary and a competent understanding of a number of other architectural styles. Some of his early buildings were wholly conventional; but he also displayed a restlessness that was expressed in experimentation and some mildly unconventional work. As Scheibler himself put it, "I went through a half and half period."[1] While he established himself in his profession, Scheibler began to create a personal vocabulary and lay the groundwork for his future direction as a designer.[2]

Scheibler was his own first client, but Antonia Oehmler provided the occasion. Their impending marriage in 1897 inspired Scheibler to design a small cottage for their life together. Scheibler drew up two alternative designs for a frame house, one with a simple gable roof, and one with a partially gambreled roof and twin cross-gables (fig. 5). The latter more complex design, a Colonial Revival–Shingle Style hybrid, was built. The house's massing and plan demonstrated the young architect's interest in the manipulation of form and the interplay of axes, while an aureole window provided a single decorative accent. Scheibler rendered the cottage as a suburban idyll; but neither the marriage nor the cottage endured, and a gas station now occupies the site.

The first professional commission, the only documented project completed by the partnership of Raisig and Scheibler, came early in 1901. The client, Edward A. Kitzmiller, was a Swissvale grocer and a likely acquaintance of Scheibler's. The drawings are in Scheibler's hand. The Kitzmiller house (fig. 11) is a free mixture of Queen Anne and Colonial Revival elements with cross-gabled massing and modest classical detailing. The lower story is brick laid in Flemish bond; the upper story was originally shingled. As with the Scheibler cottage, there is a single striking decorative device: here it is art-glass windows that meet at a corner of the second story. Though it later became a common feature of modernistic design, the use of glazing to turn a corner was highly unusual for the time.

Scheibler's independent career—sans Raisig—began in earnest in the summer of 1901 when Robert L. Matthews, a hotel operator in Pittsburgh's then sister city of Allegheny, just across the Allegheny River, and Joseph W. Steel, a Westmoreland County coal operator, each commissioned residences from the young architect.[3] Scheibler proved that he was up to the task of designing a formal and rather opulent house by producing for Matthews his most comprehensive exercise in academic design. Matthews must have been satisfied, since he gave Scheibler another commission for a commercial building, but the Matthews house was never realized. The Steel house commission followed soon after, and Scheibler simply adopted the unused Matthews house plans for the new site in Greensburg. The Steel house was built but was destroyed by fire in 1989.

The Steel house (fig. 12) can be loosely categorized with the contemporary neoclassical work of Longfellow, Alden and Harlow and of McKim, Mead and White.[4] A cubelike mass under a hip roof was extended outward with large porches and a porte cochère. Tile roofing and brick and stone quoins served as a textural overlay. Overt classical detail was largely confined to wood porches and eaves on the

Fig. 11. Kitzmiller house, 1901, front elevation.

Fig. 12. Steel house, ca. 1901.

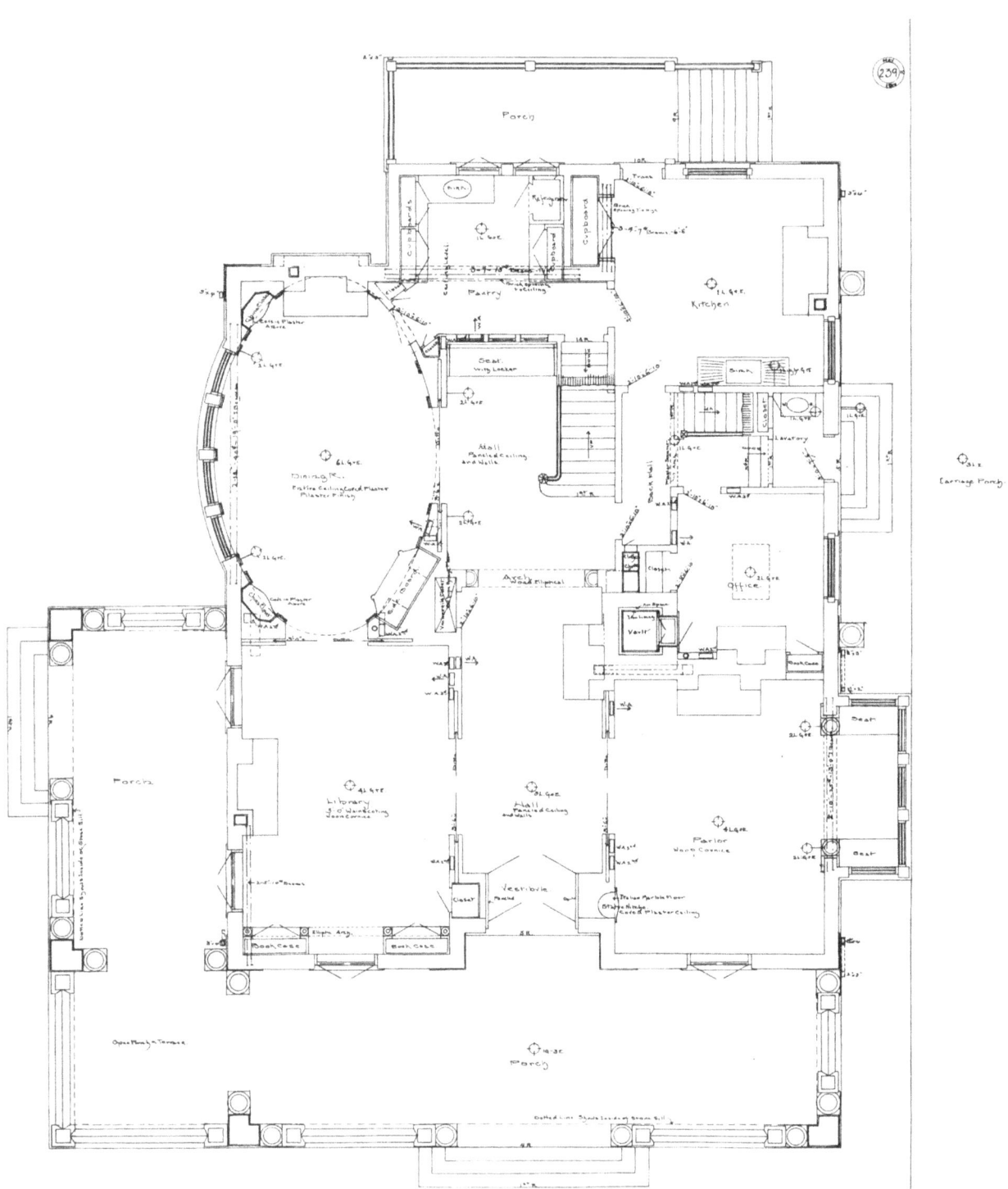

Fig. 13. Matthews house, 1901, first floor plan.

Fig. 14. Steel house, ca. 1901, dining room.

exterior, but was rampant in the richly detailed interior that included extensive built-in furnishings, wood carving, decorative painting, and stained glass. A conventional central-hall plan (fig. 13) was disrupted only by an oval dining room (fig. 14), which was nudged off-axis and subsequently formed a gently curved protrusion on the left side of the house.

Three major characteristics of the Steel house prefigure Scheibler's later progressive work. The triangular massing scheme reappeared in a different guise in some later house projects. The careful interior detailing foreshadowed the interiors of all of Scheibler's later work. And the oval dining room was an early indicator of Scheibler's interest in pure geometric form and unconventional planning.

Earlier in 1901, the firm of Raisig and Scheibler had been invited by the Swissvale Borough school district to submit drawings for the projected Longfel-

Fig. 15. Hawkins School, 1904, perspective rendering. Shows the namestone altered in anticipation of the later Wilkins School.

low School in a limited architectural competition. Scheibler ultimately submitted drawings in his own name, but lost the commission to Rieger and Currier. By 1904, the district was ready to build again, and this time the competition within the competition was even stiffer: eight architects submitted plans, including U. J. L. Peoples and Ellsworth Dean, habitual designers of Pittsburgh public school buildings, and Milligan and Miller of Wilkinsburg, then Scheibler's landlords.[5] Scheibler prepared a perspective rendering of his concept, and this time the school board minutes read: "Resolved that of the competition plans for the Hawkins School house, the sketch of F. G. Scheibler, Jr. seems to meet the ideas of the Board most closely."[6]

Hawkins School (fig. 15) was designed as a two-story brick school with eight rooms and a thoroughly neoclassical vocabulary, including a pedimented central pavilion and porticoed side entries. In satisfying his school board client, Scheibler produced the most conventional major design of his career. His school showed none of the experimentation of de Bobula's school. Elsewhere in Scheibler's practice, however, there was already evidence of new thinking.

In 1902, Scheibler received his second commission from Robert L. Matthews, this time for a commercial building in Allegheny (fig. 16).⁷ This is one of two commercial buildings that Scheibler designed as if they were episodes in an enormous classical order. Two massive pilasters frame the facade, and triglyphs and an outsized cartouche bearing the owner's initials ornament an entablature between the third and fourth stories. At a diminished scale, a layer of virtual curtain-wall construction filled the three-story void between the pilasters, consisting of bands of windows framed with thin metal mullions and divided by plain wood spandrels.

Scheibler reused this basic composition in a 1903 commission for a two-story store and office building (fig. 17) on a site just down the street from his Wilkinsburg office. The client was William E. Hamnett, a real estate speculator who established his office in the new building and later commissioned a house from Scheibler. The design improved upon the Matthews store building in two particulars: the facade was more daring in its used of five larger windows—sans spandrels—to span the void between pilasters, and it was without extraneous classical detail. Unfortunately, it is now totally obscured by a false front.

Fig. 16. Matthews store building, 1902. Shown after the first of two stages of alterations.

Fig. 17. Hamnett store building, ca. 1903.

Fig. 18. Louis Sullivan, Gage Building facade, 1898–1899.

These two commercial facades are the first substantial evidence of Scheibler's awareness of progressive architectural currents. Their open treatment reflected the achievements of the Chicago School, a progressive movement that revolved around Louis Sullivan, and prompted the rationalization of commercial architecture in the United States by emphasizing the vertical definition of tall buildings and employing broad areas of glazing between vertical piers. The Matthews building specifically recalls Sullivan's Gage Building facade (fig. 18) in its dual scales and layers, its balance of mass and void, the horizontal divisions of its window bays, and the splash of its decorative detail, if not in its neoclassical styling.[8] It is regrettable that Scheibler did not have the opportunity to further pursue these ideas in commercial work and that no intact examples of this work remain.

When Scheibler designed his first apartment building, American architects and builders had been experimenting with this type of building for only about thirty years. The late nineteenth century had placed a high value on home ownership and imbued the home with heavy symbolism. The home stood for an individual's tastes, virtues, and dedication to both family and the public order. The apartment building was widely perceived to be a threat to the life of the home. Apartments were perhaps *too* democratic, with strangers intruding upon the private sanctuary of the home, and with their thin walls, facing windows, and public lobbies that fostered lifestyles all too intimate, if not scandalous. Nevertheless, the urban pressures of high land costs and growing population dictated multifamily housing for the middle class, and apartments were readily accepted in practice. Their architects often incorporated reassuring symbols of domestic architecture such as porches and fireplaces, and their sometimes whimsical names promoted a sense of personal identification normally associated with private ownership.

Scheibler addressed this building type in a burst of activity, completing a series of five apartment buildings in Pittsburgh's far East End neighborhoods of Homewood and Park Place in 1903 and 1904. These buildings were uniformly modest in scale, at three stories and six units each, and followed prevailing conventions of apartment planning. Like the ubiquitous so-called railroad apartment, they had simple rectangular footprints and narrow units with rooms arranged in a linear fashion along long hallways (see fig. 19). All had single or twin full-height porches, and four were given unique names.

The clients for all five buildings were William Robinson and Frederick Bruckman, Homewood businessmen who shared a real estate partnership (Robinson and Bruckman) from 1902 until 1913, and who were founders and longtime directors and officers of the Hamilton Realty Company, a publicly held real estate development and holding company. Scheibler designed many projects for Robinson and Bruckman, though these were sometimes commissioned in the name of the Hamilton Realty Company, or Jesse F. Robinson (William Robinson's wife), or any of a number of other associates of the partners.[9] Together, the partners and their architect put an exceptional new face on speculative building in Pittsburgh's East End.

The first joint project was an unnamed apartment building on East End Avenue that represents an

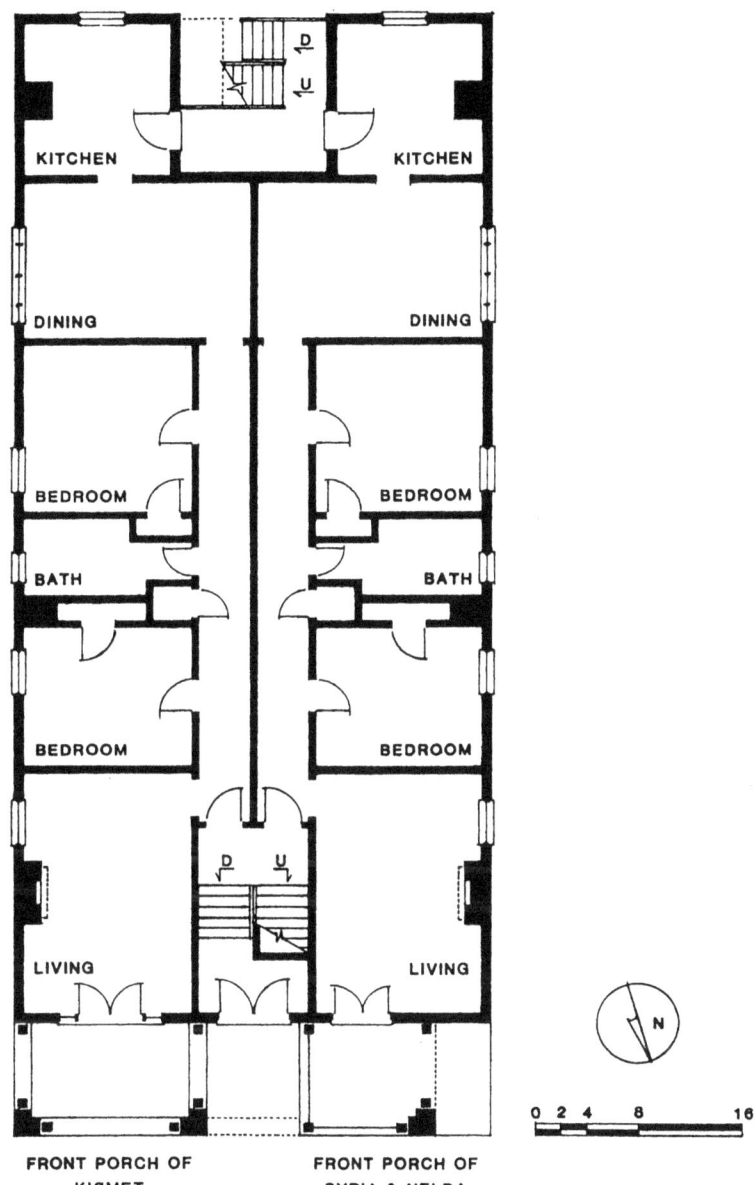

Fig. 19. Syria, Kismet, Nelda apartment buildings, 1904, first floor plan (measured drawing).

Half and Half 25

Fig. 20. Syria, Kismet, Nelda apartment buildings, 1904.

adaptation of Scheibler's neoclassical manner to the apartment building program.

More revealing are a trio of apartment buildings of complementary design known as Syria, Kismet, and Nelda (fig. 20). These curious names had meaning for the clients as well as for the tenants: Syria and Kismet were reportedly inspired by William Robinson's Masonic associations, and Nelda was the name of Fred Bruckman's sister. Flemish-bond brickwork recalls Scheibler's earliest house designs, but the character of each building's twin three-story porch towers is new. The first story of each porch is brick masonry cut through with large openings framed by angled wood inserts. The upper stories are open framework with multiple square-cut wooden posts at the corners. Syria and Nelda have a single gable over both porch towers, while Kismet has a pronounced division at the center of the facade and a gable over each porch tower.

The Arden apartment building (fig. 21) is similar in concept. Here, however, the twin porch towers rest on a masonry arcade with three rounded archways, and the open framework above terminates in nearly invisible hip roofs instead of gables.

These apartment buildings were rather unsophisticated, but they demonstrated Scheibler's ability to give new shape to established forms. Classical features quickly gave way to a refreshingly styleless architecture. Wooden members were handled vigorously, taking on some of the qualities of trees and branches in the exposed structure of the openwork porch towers. But it was decorative elements that represented the most telling departure from convention. At Syria, Kismet, and Nelda, art-glass transoms had oversized floral motifs that were apparently de-

Fig. 21. Arden apartment building, 1904.

rived from designs by M. H. Baillie Scott, a major figure in the English Arts and Crafts Movement.[10] The dining room and living room windows had exposed steel I-beams for lintels and art glass with vinelike motifs copied from Olbrich.[11] At the Arden, an art-glass lunette depicting a sailing ship was copied out of a book on contemporary English architecture and decoration.[12]

This art glass may have been Scheibler's first custom-fabricated glass, and the I-beam became a Scheibler trademark. But more important, these details represented Scheibler's first known direct borrowings from progressive European sources. From now on, Scheibler's designs would be based on such unconventional models, as promptly demonstrated in a sixth apartment building for Robinson and Bruckman.

3 Old Heidelberg

TO ALL IMMEDIATE APPEARANCES, the Old Heidelberg apartment building (fig. 22) sprang full-blown and with great suddenness from the mind of the architect in the spring of 1905. There had been intimations of a new direction in Scheibler's previous work, but nothing to indicate the thorough transformation represented by the Old Heidelberg.[1]

According to one published report, clients Robinson and Bruckman wanted "something unique, and of a worthy appearance to occupy [the site] in one of the most aristocratic [sic] neighborhoods of the city [i.e.,

Fig. 22. Old Heidelberg apartment building, 1905. Open space in front of the building is foreshortened by the photograph.

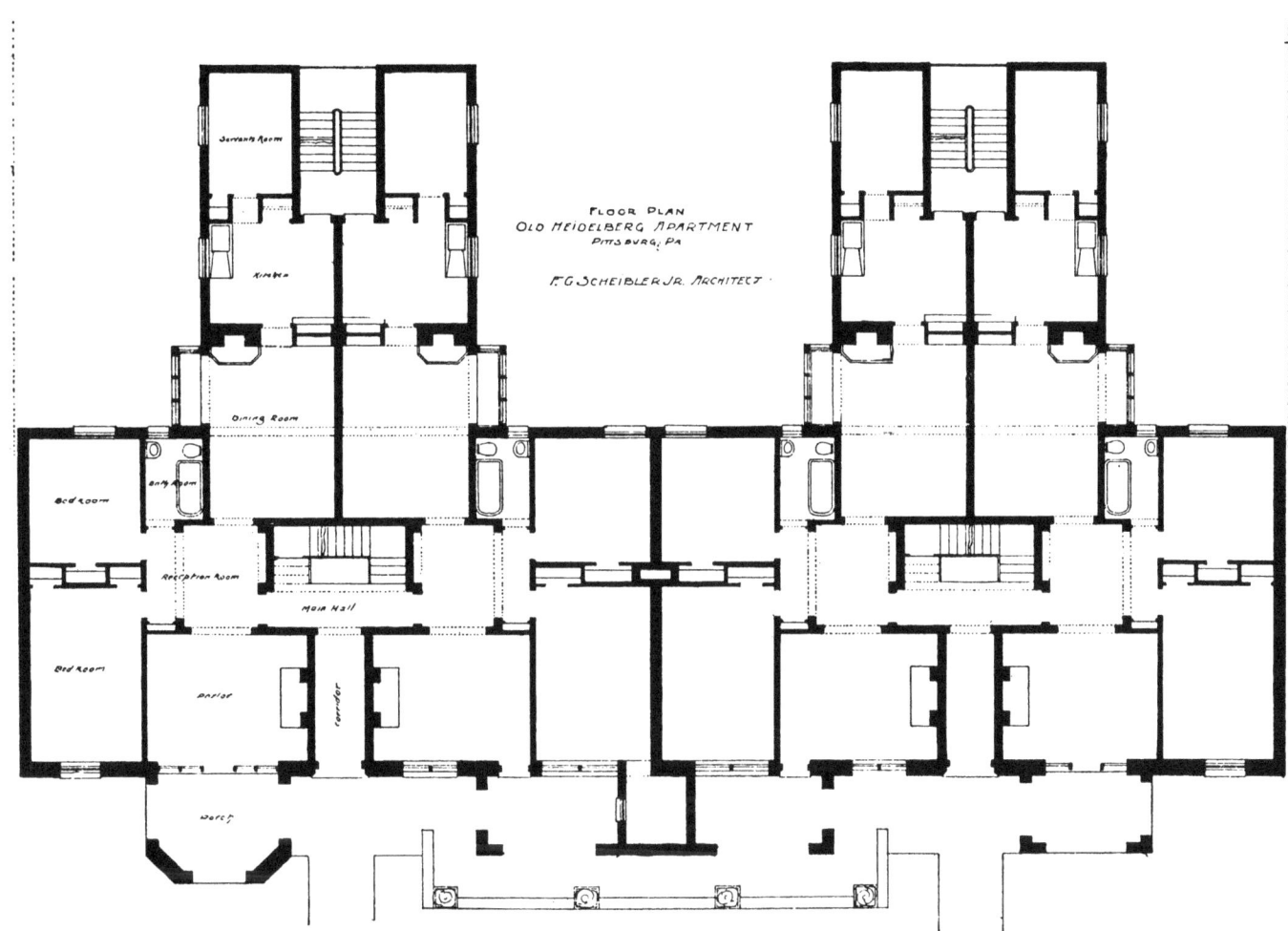

Fig. 23. Old Heidelberg apartment building, 1905, first floor plan.

Park Place]."[2] Fred Bruckman provided the name Old Heidelberg because his family had emigrated from Heidelberg, Germany. This Germanic theme would have found sympathy with Scheibler as well. A published announcement of the project, written prior to construction, stated that the building was to be "of the old Dutch [Deutch?] type," built of "bright red pressed brick, tastefully trimmed with gray brick, terra cotta, and stone," with great porches, gables, and dormers.[3] Since only the "great porches" charac-terize the executed building, a preliminary version of the design must have been significantly altered in the course of the design process. Scheibler's moment of progressive realization may indeed have been sudden. Robinson and Bruckman must have monitored this process and approved the final design, taking comfort in the building's Old World flavor while sanctioning its more unconventional aspects.

In plan the Old Heidelberg consists of two T-shaped halves joined along a shared a party wall (see fig. 23). Each half has its own entry and stair hall and could theoretically stand alone. There are four L-shaped apartments on each of three floors—each apartment occupying half of a T. The T-shaped forms afford a continuous street front, permit light and air to penetrate into courts at the rear, and allow for a more centralized arrangement of rooms. Each apartment has a living room, dining room, and two bedrooms that radiate from a reception room that is entered from the public stair hall. A kitchen, a bathroom, and a maid's room are logically subordinate in the plan. This layout was not in itself particularly innovative, but it was a step removed from the linear long-hall plan, and Scheibler took maximum advantage by creating axes and cross-axes from room to room to foster an open feeling.

The main elevation (fig. 22) belies the dichotomy of the overall plan. The facade is bilaterally symmetrical, focused not at the twin backbones of the Ts but at a central axis corresponding to the party wall. Scheibler obtained a single unified image by subordinating the dual entrances and manipulating two key elements: the roof and porches. The roof accounts for a full one-third of the height of the elevation, and Scheibler gave it a central focus by raising it at the center and accenting it with a small dormer. Four three-story porch towers are paired A-B-B-A. The outer ones stand independently and are largely of openwork timber; the inner ones are combined into a single masonry unit, at one with the fabric of the building. By their respective materials and positions, the porches bracket and accent the center of the facade. A name panel on the central axis forms a visual link with the dormer directly above.

Previously, Scheibler might have chosen a neoclassical means to this same end. In fact, the tripartite compositional scheme is rooted in Scheibler's classical training, and the mass of the central porch towers acts not unlike a portico, as at Hawkins School. The classical analogy breaks down quickly, however, and even formal aspects depart significantly from classical precedent. Symmetry, for example, though present in gross forms, is disturbed in detail. The outer porch towers differ in both plan—one is polygonal and one is rectangular—and detailing, and fenestration includes a wide variety of window types, sizes, and placements differing both from side to side and floor to floor. If the twelve units were to be broken out of the facade and viewed independently, nearly every one would differ in elevation. Van Trump noted that the disposition of openings and ornament creates a "feeling of asymmetrical movement."[4] Beyond gross forms, the composition is quite free.

A large measure of the building's coherence comes from the constant white surface of walls that are uniformly coated with a layer of white cement or stucco.[5] A hallmark of the European vernacular cottage tradition, stucco was economical, easy to use, and offered effective weatherproofing. It could provide surface continuity and sculptural plasticity, while heightening the contrast between solids and voids: windows in a stucco wall, for example, may appear as dark cutouts, especially when recessed and used without surface moldings. All of these qualities made stucco attractive to the European progressives.[6] Said M. H. Baillie Scott: "When in doubt, whitewash."[7]

This first use of stucco was an important breakthrough for Scheibler. He quickly apprehended the qualities of the material and used stucco extensively for the next five years—so much so that stucco buildings in Pittsburgh from the period are attributed to Scheibler almost as a matter of course. At the Old Heidelberg, stucco provides the building with sufficient continuity and closure to withstand the disintegrative effects of the fenestration. It also counteracts the structural expressionism of the outer porch towers, where the exposed timber framing and I-beam lintels speak boldly of things that stucco adeptly hides.

Scheibler's task was to design an apartment building that would fit into a suburban neighborhood of private homes and attract "aristocratic" residents to apartment living. Scheibler addressed these requirements by obscuring the compartmentalized nature of the program and cloaking a rather large multiunit building in the guise of a country house. The steep sheltering roof, timber-framed porches, free composition, and stucco surfacing were all traditional domestic features highly evocative of Old World housing. An early discussion of the building mentioned the Old Heidelberg's resemblance to a freestanding house, and an early advertisement remarked upon the prevailing "atmosphere of rural Germany" and "the cozy, homelike aspect of the Fatherland's treasured homes."[8]

Another published discussion of the building stated that the Old Heidelberg drew "its inspiration from the Art Nouveau movement as it is understood in Germany."[9] In fact, it was apparently modeled after a house designed by Joseph Maria Olbrich in Darmstadt, Germany.

Joseph Maria Olbrich (1867–1908) was a founding member of the Viennese Secession, an association of architects, painters, and sculptors who seceded from the conservative control of the Vienna Kunstlerhaus in 1897.[10] The Secessionists held that every age has its own "sensitivity" and worked to encourage and disseminate the art of their age. They advocated the introduction of foreign art into the previously inwardly focused Vienna art world and introduced the English Arts and Crafts Movement, the Glasgow Secession, and Art Nouveau to Viennese audiences. The foreign progressive movements were well received; but Secessionist art was deeply rooted in Viennese culture and its most prominent architect practitioner, Otto Wagner, crafted an indigenous marriage of classical austerity and baroque flair in his progressive work.

Olbrich's leadership in the Secession was short-lived, for in 1899 Prince Ernst Ludwig of Hesse asked him to come to Darmstadt to join an artists' colony that he was establishing to promote utopian reform through an intermingling of art and life.[11] Here Olbrich designed a large exhibition hall complex, a studio building, and seven houses for resident artists, including the Christiansen house. A conscious field for experimentation, the Darmstadt houses were derived from Germanic vernacular dwellings "cleaned up and given a more elegant silhouette, then garnished with lively details."[12] This development of contemporary domestic design from traditional rural sources was comparable to the practice of the English Arts and Crafts Movement, with which Olbrich had a growing acquaintance.[13]

Olbrich composed his houses of fairly simple geometric volumes with flat stucco surfaces, but he cut them through with numerous openings and decorated

Fig. 24. Joseph Maria Olbrich, Christiansen house, 1901, perspective rendering.

them both inside and out with an extraordinary variety of colorful patterns and ornaments of his own invention. Like other progressives, Olbrich designed nearly every aspect of his buildings, from teapots to gardens. Each building was itself an ornament in the landscape.

Scheibler may have discovered Olbrich at the St. Louis world's fair, where an ensemble of rooms by Olbrich was exhibited. He almost surely found a published portfolio of Olbrich's work at the Carnegie Library, for he soon acquired his own copy, and referred to it extensively in designing the Old Heidelberg. Scheibler never again modeled a project directly after one of Olbrich's own (of which there were not many, owing to Olbrich's premature death), but Scheibler discovered a natural affinity for this free spirit. He made free use of Olbrich's decorative details at the Old Heidelberg and elsewhere, and Olbrich's feel for simple composition and inventive detail, and his sense of gaiety and charm, never left Scheibler's work.

Viewed from the proper angle, the facade of the Old Heidelberg corresponds closely with Olbrich's perspective rendering of the Christiansen house (fig. 24), published in the Olbrich portfolio.[14] Here is the Old Heidelberg's stucco surfacing and high tile roof, its projecting central mass with porch openings, its dormer and its chimneys, and the source of its name panel. Scheibler adopted and adapted Olbrich's design for his own purposes, flopping it into bilateral symmetry, extending it at both ends with his own devices, and moving the name panel to a position of centrality. Notably, this name panel departed from Olbrich's model in detail. Scheibler's drawings show that a geometric treatment was planned for a time;

but the executed design included depictions of a waterwheel and a village street executed in mosaic tile—more Old World atmosphere. Unfortunately, these lower portions of the panel have since been obliterated, and only the name remains.

Many other elements of the Old Heidelberg's decorative program can be traced to projects in the Olbrich portfolio. The exposed brick imposts and I-beams on the left-hand porch, the raised plaster heart and wave trim around the third story of the central porches, and the wood trim under the eaves are taken from Olbrich's Blaue house (fig. 25).[15] The checked impost blocks and exposed I-beams of the right-hand porch, the timber-framed window bay on the left side of the facade, and the cyma-curve bases of the projecting dining room bays at the rear of the building are all borrowed from Olbrich's Stade double house (fig. 26).[16]

For the public halls (see fig. 27), Scheibler planned art-glass doors and painted decorations taken from Olbrich's design for the hall at his Kuntze house (fig. 28), although ultimately a different door design was used and the painted decorations may or may not have been executed.[17] In the apartment inte-

Fig. 25. Joseph Maria Olbrich, Blaue house, 1903–1904.

Fig. 26. Joseph Maria Olbrich, Stade double house, ca. 1902.

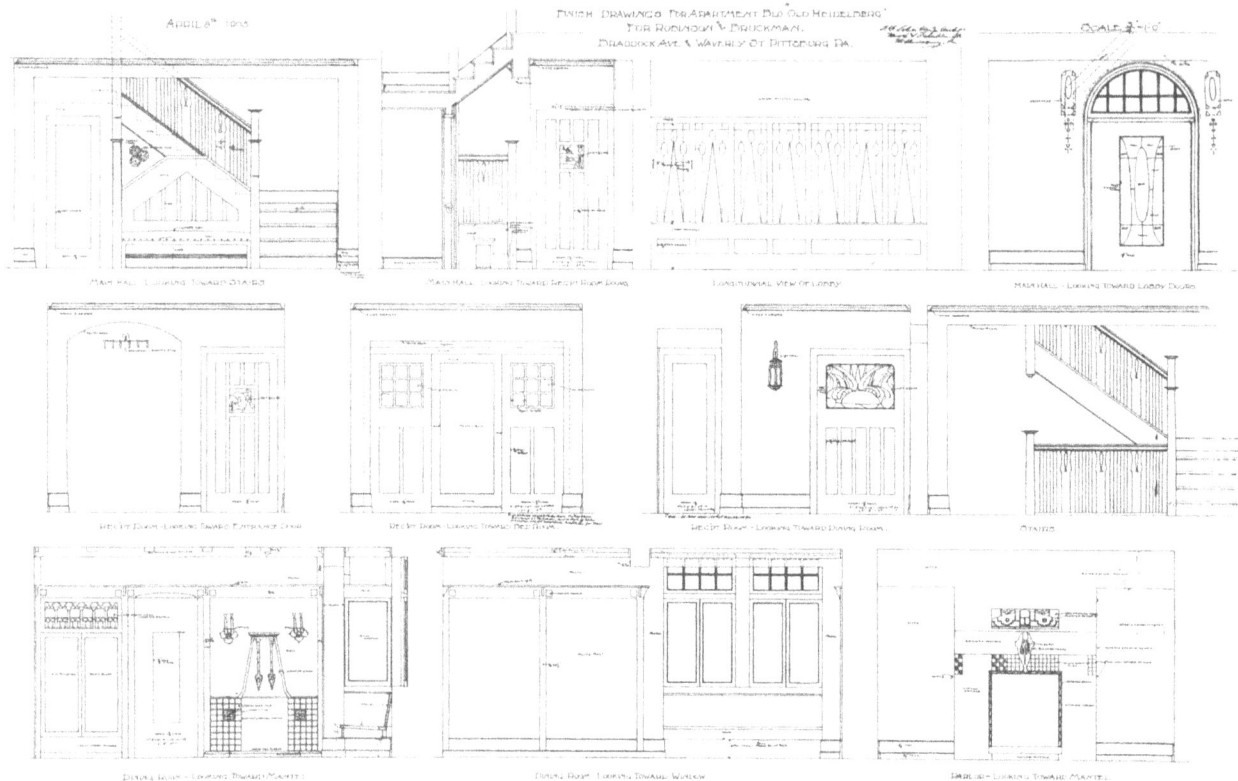

Fig. 27. Old Heidelberg apartment building, 1905, interior elevations. Not all of these details were executed.

Fig. 28. Joseph Maria Olbrich, Kuntze house, 1902–1903, hall, perspective rendering.

riors (see fig. 27), white plaster walls and simple wood trim prevail; but the living rooms are refined and elegant with parquet floors and marble fireplaces. The fireplaces were copied from the one in Olbrich's "Tea Salon," one of the rooms at the St. Louis fair. Scheibler may have seen this room if he visited the fair; he certainly knew it from the portfolio. Scheibler's version utilizes light gray marble for the fireplace surround, inset with dark gray checkerboard squares.[18]

Olbrich wasn't Scheibler's only progressive source, however, even at this early stage. The dining rooms (fig. 29) are finished in a more casual and even rustic manner typical of the English Arts and Crafts Move-

Fig. 29. Old Heidelberg apartment building, 1905, a dining room.

ment. Built-in wood furnishings include cabinets and a window seat; the walls have vertical strips of wood reminiscent of half-timbering, topped by a plate rail; and the ceilings have exposed wood beams. The fireplace has a specific English source—it replicates the raised polygonal hearth, the copper hood, and the tile surround with figural motifs of the fireplace at Baillie Scott's House at Crowborough. Square cutouts in the plate rail came from the Studio Flat of Scottish architect Charles Rennie Mackintosh. Both sources were illustrated in a book in Scheibler's library.[19]

There were other more random sources as well. Art-glass lunettes above the entry doors, featuring birds and telephone wires, were borrowed from a design by Arnold Lyongrun.[20] Art glass with a green balloonlike motif came from a published design by British designer A. Wickham Jarvis.[21]

And then there are the mushrooms. Decorative natural motifs such as plants and animals were much favored by progressive designers of all persuasions. Such motifs were generally freely devised and employed in a flat stylized manner, although Olbrich, among others, also integrated more organic plant forms into the surfaces of his buildings. Trees and other foliage seem to grow out of the stucco walls or wood trim of his houses. The Old Heidelberg's mushrooms proceed from this context. The mushrooms are modeled in plaster relief and contained within a spandrel in the two-story window bay on the left side of the facade. They are not stylized, nor are they as integral to the design as was Olbrich's foliage. In fact, they are rather clumsy in execution. But they are Scheibler's own, dedicated to his daughter, and they are memorable.[22]

The Old Heidelberg's decorative motifs are both playful and romantic, recalling, in Belnap's words, the "nostalgic environment of picture books."[23] But the detailing is not arbitrary. Decorative elements are integrated into the architectural design: art glass fills windows and transoms; decorative tiles and marblework appear in fireplace surrounds; mushrooms fill spandrels; and hearts act as capitals. In this way, Scheibler places an extensive and wide-ranging decorative program at the service of his architectural concept.

The Old Heidelberg was sited to great advantage within its suburban context, being recessed considerably behind and slightly below the streets that run in front and to one side of it. The green open space in front provided a suggestively pastoral setting and an advantageous perspective for viewing the architecture—characteristics that persist to this day. Open space to the sides, however, was a temporary amenity.

There is no evidence that the Old Heidelberg was designed to be extended. Robinson and Bruckman didn't own all of the key property flanking the building until after the original section was built, and the practice of designing the side walls without windows was common. But the blank walls and neighboring vacant properties welcomed further construction, and in 1908 and 1909 Scheibler designed four cottages for the building's north end, a single cottage for its south end, and a freestanding house for an adjacent property (see fig. 30).[24]

The four cottages at the north end are collected all under one roof and are ambiguous in composition, and thus they are difficult to distinguish one from another without reference to plans. Since the entire site slopes gently toward the rear, the first level of the two cottages facing Braddock Avenue corresponds with the second level of the two cottages facing Waverly Street. The Waverly Street elevation is animated in profile, but starkly detailed. The single cottage at the south end is more straightforwardly composed: its narrow, focused facade recalls a townhouse. The adjacent freestanding house, built for William C. Hoffman, is linked to the south cottage by a gateway, and its materials and detailing render it part of the larger whole.

These new elements added a low, rambling, and asymmetrical quality to the original high-shouldered and carefully balanced Old Heidelberg (see figs. 31–32) and contributed a sense of closure to the site by extending the architecture toward the street

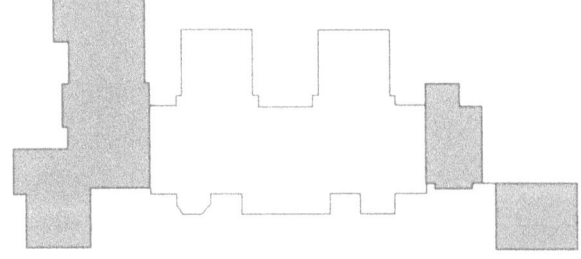

Fig. 30. Old Heidelberg apartment building, 1905, schematic plan. Shaded areas represent cottage additions and adjacent Hoffman house.

Fig. 31. Old Heidelberg apartment building, cottage additions, and Hoffman house, 1905–1909.

Fig. 32. Old Heidelberg apartment building, cottage additions, and Hoffman house, 1905–1909, postcard.

frontages. The resulting complex is dynamic in the variety and complexity of its architecture and in the relationship of the architecture to the landscape.

The Old Heidelberg is derivative in many aspects. But Scheibler's effective adaptations of Olbrich's original scheme, skillful manipulation of surface and structure, and artful ornamentation of the whole are a credit to his ingenuity and skill. Scheibler molded sometimes disparate elements into an unconventional but exceptional design, leaving the conventions of the railroad apartment behind.[25] The Old Heidelberg is the near ideal of a suburban apartment building. Like Olbrich's houses, it is an ornament in the landscape. There was, and probably still is, nothing quite like it short of Darmstadt.[26]

Scheibler solicited and received considerable attention for the building in the architectural press. It was published in the American journals *American Architect and Building News*, *Architecture*, and the *Brickbuilder*; in the regional American journal *Western Architect*, published in Minneapolis; and tellingly, in *Der Architekt*, a journal published in Vienna.[27] Belnap notes that "Scheibler's publication of Old Heidelberg in the Viennese journal *Der Architekt*, where a resemblance to contemporary Austrian architecture was noted, may have been a discreet acknowledgement of his debt to Olbrich."[28] It was also, it would seem, an effort to establish a role for himself in the international community of progressives, though Scheibler never again sought or received international attention.

Built in the same year as the establishment of a Beaux Arts curriculum at the new school of architecture at Carnegie Tech, the Old Heidelberg represented Scheibler's burgeoning interest in progressive architectural ideas.

4 ❦ The New Manner

FOLLOWING THE SUCCESS OF THE Old Heidelberg, Scheibler received commissions from new clients for four major apartment buildings over the next three years. These clients were doubtless acquainted with the Old Heidelberg, and their commissions suggest their approval of Scheibler's new manner and their willingness to promote it. The buildings that resulted achieved a high level of sophistication and demonstrated Scheibler's rapid assimilation of progressive ideas and principles.

The first two new apartment buildings, the Whitehall (fig. 33) and the Linwood (fig. 34), were each located not far from the Old Heidelberg. They were evidently designed concurrently, and were virtually a joint commission. Both were announced on March 24, 1906, and their building permits were issued within weeks of each other.[1] Harry D. Hasson, the client for the Whitehall, had a real estate office in Wilkinsburg. Daniel L. Dillinger, client for the Linwood, operated a coal and gas company in Westmoreland County and served as a bank official in Greensburg. He was an active speculator in Pittsburgh area real estate and was probably Hasson's uncle.[2] Hasson, Dillinger, and Scheibler would have numerous future involvements culminating in the Highland Towers apartment building.

Like the Old Heidelberg, the Whitehall and the Linwood are three-story buildings of moderate size, but their T-shaped plans correspond to one half of the Old Heidelberg, and they each contain only six units. The apartments in all three buildings are essentially identical in size and layout. Only the Linwood's ninety-degree angling of the maid's rooms at the rear deviates. All three buildings also feature stucco surfaces, irregular fenestration, paired timber-framed porch towers, and high roofs. The Whitehall and the Linwood are compositional dualities, however, without strong central axes, massed as if the central section of the Old Heidelberg had been removed and its outer sections brought together.

The Whitehall is rather traditional in feeling, primarily because the twin porches are gabled, as at Kismet. The stucco gables float free from the rest of the building's wall surfaces and are given extra wood posts for visual support. The gables provide vertical emphasis, and actually exacerbate the duality of the facade. This duality is addressed but not quite resolved by a prominent central entry, the most unconventional element of the facade. An entry surround of concentric pointed arches echoes the gables above and attempts to swell the doorway and to tether the eye at the building's midpoint, but without complete success. These arches may have their source in Olbrich, but their distorted shape has the flavor of Eastern Europe. Birds in flight add movement to the art-glass transoms of second-story windows; a color-

Fig. 33. Whitehall apartment building, 1906.

ful art-glass parrot once held forth over the front door.[3]

Scheibler gave the Linwood a more disciplined and more abstract treatment. Here, a pergola carried on piers joins the porches and resolves the duality of the design, and horizontal elements in the pergola, the porches, and the roofline counteract and balance the verticality of the massing. A rectilinear grid of horizontal and vertical lines accounts for most of the delineation of the facade, and special emphasis is placed on the crisp relationship between the strong lines of exposed structure and the flat white wall surfaces.

The tapered wood posts—with their exposed mortise and tenon joints, the exposed I-beams, and the checked impost blocks of the porches were directly appropriated from the Old Heidelberg. A historic photograph shows that the Linwood's front door orig-

Fig. 34. Linwood apartment building, 1906.

inally had an art-glass panel with one of Baillie Scott's oversized floral motifs, as previously employed at Syria, Kismet, and Nelda, and that domed lamps once flanked the entrance.

In both buildings, the individual apartment doors have art-glass panels with floral motifs, including irises. The apartments themselves have plaster walls, simple wood trim, and built-in window seats and cupboards. The living room fireplaces have brass hoods that are similar to those in the dining rooms of the Old Heidelberg, but here there are surrounds of white glass, instead of just plaster.

The Whitehall and the Linwood achieve the same general effect as the Old Heidelberg without some of its more nostalgic qualities, and the Linwood in particular suggests future directions in Scheibler's work. The ultimate significance of both buildings lies in their indication that Scheibler would shape a pro-

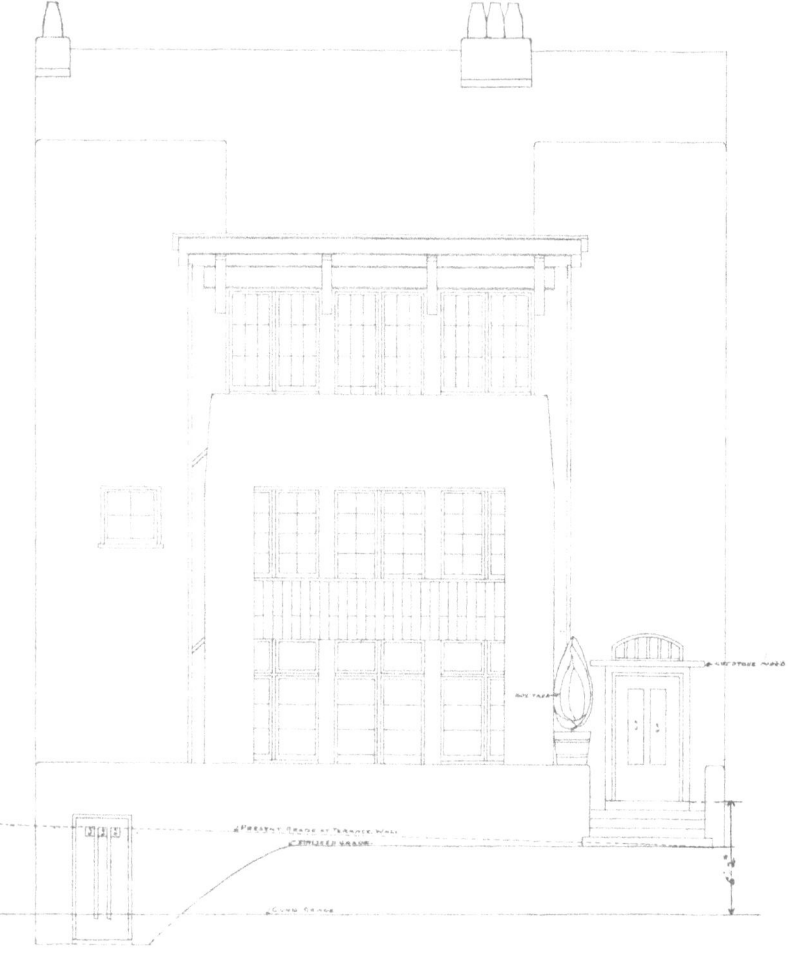

Fig. 35. Coleman apartment building, 1906, front elevation. The potted bush is drawn in a characteristically Secessionist manner.

gressive manner that would define his career. The Old Heidelberg would not be an anomaly.

The Coleman apartment building of 1906 (figs. 35–36) followed closely after the Whitehall and the Linwood.[4] Here the Old Heidelberg's plan is halved and halved again to produce L-shaped units, one on each of three floors. The floor plans and interior detailing echo its predecessors, and the narrow stucco facade has a single central porch tower flanked by tall blocky masses, recalling the porch towers of Scheibler's previous apartment buildings and the forms of enframement in his early commercial work. The facade departs from precedent, however, in the sheer strength of its massing, and in its near total lack of common domestic imagery—even a cornice. The porch tower has little of the exposed timber of previous versions. There is virtually no exterior ornament at all. The Coleman facade continues a process of abstraction begun at the Linwood, but the leap forward in Scheibler's developing style is sudden. The key is seemingly found in the influence of Charles Rennie Mackintosh (1868–1928) of Scotland.

Mackintosh, architect and graphic designer, was the key figure of the Glasgow Secession. The quartet of Mackintosh, Herbert McNair, and Frances and Margaret MacDonald were known as "the Four" when they proclaimed their independence from the local art scene and struck out in new directions.[5] Mackintosh was said by Muthesius to be on the short list of "truly original artists, the creative minds of the modern movement."[6] His exteriors were bold essays in stone or stucco with strong lines and planer surfaces, deeply rooted in the Scottish vernacular, but

Fig. 36. Coleman apartment building, 1906.

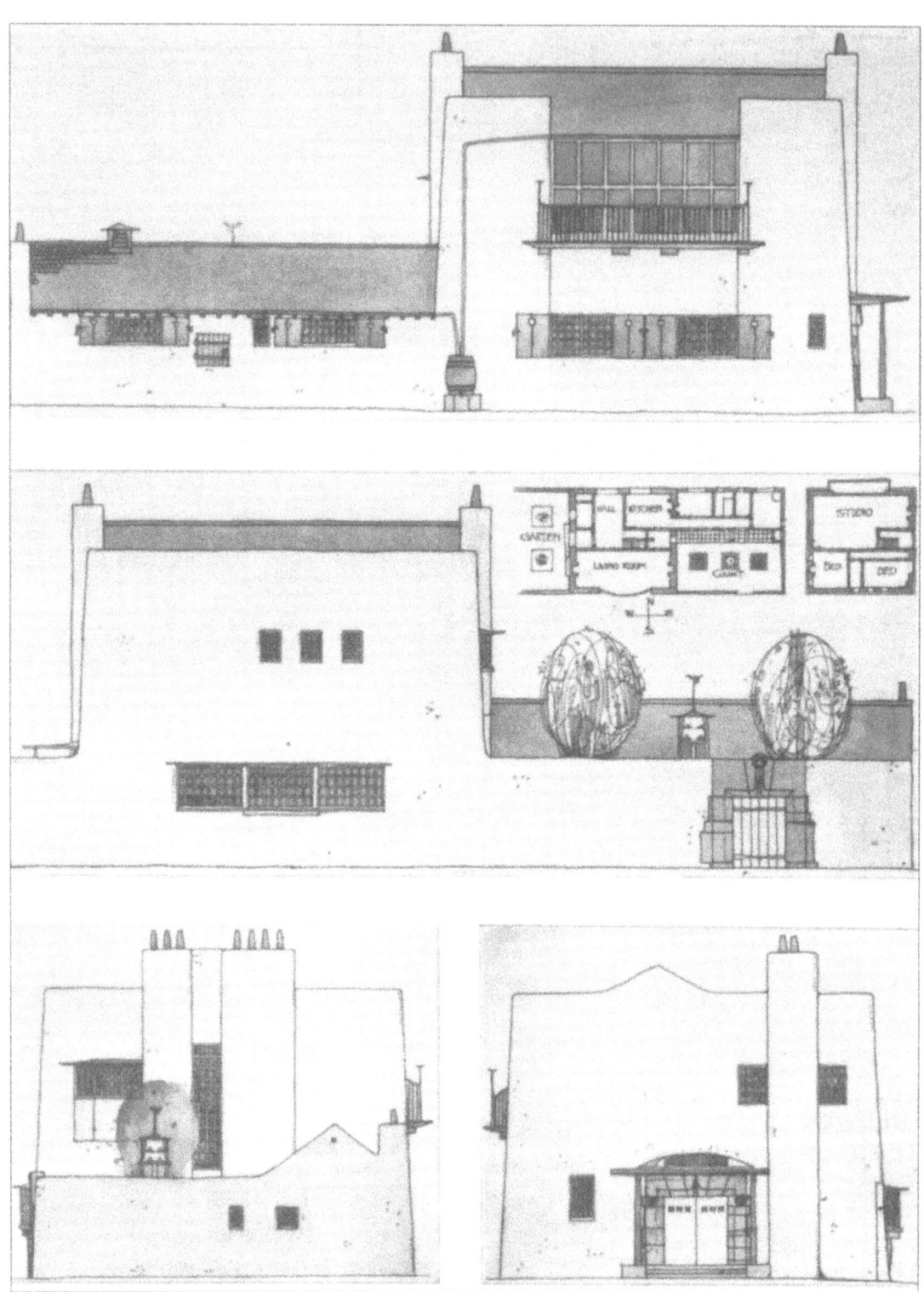

Fig. 37. Charles Rennie Mackintosh, design for an artist's country cottage and studio, 1901, elevations.

uniquely expressive all the same. His interiors were delicate and totally unified in concept. His decorative work favored floral motifs in a flowing but essentially linear manner derived from his experience in graphic design. Mackintosh's interiors were influential for a time, but his architecture had virtually no lasting impact either in Scotland or on the Continent, and certainly none in the United States.[7]

Mackintosh's 1901 design for an artist's country cottage and studio (fig. 37) was never built, but its elevations demonstrated Mackintosh's strengths as a designer. Its planer stucco surfaces achieved a highly plastic look, but Mackintosh the graphic artist was readily apparent in the project's delineation and detailing.[8] Scheibler probably knew this project from drawings published in *Dekorative Kunst*, a journal that he evidently consulted often, and referred to while designing the Coleman apartment building.

The framing wall sections, the glazed central void, the asymmetrical fenestration (with a single small window to one side), and the entry configuration of Scheibler's facade all have specific referents in Mackintosh's front and left side elevations. The peaked roofs, almost hidden in Scheibler's work, are a less obvious parallel.[9] Most important, Scheibler absorbed the inherent simplicity and strength of Mackintosh's design. In choosing Mackintosh over Olbrich for this design, Scheibler opted for greater abstraction. In fact, the elimination of extraneous detail is even greater in Scheibler's building than in his model. He did more than trade one vocabulary for another, however. The elements borrowed from Mackintosh, though recognizable, are integrated into a framework equally recognizable as Scheibler's own.

The Coleman apartment building was both a rare

Fig. 38. Adolph Loos, Steiner house, 1910.

American reflection of Mackintosh's craft and one of the first minimalist buildings in United States. It appeared a few years before Irving Gill's exercises in the simplified Mission Style in southern California, and only the Larkin Building (1904) and Unity Temple (1906–1907) are of comparable abstraction among Frank Lloyd Wright's early works. It also predated Adolph Loos's celebrated Steiner house in Vienna (fig. 38) of 1910, which is only marginally more abstract.

A tendency toward austerity persevered in Scheibler's work, but never again reached this intensity. Nothing is known to explain the Colemans' interest in (or tolerance of) such a building—James H. Coleman was in real estate. Perhaps economics played a role; but this sort of thing was too severe for the average client.

Scheibler found another adventuresome client in Edward C. Wefing, a real estate man in Pittsburgh's Shadyside area who had visionary plans for that neighborhood's commercial district along Walnut Street. When Wefing's store and apartment building was erected in 1908 it was by far the largest structure on a street that boasted only a few shops. His faith was well placed, however, for today the building is at the center of a fashionable shopping district.

With its four storefronts and one-bedroom apartments, the so-called Minnetonka Building (fig. 39) is distinctly urban architecture. The building entirely

Fig. 39. Minnetonka Building, 1908. Shown with alterations.

fills its lot. The shallowness of the lot dictated a rectangular footprint, and its breadth ensured horizontal massing, departures from the T- or L-shaped plans and strong verticality of Scheibler's recent apartment buildings. The horizontality and the arrangement of the apartments around two entries recall the Old Heidelberg, but here the roof is flat and the entries are accented rather than minimized.

White brick replaces stucco on the Minnetonka Building's upper stories, yielding a harder surface and more urbane appearance. The brick is used in broad flat surfaces, however, almost as if it were stucco. A half-timbered panel at the center of the facade and the nearly flush casement windows used throughout reinforce the sense of flatness and introduce a strong sense of line. A pair of metalwork light fixtures originally broke the plane of the facade, but their linear construction was in keeping with the prevailing character.[10] Stucco *is* used between the vertical timbers of the central panel and on the building's rounded corners where it alternates in bands with arcs of glazing. The rounded corners unify the front and sides of the building and give a sense of wrap and closure to the planer elevations.

Such rounded corner treatments were popular urban foils in contemporary Vienna; the precise form used here—which incorporates a hingelike indentation at the parapet—is related to that used by Otto Wagner in his apartment house with shops at Link Wienzeile 38 (fig. 40).[11] Scheibler may have referred to buildings such as this one in developing his design, but he greatly simplified the concept by stripping the rounded form of all extraneous detail.

If the upper stories of the Minnetonka Building are closed, the first story is open. If the upper stories

Fig. 40. Otto Wagner, Linke Wienzeile 38 apartment building, 1898–1899.

The New Manner 47

Fig. 41. Minnetonka Building, 1908, detail.

show an inclination toward flat surfaces and strong lines, the bottom story is an exercise in contrasting solids and voids. Here heavy surrounds of cut stone alternate with plate-glass display windows (fig. 41). The surrounds are dramatic compositions of projected and recessed blocks assembled as tapered square columns and heavy lintels. The surrounds are equivalent to porch towers, compressed and made integral with the mass of the building. They have a quality at once skeletal and massive: they are columnar in relation to the stories above, but act as solids in contrast to the voids of the adjoining windows and doorways.

The entry surrounds serve as a frame for heavy wood doors and delicate art-glass transoms with a design of abstracted roses that is pure Mackintosh (see figs. 41–42).[12] Inside these doors, Scheibler imparts extraordinary drama to the stair hall (fig. 43). As the world of the street is left behind, the southern sun streams through the transom, casting blotches of color on white surfaces. The wainscoted walls, the flooring, and even the steps are milky-white marble. The steps are very steep and the first flight is long. Beyond the first landing, the stair turns, then turns again. By the upper landing, balustrades have taken on rounded profiles set with colorful glass mosaics that glisten in blue light streaming through an art-glass skylight, a window into heaven.

Wood doors with bright panels of floral art glass again mark the apartments, but the interiors are a little anticlimactic. The apartments are arranged in an A-B-B-A pattern of mirror-image pairs on each floor. Their plans (fig. 44) are necessarily more centralized and complex than Scheibler's previous efforts. The slightly larger inner units have continuous circu-

Fig. 42. Charles Rennie Mackintosh, Windyhill, 1901, rose motif.

The New Manner 49

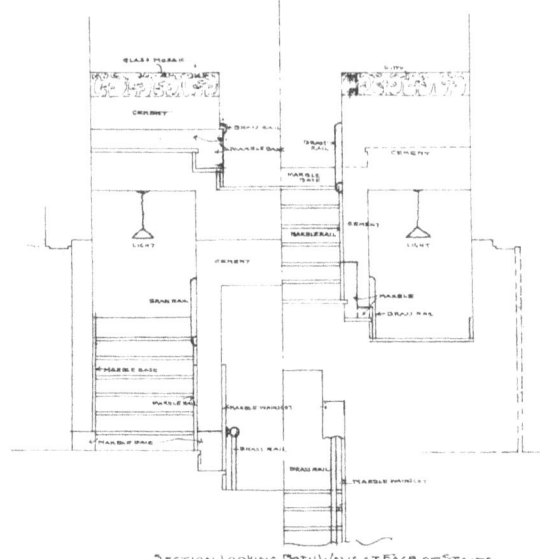

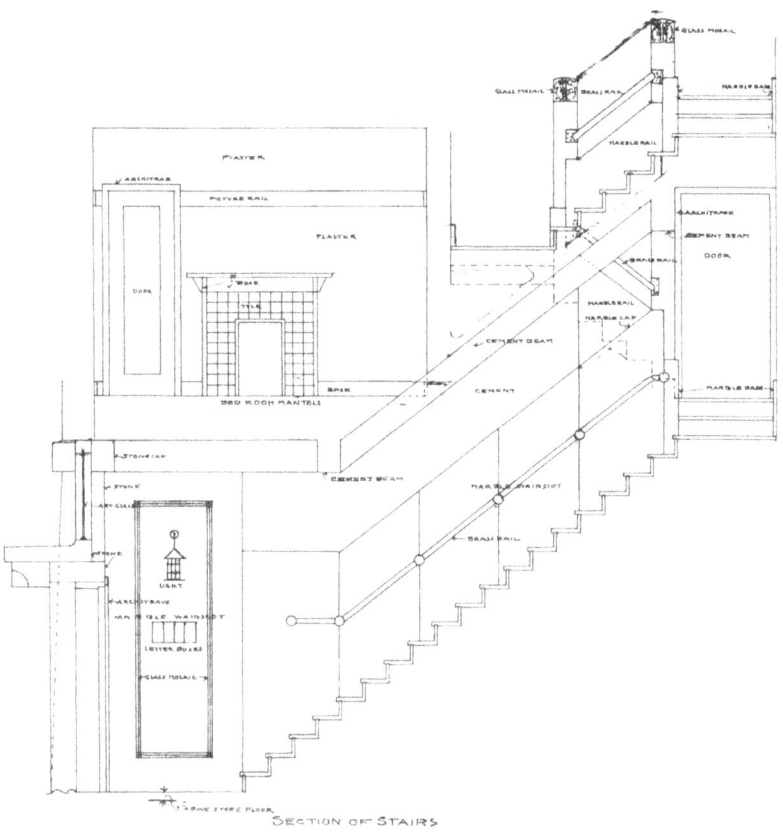

Fig. 43. Minnetonka Building, 1908, stair sections.

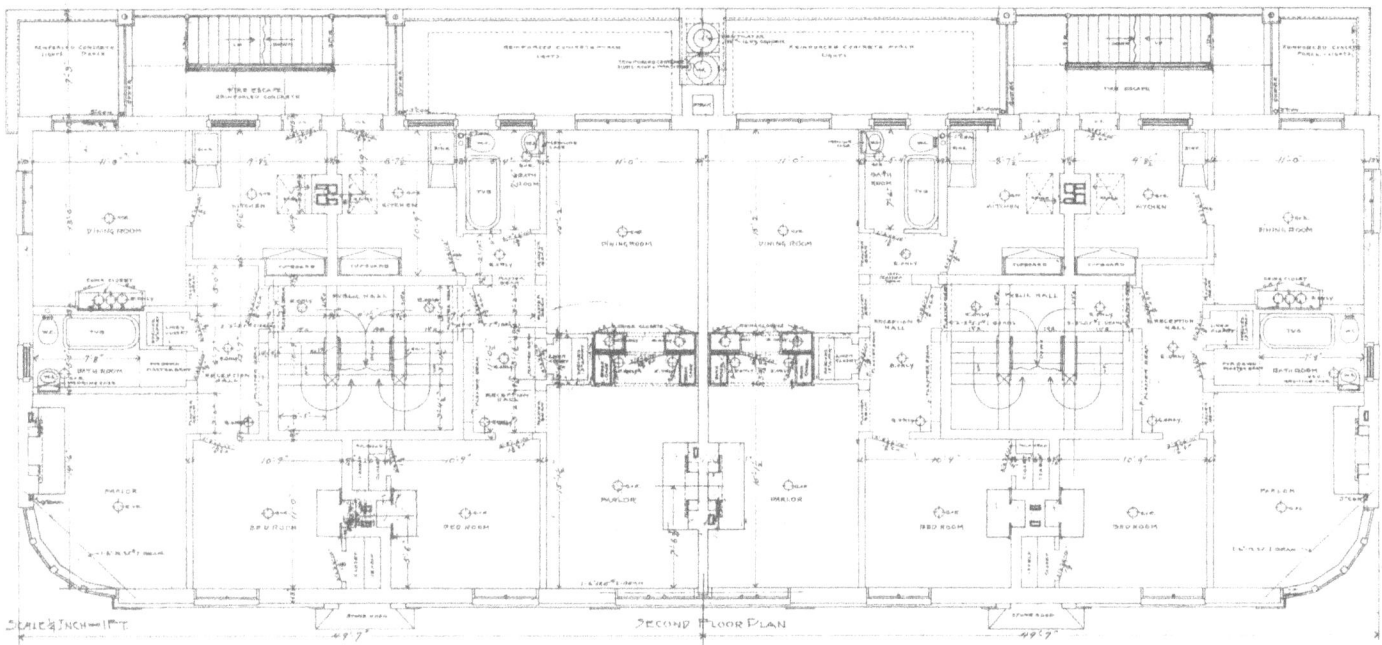

Fig. 44. Minnetonka Building, 1908, second floor plan.

lation and feature virtually freestanding bookcase and cupboard units between the living and dining rooms—where the outer units have their bathrooms. The "parlors" of all units feature fireplace surrounds of marble and tile that are austere and rectilinear and derived from Mackintosh.[13] The bowed corner windows survey Walnut Street.

There were also several public and quasi-public commissions during the early period of Scheibler's new manner. In the case of the Wilkins School (fig. 45), an earlier Scheibler design was quite literally transformed by the architect's newfound approach to design. The commission dated back to 1904, when the Swissvale Borough School Board, upon the motion of Dr. William T. Pyle, who later commissioned a house from Scheibler, decided that that the plans that Scheibler had drawn for the yet unbuilt Hawkins School would be used for the proposed Wilkins School as well.[14] This decision simplified the board's planning process and made economic sense, theoretically requiring only the change of three letters on the name stones, a change actually made on at least one rendering of Hawkins School (see fig. 15).

The Wilkins School project went forward, how-

Fig. 45. Wilkins School, 1907, postcard. Antonia Oehmler Scheibler sent this post card to her mother in Pasadena, California, in 1909.

ever, only after Hawkins School opened in the fall of 1906.[15] By this time Scheibler was using an entirely different design vocabulary. As built, Wilkins School was virtually identical to Hawkins School in plan and massing, housing eight classrooms on two floors in a rectangular brick box under a hip roof. It was the detailing that was new. Classical ornamentation gave way to clean wall surfaces and loosely Secessionist detail. Classical porticoes gave way to round-arched side entries flanked by tapered square columns with blocky capitals. Exposed I-beam lintels replaced flat arches.

The school's main entry was set within a masklike overlay of white stone crowned with a peak, a progressive reinterpretation of the pedimented classical pavilion at Hawkins School. Openings were crisply cut into the sheer stone surface. The only detail, a namestone orb inspired by Mackintosh, was as if drawn with a pen on the white stone.[16] This overlay recalls both the facade of the Coleman apartment building and the white-glass fireplace surrounds at the Linwood and the Whitehall. Unfortunately, Wilkins School was destroyed in a gas explosion in 1925.

In the case of the Wilkinsburg Natatorium (fig. 46), Scheibler brought his new manner to what was for him a brand-new building type. The natatorium was an ultimately unrealized 1907 project of the Wilkinsburg Natatorium Company, a quasi-public organization formed at a time when the indoor swimming pool was becoming a common urban amenity. Scheibler's drawings show a scheme that incorporates a pool on the first floor and locker rooms and bathing rooms on the second floor. The building's sides are party walls, recessed at the second story to allow for fenestration. The facade is essentially a stage set that formally presents the building to the urban streetscape while screening the utilitarian box behind.

At Wilkins School, a planer mask was overlaid on the building. Here, it essentially *replaces* the building. The facade is sheer and stark, with no base and no cornice, its plane broken only by the disparate geometric shapes of a central entry, two windows groups, and hanging lamps. The entry is set in a low-springing half-circle arch (or omega arch) of the sort found in the work of both Olbrich and Frank Lloyd Wright.[17] Windows are vertically grouped and divided by spandrel panels with swirling female figure motifs, an arrangement identical to the mushroom bay at the Old Heidelberg. These spandrels are the purest incident of Art Nouveau in Scheibler's work. Each lamp, a halved cone in shape, is like a brass fireplace hood, hanging from its flat surround.

Fig. 46. Wilkinsburg Natatorium, 1907, front elevation.

This facade has its weaknesses. It is a loose and somewhat awkward assembly of parts rather than an integrated concept. The design is remarkably fresh, however, with none of the architectural baggage of Wilkins School. It would have been an astonishing presence in the Wilkinsburg streetscape; but the project never swam, and Scheibler's only natatorium was never built.

Nevertheless, in three short years Scheibler had demonstrated the strength of his new progressive manner.

5 Group Cottages

ONE MANIFESTATION of the progressive movements was a reformist effort led by architects and planners to improve living conditions for the working and middle classes. This effort took shape most prominently in England as the Garden City Movement, which promoted the creation of new self-sufficient towns that would realize the amenities of urban life in semirural and healthful surroundings. Garden City housing was intended to be a vast improvement on the crowded conditions and architectural monotony of typical urban housing. The remedy called for houses and broken housing rows that would be varied in architectural composition and set back behind gardens or courts. Special emphasis was laid on plantings and the provision of pleasant views and sunlight. In the hands of English architects such as Parker and Unwin and M. H. Baillie Scott, these buildings generally adopted the vernacular cottage idiom of the English Arts and Crafts Movement. Directly influenced by William Morris, the Arts and Crafts designers emphasized traditional building materials and techniques and functional simplicity in plans and massing, time-honored characteristics of the vernacular buildings of the English countryside.[1]

The Garden City and the Arts and Crafts Movements together produced a turn-of-the-century revival of English domestic architecture and were influential on the European continent and, to a lessor extent, in the United States as well. The architectural ideas appealed to certain American architects to whom other progressive modes may have seemed inordinately foreign and exotic. The planning ideas were belatedly employed in the so-called garden suburbs of the 1920s and 1930s, including Pittsburgh's own widely acclaimed Chatham Village.[2]

Years earlier, however, between 1907 and 1914, Scheibler was applying Garden City planning principles to multifamily housing in Pittsburgh. As the English sought to translate terrace housing into the Garden City context, Scheibler pursued the suburbanization of the American row house. Scheibler's term for his projects—group cottages—even has an English ring to it. Unlike some of his English colleagues, Scheibler left no clear evidence of social activism, but he must have shared some of their concerns. His group cottages demonstrated a willingness to address the need for multifamily housing and to seek worthy solutions. Scheibler must have advocated the concept to clients such as Robinson and Bruckman. Many of the group cottages proved to be successful speculative ventures for their clients, while they also supplied decent affordable housing at a time when many Pittsburgh-area residents were notoriously ill-housed.[3]

Scheibler's group cottages are comprised of row

Fig. 47. Titus de Bobula, row houses, 1905. Shown with alterations.

houses that are arranged in small groups and either aligned in a linear sequence or organized around a central court. Projects such as Hamilton Cottages and the Singer Place row houses take maximum advantage of their natural siting, and even the simplest groups have porches or sun porches and are set back behind front yards. Open green spaces are variously defined by walls, piers, and plantings.

Surprisingly, however, with few exceptions, the cottages themselves stand in considerable contrast to the vernacular cottage idiom of the Garden City architects. Specific sources for this work, if any, are not readily apparent. Titus de Bobula's design for a group of flat-roofed poured-concrete row houses (fig. 47) for Pittsburgh's Frank Avenue in 1905, although rather clumsy, is extraordinary in its reductionist qualities.[4] Scheibler could have known of these houses and might have received from them some of the inspiration and vocabulary for his group housing. In any event, Scheibler's immediate response to the group housing program was reductionist forms and flat roofs.

Between 1907 and 1909 Scheibler produced three types of row houses. All had planer brick walls, minimal detailing, and flat roofs. Five groups of the first and simplest houses (fig. 48) were built on Inglenook Place, in Pittsburgh's Homewood neighborhood.[5] The single plane of the facades and the continuous

Group Cottages 55

post-and-lintel construction of the porches emphasize the unity of each group, and indeed of the street as a whole, while shoulder-height stucco walls demarcate the porches of individual units. The only exterior decoration is a checkerboard motif incised into the butt ends of timbers at the eaves of the porch roofs.

Houses of the second row house type (fig. 49) were added to the original Inglenook Place development, and others were built separately a few blocks away on Bennett Street. These houses are simple in content but complex in their relationships. Each housing group consists of four units composed as a *single* integrated design; but the fenestration of the second story represents a *duality*; the piers and I-beams of the post-and-lintel porches divide the facade into *three* sections; and shoulder-height walls demarcate *four* individual porches. The result is a sophisticated if somewhat ambiguous composition of multiple, almost musical, rhythms. The group housing dichotomy of unity versus individuality is purposefully thrown into confusion. In the parlance of Robert Venturi, the design is an experiment in "juxtaposed contradictions."[6]

Fig. 48. Inglenook Place row houses, 1907.

Fig. 49. Bennett Street row houses, 1909.

All of this polyrhythmic activity effectively takes place within a single plane (or musical staff). Even the projecting porches read as lines instead of volumes. The I-beams, Scheibler's longest with clear spans of twenty-one feet, are employed solely to make possible the desired linear divisions.

In Scheibler's third row house design (fig. 50), first built on Pittsburgh's Aurelia Street, the porches become three-dimensional enclosed spaces, and the composition is active on two planes: the familiar plane of the brick front wall and a plane newly established by the projecting sun porches. The linear definition of the earlier houses has been replaced by the forceful manipulation of solids and voids. The planer surfaces are themselves broken down by the glazing of the sun porches and by window groups that appear larger than they are from being set into recessed stucco panels. These devices contribute to a more complex and more open treatment of the flat-roofed brick box.

The sun porches are an amenity, for they complement rather than replace living rooms. There are decorative art-glass transoms with lovely rose and calla lily motifs above the paired entries. But this is still very modest construction—the sixteen-foot wide units are even smaller in floor area than the first Inglenook Place houses. As a further statement of economy, Scheibler used this design for at least three other group cottage projects.

Closely related to this work is a group of workers' houses that Frank Lloyd Wright designed for the Larkin Company (fig. 51) in 1904.[7] But by the time this project was published, Scheibler's experiments with planer brick walls, sun porches, and paired entries were already well under way.

Hamilton Cottages (figs. 52–54) was designed for a familiar client, Robinson and Bruckman's Hamilton Realty Company, in a distinctly modest manner, but the project's scale and its location in Pittsburgh's Squirrel Hill neighborhood were a step up from Scheibler's previous group cottage projects. A watercolor perspective rendering (fig. 52) shows

Fig. 50. Aurelia Street row houses, 1909.

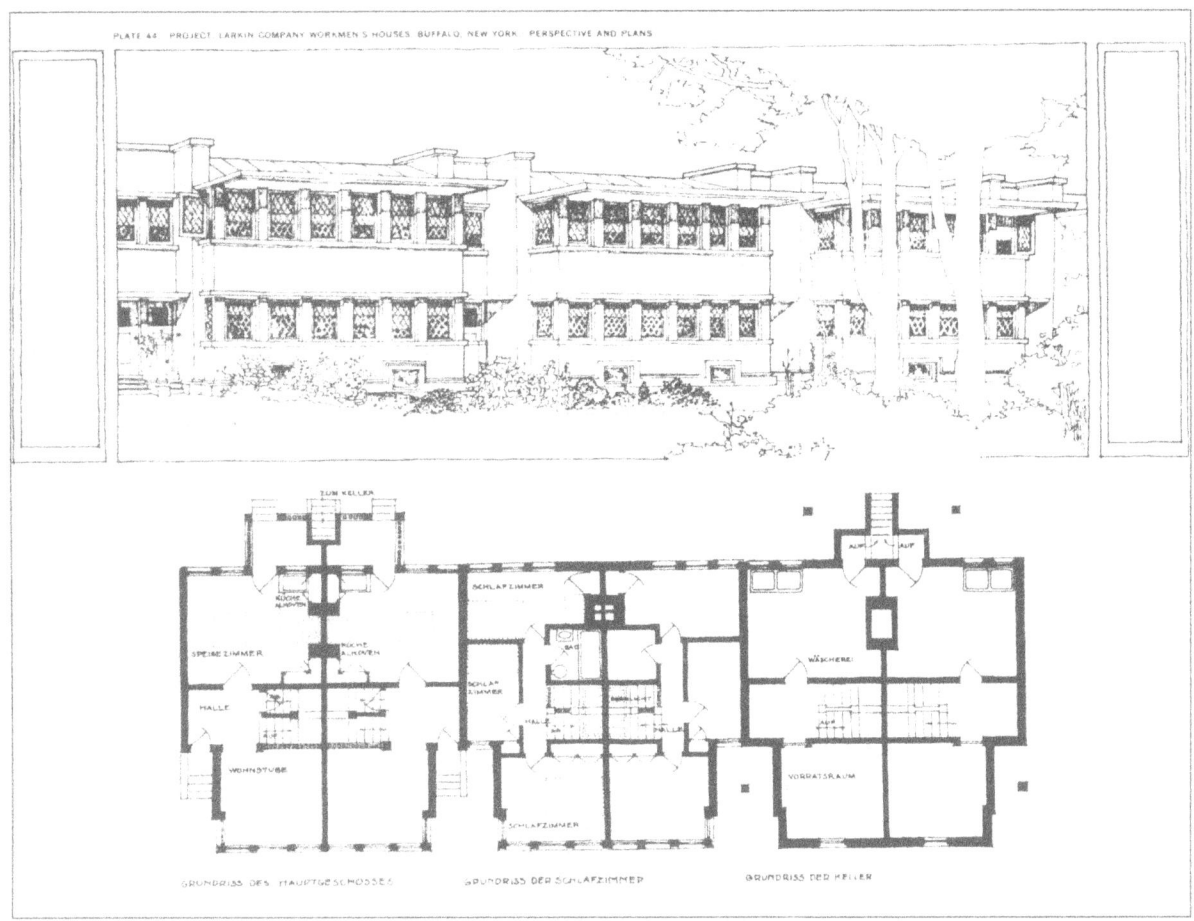

Fig. 51. Frank Lloyd Wright, Larkin Company workmen's houses, 1904, perspective rendering and plans.

that the original concept called for nineteen row houses grouped around a large central court. Six of these houses were built in 1910 in two groups of three facing Beacon Street. When the remainder of the houses were undertaken a year or so later, however, their design had been changed somewhat and the total number had grown to twenty-one. The new houses were organized in three groups of five around three sides of the court.[8]

All of the houses are of brick veneer construction with six rooms in two stories. The earlier houses have planer brick facades, broken only by their entries, shallow projecting sun porches, and paired windows that abut the eaves of a hip roof—just as depicted in the perspective rendering. The later houses, however, are more complicated configurations of geometric shapes and solid and glazed wall areas. With these it is as though gabled entry pavilions had been grafted onto the Aurelia Street houses and the second-story windows of Aurelia Street had

Group Cottages 59

Fig. 52. Hamilton Cottages, 1910–1911, perspective rendering.

then been countersunk deeply into the facade. The resulting composition is a sequence of three planes established by the projecting sun porches, the gabled wall sections, and the recessed window groups.

With this latter scheme, Scheibler progressed from his earlier experiments with unity and ambiguity to embrace the dichotomy inherent in group housing. At Hamilton Cottages, individual units remain subordinate to the whole in terms of siting and function, and the horizontal continuity of sun porches, window groups, and shared roofs ensures compositional unity. But the need for individuality is satisfied by the articulation of the gabled entry pavilions, replacing the continuous flat roofs and understated entries of Scheibler's previous group housing projects.

Hamilton Cottages is set back from the street behind plantings and a rubble stone wall. The central court, which measures a generous 150 by 200 feet, is common outdoor space landscaped with naturalistic groupings of trees and other plantings.[9] The houses facing the court can be reached only on foot along meandering walks. Sun porches project to catch the southern sun. Scheibler here accounts for all Garden City requirements, and the architecture, though noteworthy, ultimately takes a back seat to these concerns.

Willo'mound (fig. 55) and Meado'cots (fig. 56) are Scheibler's most artfully picturesque group cottages,

Fig. 53. Hamilton Cottages, 1910–1911.

Fig. 54. Hamilton Cottages, 1910–1911.

Fig. 55. Willo'mound, 1911, perspective rendering.

Fig. 56. Meado'cots, 1912.

and not in name only.[10] Here, the architecture and the environment are on more even footing. Both projects were designed to extend across entire blocks and face onto three streets. These sites encouraged Scheibler to develop more studied siting schemes that took advantage of all three frontages, resulting in increased architectural complexity and less naturalistic environments. Both projects have central courts, but these are architectural rather than naturalistic settings, and stucco piers frame formal entrances to the sites, replacing the rubble stone walls and meandering walks of Hamilton Cottages.

Willo'mound, which was never built, called for eighteen cottages, with pairs of units facing the two streets that flanked the site, three-unit groups pulled forward on the site at its front corners, and eight cottages spread along the rear of the site. The lot for Meado'cots was somewhat deeper and less broad, so that four units were planned to face each of the side streets, groups of three were again placed at the front corners, and six cottages were aligned across the center of the lot (see fig. 57). Of the twenty cottages planned for Meado'cots, however, only sixteen were built, unbalancing but not otherwise altering the scheme. In both projects, the cottage groupings were joined to each other by walls and gateways, strengthening the architectural definition and compositional unity of each site.

Scheibler's design for Willo'mound is known only through a watercolor perspective rendering (fig. 55) that depicts the development on a slight rise of land marked by a pair of willow trees. Though arranged in linear sequences, the cottages display a studied irregularity in composition. Both sun porches and open porches project capriciously from the facades. A con-

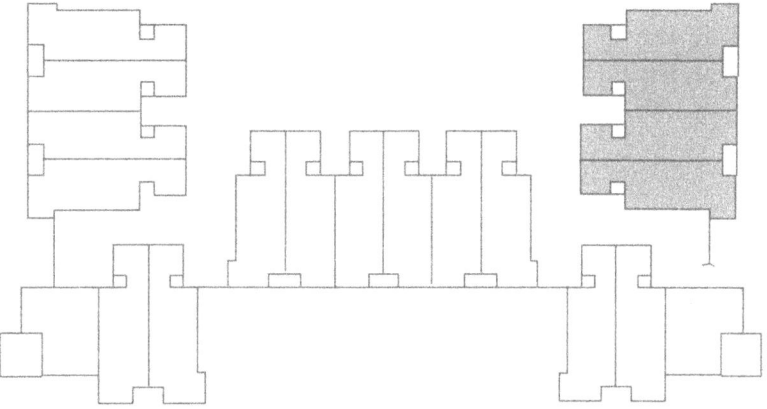

Fig. 57. Meado'cots, schematic plan. Shaded area represents unbuilt units.

tinuous sloping roof that variously extends downward over projecting elements below, or recedes along gable ends, is far from flat.

Willo'mound is the most English of Scheibler's group cottages and would seem to be most at home in an English Garden City. The irregular rooflines, stucco surfaces, and casement windows are worthy of Parker and Unwin or Baillie Scott (see fig. 58).[11] The irregular roof planes are specifically Voysey. But none of the English models is quite this picturesque, and there is no evidence that Scheibler had a specific English model in mind.

The freedom of the composition is most closely related to the cottages that Scheibler had added to the Old Heidelberg a few years earlier, transforming it from a freestanding apartment building into a semblance of a group cottage development. Willo'mound's two-story window bays with mushroom reliefs are direct quotes from the Old Heidelberg. The design for Willo'mound, then, was an attempt to integrate an earlier Scheibler vocabulary into a group housing format. But there are also elements that rep-

Fig. 58. M. H. Baillie Scott, workmen's houses, ca. 1908–1910, perspective rendering.

resent Scheibler's ongoing experiments with reductionist forms and structural expression. The sun porches are minimalist boxes grafted onto the picturesque whole, and the two units that turn the outer corners of the lot do so with porches that are sharply undercut into the body of the building. This latter device was soon exploited at Meado'cots.

Meado'cots' architectural vocabulary is similar to that of Hamilton Cottages in the arrangement of three planes established by projecting sun porches, gabled wall sections, and recessed window groups. But the light-colored brick and hip roofs are more open in feeling, and the two units that turn the outer corners of the complex have inset corner porches, like Willo'mound. The porches are formed by jutting gables that ride out on lengthy exposed I-beams to rest on rounded columns. This is Scheibler's most dramatic use of his trademark I-beam and his ultimate exploitation of this structural tool for aesthetic ends.[12]

These later group cottage projects were distinctive and progressive, but they had moved away from the early minimalist experiments of Inglenook Place, Bennett Street, and Aurelia Street. The architecture deferred to, or at least accommodated, the landscape, while gable and hip roofs and individualized entries supplied a measure of traditional domestic feeling. A 1914 double house built for Daniel L. Dillinger (fig. 59) epitomizes this trend. Though it shares the language of Scheibler's group cottages, it has the unified conceptual quality and quiet dignity of a single-family house. A projecting hip roof, a low bowed wall that forms a small front terrace and a trellis that extends from the facade blur the distinction between the two units and foster domestic feeling.[13] In one final group cottage project, however, Scheibler rejected compromise with the landscape, discarded domestic feeling, and unequivocally gave architec-

Fig. 59. Dillinger double house, 1914.

ture center stage in a jarring return to minimalism.

Vilsack Row (fig. 60) was commissioned by the estate of Leopold Vilsack, a prominent Pittsburgh businessman and entrepreneur, late in 1913. At the time, Scheibler was renting office space in a building in East Liberty that was owned by Vilsack family interests, and the commission for a site in the nearby neighborhood of Morningside may derive from that association. There is no evidence that Scheibler or his client intended a radical undertaking; indeed, the commission was extremely modest in its program of eighteen row houses, each just fifteen feet wide, with only five major rooms each (see fig. 61). The design was an outgrowth of Scheibler's early low-budget row house projects in both its siting and its design. Like the earlier projects, the houses are organized in a single linear sequence of housing groups, here consisting of four, eight, and six units. But here, key architec-

Fig. 60. Vilsack Row, 1913. Shown upon completion and "open for inspection," according to a sign in one window.

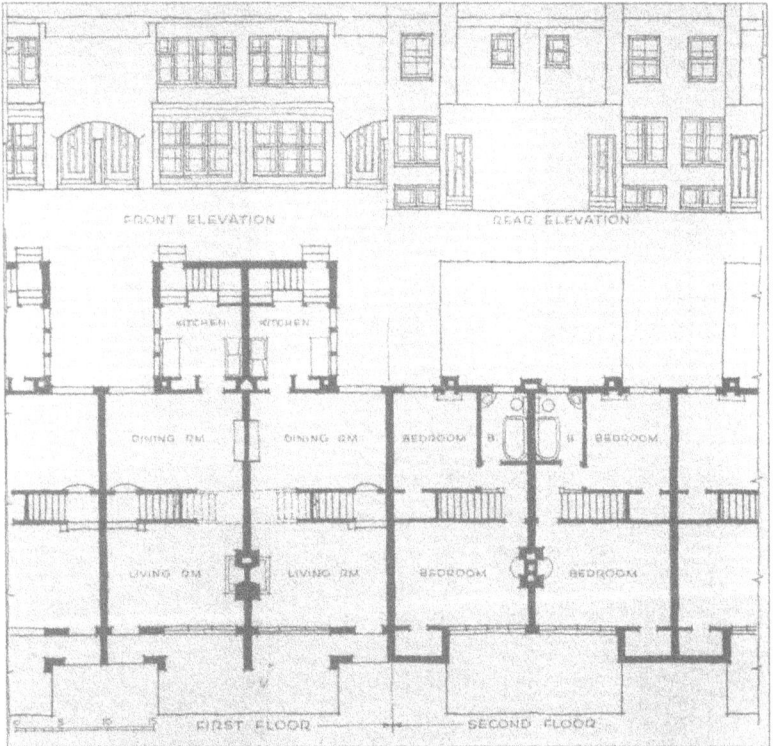

Fig. 61. Vilsack Row, 1913, front and rear elavations, plans (measured drawing).

tural elements are further abstracted into basic geometric shapes, and the composition embodies stark and startling contrasts of solid and void, line and arc, brick and stucco.

At first glance, the composition seems familiar: the brick entry pavilions, the porch projections, the extensive glazing, and the flat roofs are common to many Scheibler row house projects. Here, however, "sun porches" project inward rather than out and form two-story window cavities that are more than twenty feet wide and eighteen feet tall. These cavities contain all of the glazing—save for the rear elevation—and are not unlike the curtain-wall experiments of Scheibler's early commercial buildings. The porches themselves consist only of concrete slab roofs that project dramatically *from the void of the window cavities* as virtual cantilevers resting on single thin center posts. Sharply cut arches mark the entries, and where two entries share a single arch, the doors are deeply recessed and the segmental arch drops down *in front* of them to visually cut off their upper corners and emphasize the depth of the opening through visual layering.[14]

Scheibler had previously developed facades composed of up to three planes arranged in sequence; but here, two planes are arranged as distinct layers: an inner layer of windows and doors, and an outer layer of solid wall at an unconventional distance out in front. The voids of the facade are of such size and depth that the brick wall stands out like a template. It almost seems like an exploded diagram; you expect to see dotted lines tying the wall back to the plane of the windows and doors. Scheibler combats the visual stress of detachment by crisscrossing the battered ends of the front and side walls to lock them into place. Coving at the top of the window cavities also serves to hold the front wall tethered, like one of those dotted lines. These relationships are highly dynamic. And the porches, suspended in space, are just plain unnerving!

The contrast of solid and void is so severe that the edges of both walls and openings take on highly linear qualities and enable a composition of three-dimensional tension to assume linear definition. Edges form massive squares, slivers of triangles, segments of circles. Vertical lines contrast with horizontal lines and slanted lines, arced lines contrast with straight. In elevation, the porches read simply as perpendicular lines (as at Bennett Street), and the complex muntins of the windows comprise a flat grid of squares and rectangles.

The materials add their own measure of contrast. This is a three-color job of bluntly adjoining red brick, white concrete and stucco, and glass. No other colors or textures intervene.

The simple interiors are not so unique as the exteriors, but are thematically consistent. The cut-out parapet of the stair and a segmentally arched passage between the living room and dining room form another strong-edged template, and the ceiling arch, fireplace arches, and even steps and hearthstones are shaped to echo the arcs of the exterior entries.[15]

Vilsack Row culminated the thrust of rational simplification in Scheibler's group cottage work and demonstrated his capacity for expressive design within a minimalist framework.[16] Only Irving Gill's Lewis Courts (fig. 62) in Sierra Madre, California, built in 1910, is comparable among contemporary work. The houses of Lewis Courts had flat roofs and stark white surfaces broken only by large glazed openings and loggia arches.[17] Lewis Courts was published in the December 1913 *Architectural Record*, when Scheibler was designing Vilsack Row; but the similarities between the two projects are more a matter of conceptual affinity than a commonality of elements.[18]

When the editorial voice of the *Architectural Record* remarked in 1949 that the cottages of Vilsack Row "escape their time altogether as good architecture regardless of date," it paid Scheibler a prime compliment.[19] Indeed, there is an uncanny resemblance between Vilsack Row and Le Corbusier's Maisons Jaoul of 1951–1952. The Maisons Jaoul were a key source of the so-called New Brutalism, and their concrete lintels and brick walls became a common vocabulary for America architecture of the 1960s.[20] It is implausible that Vilsack Row played any

Fig. 62. Irving Gill, Lewis Courts, ca. 1910.

role in stimulating these later developments, but its aesthetic anticipation reveals how remarkably forward-looking Scheibler's work was in 1913.[21]

Among the group cottages, Meado'cots and Hamilton Cottages, at least, had middle-class tenants, and both may have had tennis courts.[22] Shear and Schmertz noted back in 1948, however, that Vilsack Row was "gotten up on a most restricted budget" and reported deterioration even at that date. Many of Scheibler's group cottages were, in fact, cheaply built, and have deteriorated appreciably. This is, of course, unfortunate. Nevertheless, such economic strictures may have provided Scheibler with his greatest opportunity. According to Barry Parker, writing in 1901:

One of the definite requirements which an architect should welcome most heartily is the necessity to consider real economy, for not only will this give him an added satisfaction in his work; it will increase his chances of artistic success by tending towards that element of simplicity and directness so necessary, and lessening his risk of falling into the vulgarity almost inseparable from superfluity.[23]

In embracing "real economy," Scheibler could be reductionist without apology. In this way he did some of his most advanced work and showed that he could be an innovative designer without close dependence on specific sources. Scheibler also fulfilled both the economic and the social requirements of the task. His group cottage designs were highly versatile—some were reused at multiple sites, and others were adapted for programs ranging from double houses to groups of more than twenty units. They proved economically viable—some were owned by their original clients for nearly eighty years.[24] And they affirmed their residents and their needs, both individually and communally.

Many of the housing schemes of the progressive age were just schemes; it was easier to talk about such housing than to build it. With the exceptions of Baillie Scott and Gill, Scheibler was alone in executing a substantial body of multifamily housing. His work predated Chatham Village by many years, and as noted by Van Trump, Scheibler's group cottages "must have been almost unique in America in their day."[25]

6 Highland Towers

IN 1913, AT THE HEIGHT OF HIS POWERS, Scheibler returned to the medium-sized apartment building one last time when he designed Highland Towers (figs. 63–64) for Daniel L. Dillinger in Pittsburgh's East Liberty–Shadyside district.[1] Harry Hasson, then manager of D. L. Dillinger Properties, was the rental agent for Highland Towers, and his office may have been the source of a marketing brochure that included a rendered image of the building (fig. 65), a floor plan (fig. 66), and effusive prose (see fig. 67):

In this splendid apartment, owner, architect and builder have worked together to give not only the utmost of modern comfort but also that beauty which adds so much to the enjoyment of a Home. Highland Towers comprise a few select **Homes** as attractive in appearance, as satisfying in arrangement and as perfect in construction and equipment as modern art and science could make them.[2]

Like the Old Heidelberg, Highland Towers offered a domestic image to prospective tenants who were leery of apartment living. But this was a very different image of the home. The Old Heidelberg's "cozy, homelike aspect of the Fatherland's treasured homes" was replaced by a home environment billed as the product of modern art and science. Scheibler dispensed with the wooden porches, overhanging eaves, high roofs, and prominent chimneys—traditional symbols of domesticity that had served him in the past. Here the domestic image emphasized values of efficiency and abstract beauty—an outlook consistent with modern life.

The marketing brochure went on to note that the building was equipped with a host of modern conveniences: telephones, electrical connections in each room, refrigerators, clothes dryers, a Modulated Vapor System adjustable for each room, a vacuum cleaning system, and a refuse incinerator. Exposed steel windows and solarium doors, tile flooring, metal cabinets, Cararra glass in the bathrooms, and a "sanitary material" on the kitchen floor were chosen for their clean lines and ease of care.

Apart from a lack of elevators, Highland Towers was a consummately modern high-class building. The marketing effort met with some success: this was eas-

Fig. 63. Highland Towers apartment building, 1913–1914, sketch. The sketch is a combination of two two-point perspectives. The point of view changes from the left two-thirds of the sketch to the right third of the sketch.

Fig. 64. Highland Towers apartment building, 1913–1914.

Fig. 65. Highland Towers apartment building, 1913–1914, perspective rendering.

Highland Towers 71

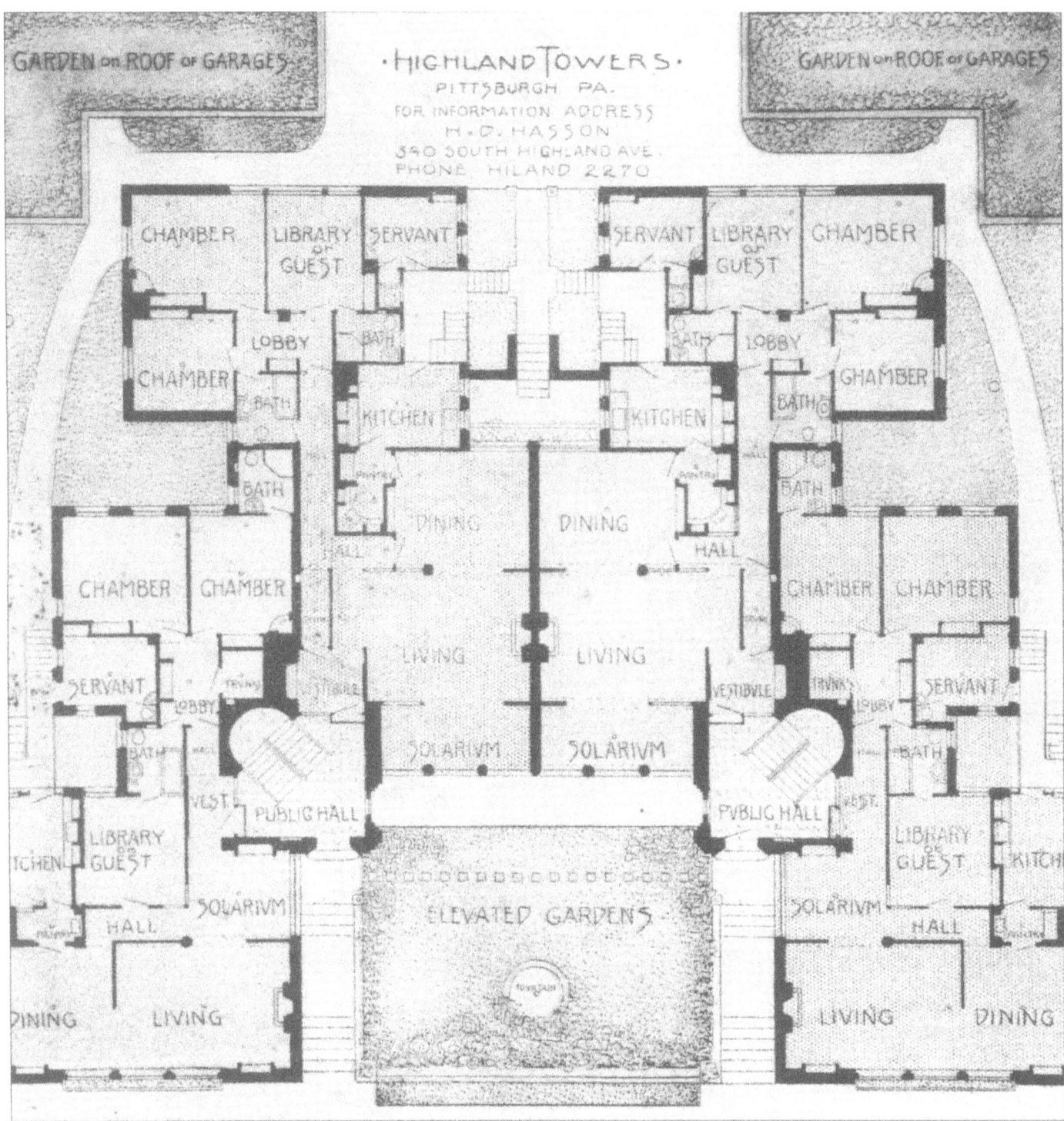

Fig. 66. Highland Towers apartment building, 1913–1914, first floor plan.

HIGHLAND TOWERS
Apartment Homes

IN this splendid apartment, owner, architect and builder have worked together to give not only the utmost of modern comfort but also that beauty which adds so much to the enjoyment of a Home. Highland Towers comprise a few select Homes as attractive in appearance, as satisfying in arrangement and as perfect in construction and equipment as modern art and science could make them. In beauty and comfort you will not find an apartment anywhere which excels them.

The Touch of Home Beauty

The Towers was built with the object of attracting those who appreciate the real beauty of home. Its standards in quality and artistic merit are those which a man holds when he builds a home for himself. Iron, cement, brick and hollow tile form the skeleton. It is a scientifically fire-proof, sound-proof structure. The manner in which it is finished in Tapestry Brick, Rookwood Tile, White Oak and Mahogany will give you a pleasant surprise.

"Here," you will say, "is something really beautiful."

Throughout the apartments—**the homes**—this same high standard of beauty and true quality is upheld. Through the different rooms, which constitute an apartment, the beauty and convenience the builder has provided, repeatedly wins admiration.

The decorating and finishing has been done by artists in this line and the same exacting care has been given to the selection and placing of the Lighting and to the Hardware and Electrical equipment.

Entrance

Through the elevated garden, into a Tower Hall with floor laid in random blocks of green and white Rookwood, blending into a wall of golden tapestry brick and a ceiling of stalactite effect.

Solarium

Enclosed in steel casement windows, overlooking a beautiful garden.

Garden Terrace

A mass of shrubbery and vines, a fountain and an old-fashioned garden, beautify the entrance through the elevated garden and afford a restful view from the Solarium.

A Little About the Rooms

The Living and Dining Rooms are finished in oak and mahogany and equipped with book and china cases of handsome design and finish, and with a built-in brick fireplace of logs. Electrical connections are supplied for library table lamps, fans and dining room table equipment. These rooms have an abundance of light and air by metal casement windows.

The Bed Rooms are finished in mahogany and equipped with large wardrobes with dressing mirrors, electrical attachments for adjustable light and toilet necessities, and call bells and telephone.

The Bath Rooms are equipped with built-in tubs and showers, and vitrous china fixtures and accessories, steel medicine cases, mirror and attachments for electrical appliances. These rooms are finished in tints and designs of Rookwood tile and Carara glass.

The Vestibule is supplied with a coat cupboard and large mirror. Off the lobby is a Trunk Room. A large Linen Case is also built close to the trunk room, off the lobby.

The Kitchen and Pantry have floors laid of a sanitary material of a slightly elastic nature, much easier to keep clean, and decidedly easier to stand on, than cement. The Cupboards are built of metal—thoroughly sanitary. These rooms are also equipped with the latest approved kitchen sinks and pantry sinks of copper. Built into the pantry is a glass-lined Refrigerator, mechanically cooled, of the latest and best type. This dispenses with the ice man. The kitchens are also fitted with attachments for any necessary electrical equipment. A high grade Cabinet Range, and a Refuse Incinerator complete the kitchen equipment. This latter article eliminates the garbage can from your back porch, and adds to cleanliness.

Comfortable and convenient Servant Room and Bath a part of each suite.

Noteworthy Features of the Construction

Division Walls and Floor between Suites—Between your apartment and that of your neighbor in this building are walls of the same construction as the outside walls—fire-proof and sound-proof—not merely the narrow partition walls which you almost invariably find, even in fire-proof construction. Those who have lived in apartments will appreciate the rarity and benefit of this feature. The floors are also sound-proof.

The Laundry is equipped with a series of triple wash trays and built-in Copper Wash Boilers. These wash boilers are hooded to a flue from the laundry and all steam or odor from the washing is taken up the flue to the outside air. Individual Steel Lockers are supplied for washing and ironing equipment. The latest improved Clothes Dryers, Ironing Room Stoves and Sinks, and Ironing Boards with attachment for electric irons are also supplied. Individual Lockers are installed in the basement for the use of each tenant.

Other Things Which Count for Comfort

A thorough vacuum cleaning plant is installed and is a part of the building equipment. A Refrigerating Plant supplies a cooling system to each refrigerator, as well as a limited supply of ice for sickness or table use.

Heat is supplied by the Modulated Vapor System, adjustable to the heating conditions of each apartment or each room. This is far superior to steam or hot water, and much easier regulated.

Particular attention has been paid to parts that are hidden in the walls and floors—for instance, the Sewering, which is properly laid and carefully taken care of, and the Plumbing—all pipes and tanks wherever water touches them are Brass or Copper, thus insuring you against rusty, dirty water and adding to cleanliness. A Burglar Proof Safe is built into the brick walls of each apartment. Copper Screens and Weather Strips are a part of the window and door openings.

The Roof Garden

A large, open Roof Garden overlooking the Elevated Garden in the front of the building and accessible through the Tower Entrance will be maintained for the convenience of the tenants.

Garage Garden

There is a Garage in the rear for tenants having cars. It is steam heated and electric lighted. On the roof is a mass of shrubbery and flowers, making a delightful view from your rear windows.

Reception Room

A large Reception Room, appropriately decorated, furnished and equipped will be at the disposal of the tenants by appointment for certain social functions.

The Office and Janitor's Apartment

These are located in the basement and are kept in close touch with each apartment and with the Main Hall through a complete telephone system.

Accessibility

Highland Towers is easily accessible from all parts of the city by a dozen different car lines and is within eight minutes walk of East Liberty Station.

We Invite You to Call
We Challenge You to Compare

Highland Towers is, we believe, the most nearly perfect building for the purpose that you have ever seen; results have been achieved that have never been seen before in Apartment Home construction and equipment. This is a strictly high grade Apartment Home, under the constant supervision of expert property management, together with efficient and courteous janitor service. We solicit your careful consideration and challenge comparison with other apartments anywhere.

Fig. 67. Text of Highland Towers advertising brochure.

ily the most prestigious address of any of Scheibler's multifamily commissions and it housed its share of society-register tenants.³

Unlike Scheibler's previous work in this genre, Highland Towers imposes on its neighbors. It utilizes its full lot out to the sidewalk, disrupting the prevailing streetscape of houses set back behind yards. Its four floors of apartments and raised basement—in effect, five stories—literally tower over the street despite the relatively small scale of its individual elements. The building has a U-shaped footprint, and forward portions of wings are upended brick boxes that appear as elemental geometric forms. The virtually faceless side and rear elevations and the flat roof are severe.

The otherwise blank front faces of the wings are broken, however, by large rectangular cutouts filled with alternating rows of casement windows and decorative tile spandrels. Elevations of the three-sided court that opens up the building at its center are even more open and animated. Here the building's reinforced concrete structure is exposed as stacked series of rounded concrete columns. The columns frame the glazed outer walls of solaria, in front of which narrow concrete balconies ring the court in tiers. This is pseudo–curtain wall construction, with floor-to-ceiling glass panels hung between the columns from overhead beams. Thin steel window frames are integral with the columns, which are rendered half external and half internal to the building.

At the rear corners of the central court, squarish stair towers act as hinges between the wings and the base of the U. The towers' strongly vertical brick masses project outward from the adjacent solaria walls and extend above the prevailing roofline, anchoring the building at points where the walls have become mostly glass, and providing counterweights to the heavy forward masses of the wings. But whereas the wings are sheer and elemental, the towers are textured and picturesque: here the brick is laid in Flemish bond and there are octagonal mini-towers at the projecting corners with a sawtooth brickwork pattern on alternate faces. The emergent octagonal masses and adjacent slits of glazing are somewhat reminiscent of details on the side elevations of Mackintosh's Glasgow School of Art.

The glazing of the court elevations allows light and air to penetrate the building, and an elevated garden within the court provides pleasant views from the interior. The garden also softens the building's hard-edged masses, and urns and planters further garnish the architectural forms with foliage. The roof gardens that were originally planned for the building and its adjacent garages would have reinforced this effect. This is gritty urban architecture, but with a suburban sensibility.⁴

At the Minnetonka Building six years before, Scheibler had employed two different treatments on the front elevation, isolated on different stories. At Highland Towers (and Vilsack Row), Scheibler simultaneously exploited the interplay of solids and voids *and* two-dimensional linear design. Enframement is the dominant theme. At the largest scale, the solid mass of the building frames the large void of the court. This is done with extraordinary rigor, as the two wings and the rear wall of the court are pre-

Fig. 68. Highland Towers apartment building, 1913–1914. Note the two-dimensional grids of detailing.

cisely equal in width. The stair towers frame the rear solaria wall. Expanses of solid wall give way to glazed voids. The strong sense of line is found in grids of detailing. In the wings, casement windows and spandrels comprise a two-dimensional grid free of moldings or heavy mullions, and the tile panels in the spandrels are themselves flat grids of squares, rectangles, and lines. The glazed walls of the solaria hold two-dimensional grids of metal muntin strips and square art-glass medallions, overlaid with the only slightly more three-dimensional grid of half columns and balustrades (see fig. 68).

These twin treatments enabled Scheibler to eliminate virtually all standard applied ornament at High-

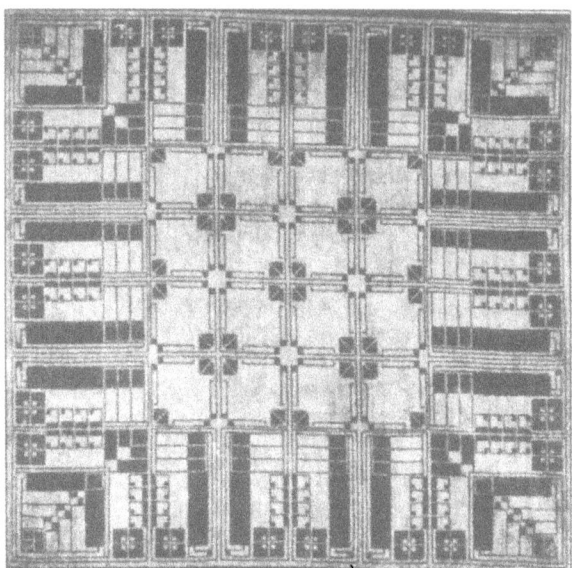

Fig. 69. Peter Behrens, fabric design, ca. 1905.

land Towers and still achieve a rich visual effect. Another important tool was tapestry brick, a building material that was praised and promoted by the great Chicago progressive Louis Sullivan late in his career.[5] Sullivan wrote in 1910:

> When [tapestry brick is] laid up promiscuously, especially if the surface is large, and care is taken to avoid patches of any color, the general tone suggests that of a very old oriental rug and differing color values of the individual bricks, however sharply these may seem to contrast at close view, are taken up and harmonized in the prevailing general tone. Composed of many colors, the general tone is, in a sense, neutral and is rich and impressive. It lends itself admirably to color selection or treatment, such as stone, terra cotta, wood, glass and the metals, and admits in these, because of its broad, supporting neutrality, a great variation in range of treatment.[6]

Scheibler used tapestry brick in precisely this manner. At Highland Towers, shades of yellow, bronze, tan, and brown brick provide a rich but neutral backdrop for a variety of other materials, forms, and colors that are carefully manipulated for aesthetic effect. The brickwork acts as a foil for expanses of glass, projecting concrete elements, grids of blue, pink, and green art glass, and the geometric blue tilework that Scheibler adapted from a fabric design by the German architect Peter Behrens (fig. 69) and distributed in swatches across his facade.[7]

Only in the public halls of the stair towers did Scheibler allow himself the flavor of domestic nostalgia. The key ingredients are materials and devices that serve to blend outside and inside and render the stair halls as garden pathways between homes. The public entrance doors, which open off of the garden court, function like arbors. Their art-glass motif of abstract green willow leaves seems to have been inspired by the decorative motifs of Mackintosh's Willow Tea Rooms.[8] Inside, Rookwood tile flooring simulates flagstone; walls are the same golden brick as on the exterior; casement windows are flanked by colored tiles that simulate shutters; and each apartment entry is a simulated facade with a step, a door, and a window. (The entries have since been altered.)

The transformation of an anonymous stair hall into a pathway to the home was a tour de force for which no known precedent exists. Baillie Scott regularly used external architectural devices such as brick walls, half-timbering, and windows in the interiors of his houses, but he created nothing so purposeful as this. Scheibler's stair halls can best be seen as an integration of Baillie Scott's romantic outside-in manner with the concept of the internal street, as realized, for example, in Henry Hornbostel's Central Building (now Baker Hall) at Carnegie Tech, where the brick-

Fig. 70. Highland Towers apartment building, 1913–1914, a living room and solarium.

work and window forms of the exterior are replicated in a public hallway. All of these devices were in marked contrast to the plush lobby decor of the common apartment building of the day.

The apartments at Highland Towers have since been subdivided and much altered. The original layout (fig. 66) accommodated four ten-room apartments on each floor arranged in an A-B-B-A pattern of mirror-image pairs. The major living spaces—living room and dining room, plus solarium—were located in the front part of the building; sleeping rooms and service spaces were located on the sides and at the back. Each outer apartment was entered near its center adjacent to a solarium overlooking the central court. The living room and dining room were placed side by side across the width of each wing, and a short hall led to the rear bedrooms. Each inner apartment was entered near its front, and a long hallway led to a rear lobby and its surrounding spaces. The solarium, living room, and dining room were aligned one behind the other on an axis that lay perpendicular to the street and extended deep into the building.

These compact and rather complex floor plans were saved by open planning in the living spaces (see

Fig. 71. Highland Towers apartment building, 1913–1914, detail of a living room. Shown with alterations.

figs. 70–71). The floor-to-ceiling glass walls of the solaria drew light and air from the court into the interiors. Some rooms were divided from one another only by partitions, some with art-glass panels and some of three-quarter height. In the inner apartments, this device facilitated a view to the street from deep inside the apartment. In the outer apartments, a library/guest room internal to the plan had one of its corners glazed so as to draw light from the solarium.

The dominant effect, however, was quite severe. The building's concrete frame was exposed on the interior, and every unit was punctuated with at least one large round concrete column and was crossed overhead by concrete beams (see fig. 71). These surfaces were coated with a cement-and-silica-gravel concrete, assuring a rough texture and dark coloration. The outer apartments have exposed brick mullions between the front windows, and all of the apartments have low-slung brick arched fireplaces with simple shelflike mantels.[9] There are plain white plaster walls and simple wood trim. Scheibler's specifications reminded carpenters, "There are no moldings on any of this work." This gritty interior architecture.

Colorful painted murals provide a lighter touch (see fig. 71). These were painted on cement surfaces above entrance doors, above mirrors in vestibules, around the perimeters of built-in cabinets, and along the tops of partitions. Scheibler had called for painted decorations previously at the Old Heidelberg, but these murals are painted in a unique manner that recalls art glass or mosaics: the gray surface on which the mural is painted is purposely exposed as if it were leading or mortar. This was a comfortable aesthetic for Scheibler, but the hand-painted manner is in sharp contrast to the crisp geometry of the rest of Highland Towers. These murals represent the hand-finishing ideals of the Arts and Crafts Movement—Baillie Scott, Mackintosh, and Parker and Unwin, among others, used and advocated mural painting—that occasionally emerged in full flavor in Scheibler's work. In their handwrought manner they are akin to the mushrooms at the Old Heidelberg.

The murals' iconography encompasses dragons, butterflies, peacocks and other birds, and a variety of flowers and foliage, including water lilies and bamboo. Both the murals and the largest of the art-glass room dividers (see fig. 72) are oriental in feeling.[10] Scheibler's Japanese designer friend Kantero Kato may have played a role in these designs (and may have even painted the murals), though Scheibler himself was much taken with the Orient, as were many other progressives. Scheibler's daughter has recalled, "At one time we were very interested in things Japanese and had a party at our house com-

Fig. 72. Highland Towers apartment building, 1913–1914, art glass.

plete with lanterns, chopsticks, Japanese food, kimonos, etcetera."[11]

Highland Towers was seemingly Scheibler's most inventive design; but it had its sources. Scheibler, who ordinarily sought inspiration in foreign lands, occasionally looked over his shoulder to see what was being wrought in the American West. This time he saw the unmistakable figure of Frank Lloyd Wright

Fig. 73. Frank Lloyd Wright, Larkin Building, 1904.

(1869–1959), progenitor of the Prairie School, perhaps the most revolutionary of all the progressive movements. Scheibler may have become acquainted with Wright through *Ausgefürte Bauten und Entwürfte von Frank Lloyd Wright*, the portfolio of Wright's work published in Germany in 1910, a copy of which could be found in Pittsburgh's Carnegie Library.[12] Wright himself denied any European influence in his own work and deprecated many of the European progressives for what he considered to be their affected naivete. But Wright saw those Olbrich interiors at the St. Louis fair, and when he visited Europe in 1909, he sought out Olbrich's work (and was introduced in Berlin as "the American Olbrich"). Olbrich's Secession Building probably influenced Wright's early Larkin Building (1904) and Unity Temple (1906).[13]

A published photograph of the Larkin Building (fig. 73) was found among Scheibler's office ephemera, and very possibly provided the starting point for Highland Towers. Scheibler may have recognized Olbrich in Wright's design, or may have been drawn to the qualities of enframement and simplification that had been characteristic of his own projects such as the Coleman apartment building. Highland Towers and the Larkin Building share an abrupt siting, a forceful integration of vertical and horizontal elements, and more specifically, massive and elemental corner masses, a central void fronted by a low wall, and tall thin verticals within the void. Although the Larkin Building was an office building in an industrial setting, Scheibler adopted these themes for Highland Towers, a high-class residential building in a distinguished neighborhood.

A second likely and seemingly more appropriate source for Highland Towers was Wright's McArthur apartment building (fig. 74) of 1906. Both buildings share a U-shaped arrangement of base and wings framing an open court. In plan, Wright's court is much deeper and his wings much longer, but the dimensions of the two plans are proportionally quite similar; the rear portion of Wright's court is simply transformed into interior space in Scheibler's plan. The perspective drawing of the McArthur building that was published in the Wright portfolio is foreshortened to suggest that the court is broader and more shallow than it really is; its *apparent* proportions are quite like the actual proportions of the court at Highland Towers. Both projects also feature an elevated garden fronted by a low wall, window groups in the wings, shallow projecting elements along the sides of the court, and a rear court elevation with horizontal bands of windows broken only by thin supports.

Wright's Francis apartment building of 1895 may have been the source for the disposition of Highland Towers' dual entries at the rear corners of its central court. The art glass of Scheibler's solarium doors has an affinity with the detailing of Wright's Coonley house of 1908. Highland Towers also incorporates generic Wrightian features like stone window sills, window boxes, and urn planters; and the tile spandrels and the low arched fireplaces, though actually of foreign origin, *appear* Wrightian. Wright's fascination with things oriental is well known.

Yet, despite this seeming dependence on Wright, Scheibler manipulated his models considerably. He used the austere forms of the Larkin Building to discipline the contributions of the McArthur and Francis apartment buildings and sometimes surpassed the Larkin Building at its own game. Whereas the McArthur apartment building has projecting bays, Highland Towers has only balconies, and whereas all of the Wrightian sources have projecting window trim, Highland Towers' is flush. Highland Towers makes a clean transition to its flat roof, dispensing not only with the overhanging eaves and parapets of the McArthur apartment building, but also with the attic beltcourse and cornice of the Larkin Building. Whereas Wright's entries at the Francis apartments are located in fussy decorative pavilions linked by

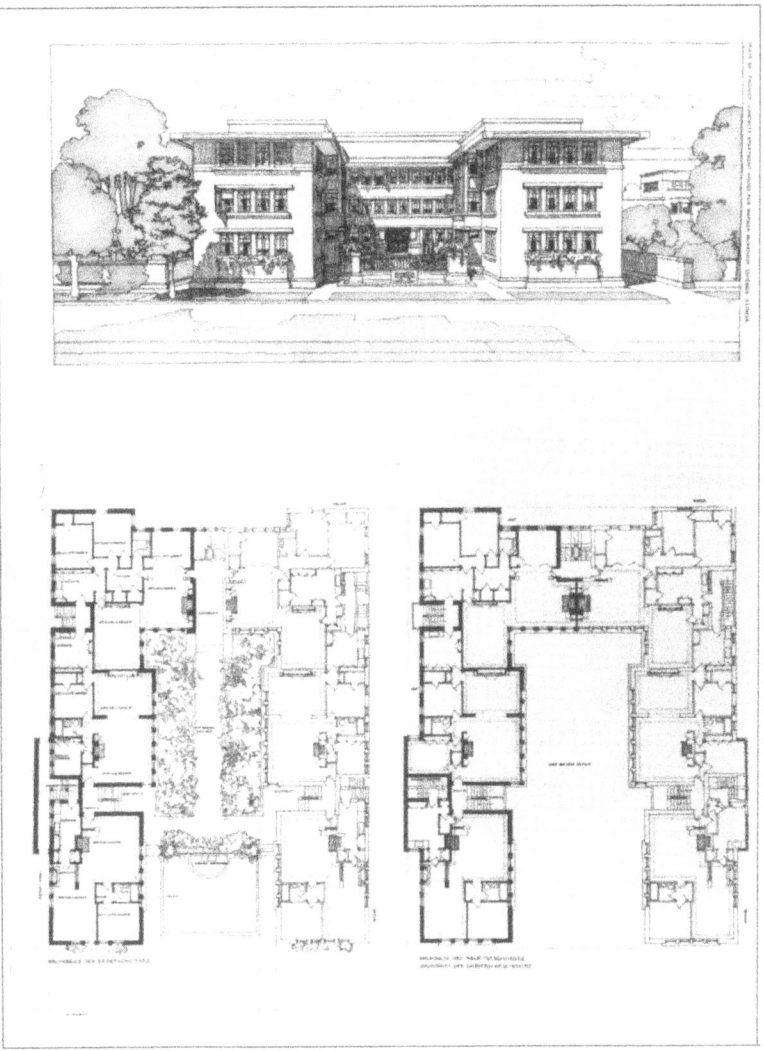

Fig. 74. Frank Lloyd Wright, McArthur apartment building, 1906, perspective rendering and plans.

hallways to internal stairs, Scheibler's entries are located in projecting but integral stair towers. Scheibler also achieved a richness of external detail that Wright did not demonstrate in any of the relevant sources (though it is present elsewhere in Wright's work). And, except for their open planning, Scheibler's interiors are not really Wrightian at all.

Once again, at Highland Towers, Scheibler successfully cloaked the requirements of communal housing in a distinctive aesthetic concept. Since the Old Heidelberg, Scheibler's artistic manner had evolved toward abstraction—to the Coleman apartment building, to the early group cottages, to Vilsack Row. At Highland Towers, abstraction was combined with richly textured polychromatic surface treatments on both the exterior and the interior. The design owed its primary debt to progressive American ideas. Highland Towers is not strictly speaking a Prairie School building, but with its affinities with both Wright and Sullivan, it would fit in quite comfortably a few hundred miles west.

Despite this grand performance, however, Highland Towers brought nothing permanent to Scheibler's work. Far from providing him with a new architectural language, Highland Towers marked a virtual halt in Scheibler's experiments in both abstraction and multifamily housing. Scheibler received no additional commissions for medium-sized apartment buildings—clearly his forte—and few for group cottages. Robinson and Bruckman ended their partnership, the Hamilton Realty Company stopped building, and commissions from Dillinger and Hasson ceased as well. Scheibler's future work was largely in the area of single-family houses, for him a less adventurous though not unsuitable arena for his skills.

According to Belnap, the multifamily projects showed that "Scheibler was not just another back-to-basics Arts and Crafts architect, but was part of a forward moving trend in which domestic architecture was being brought in tune with modern life."[14] The apartment building, in particular, represented a modern way of life, and provided a particularly appropriate and effective setting for Scheibler's progressive experiments. Highland Towers represents the culmination of Scheibler's work in this genre and the pinnacle of his career as a designer.[15]

7 · The Artistic House

IN TURN-OF-THE-CENTURY America, the growth of the middle class dramatically altered the urban landscape, not only with the introduction of apartment buildings and group housing, but also with the construction of ever increasing numbers of freestanding single-family dwellings. In a common scenario, Pittsburgh's East End filled rapidly with houses devised with an economic rather than artistic rationale. Basic plans were used over and over, and familiar details were more or less randomly applied. A typology of basic house types can account for most dwellings. Even Kiehnel and Elliott's Stengel house (fig. 75), one of few Pittsburgh houses that aspired to be progressive, was a reworking of a standard Pittsburgh house type. It staked any claim to be progressive on its Wrightian detailing and Arts and Crafts interior, not on innovations of plan or massing.[1] In this context, Scheibler's houses were consistently the exception.

In the early years of his new manner, Scheibler's freestanding houses were quite modest.[2] Part English Arts and Crafts, part Olbrich, and part Scheibler, they would have fit comfortably in an English Garden City, or perhaps an everyman's Darmstadt. Projects such as the Miller house (fig. 76), the Wright, Hoffman, Vogeley, and McNall houses, and a series of houses for William Ebberts (fig. 77), all designed and

Fig. 75. Kiehnel and Elliott, Stengel house, ca. 1915, exterior and living room.

Highland Towers 83

Fig. 76. Miller house, 1905.

Fig. 77. Ebberts house, 1910, front elevation.

built between 1905 and 1910, typify this work. Composed of one or two simple volumes, they are either brick on the first story and stucco above, or wholly stucco. Half-timbering sometimes appears as a simple sequence of vertical timbers in a window bay or a small gable end, emphasizing strong edges and the play of black against white.³ Roof forms include clipped gables and various combinations of gable and hip roofs. Decorative detail consists largely of art glass. The Miller house, for instance, has art-glass window transoms that comprise a triptych of pastoral images, and the Ebberts houses have art-glass irises on outside entry doors and on inside cupboard doors.⁴

In 1910 Scheibler designed two houses of this sort for Ebberts, to flank two other houses built a year earlier for the same client. The earlier houses are atypical, tiny and red brick, each with a street-facing gable end—they look rather like row house segments that have been detached from their neighbors. The four houses together formed a near mirror-image grouping around a central court, reflecting Scheibler's group housing practice.⁵

As early as 1907, however, Scheibler was also producing a more sophisticated domestic architecture, and after 1915 his practice turned almost exclusively to the so-called artistic house. Red House, designed for William Morris by Philip Webb in 1859–1860, is generally considered to be the first house "made artistic." For the first time, the small house became a legitimate forum for lofty architectural ideas. A later generation took up the banner of the "artistic house" about 1890, and architects such as Olbrich, Mackintosh, Voysey, Baillie Scott, Wright—and Scheibler—attained a unity of purpose and style in their concentration upon the architectural possibilities of the small house that opposed conventional practice at nearly every turn.

Still, Scheibler's mature houses are a disparate bunch. There are houses influenced by works of Baillie Scott, Mackintosh, and Voysey, and houses more freely conceived. Different economies and different aesthetic goals differentiate these houses from Scheibler's earlier houses, apartment buildings, and group cottages. Away from the demands of disguising or differentiating multiple units, Scheibler could concentrate on the whole and design in the round. He laid less emphasis on linear definition and the manipulation of solids and voids, and instead created more evenly textured sculptural objects. Without the requirement of replication, he could opt for asymmetrical compositions and more freely devised interiors.

English architect M. H. Baillie Scott (1865–1945) specialized in small country houses and made extensive use of vernacular materials and techniques.⁶ But he freely added his own imprint as well. According to Muthesius, Baillie Scott conceived of the house as "an organism which is thoroughly unified and interrelated internally and externally. Here the architect and the interior decorator step forward fused together. . . . Here, in the case of Baillie Scott, with every room it is a question of an individual creation; whole elements are not present as a matter of chance but rather are derived from the main concept. It is the new thought of interior space and an independent work of art which Baillie Scott put into effect for the first time."⁷

Baillie Scott employed an unprecedented degree of open planning. His houses often featured multi-

Fig. 78. Ament house, 1907.

Fig. 79. M. H. Baillie Scott, Springcot, 1903, perspective rendering. Shows garden facade.

room and even multistory living areas. Rooms were divided by thin panel walls or extended with intimate inglenooks. Meanwhile, Baillie Scott the interior decorator embellished walls and windows with colorful painting and art glass.

Scheibler was familiar with Baillie Scott's houses from published sources and absorbed some of their characteristics. One Scheibler house, known only by a sketch on a calendar page (see fig. 9), featured a combined living room and dining area that extended across the entire front of the house to terminate in what appears to be one of Scott's three-sided dining alcoves. Scheibler's drawings for his unbuilt Logue house show a broad wall at the rear of the living room with a clerestory of large art-glass windows along the top. These windows transmit light from a two-story stair hall which extends across the rear axis of the house and is in turn lit by an additional two-story art-glass window. Baillie Scott would have admired the spatial ingenuity and decorative richness. Two other Scheibler houses are linked to specific, if somewhat atypical, Baillie Scott houses.

In 1907, Scheibler designed a house for Silas M. Ament, proprietor of a Wilkinsburg insurance business, and one of a number of Scheibler's Wilkinsburg and Pittsburgh clients who made (or contemplated) a move to Oakmont, a pleasant residential town twelve miles up the Allegheny River. The Ament house (fig. 78) was evidently closely modeled after Baillie Scott's "Springcot" (fig. 79), designed in 1903 and published in Baillie Scott's *Houses and Gardens* in 1906.[8] Baillie Scott's house is mostly roof. Through this device, the house is visually simplified but retains strong domestic symbolism.[9]

The roof is also dominant in Scheibler's Ament

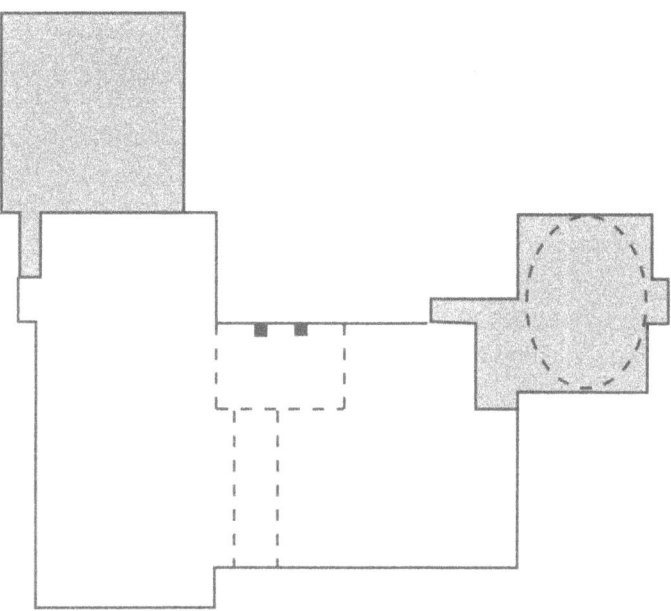

Fig. 80. Ament house, schematic plan. Shaded areas represent additions.

house, but it is not so overbearing. Two low-slung stucco wings are equally strong elements. Scheibler adapted Baillie Scott's garden facade for his street facade by shrinking the roof, projecting the gable end, and adding a formal entry. In both houses, a gallery runs through the house to connect the front entry and a three-bay rear porch on the garden facade.

Later owners Charles F. and Marie S. Blue added a garage to the house's north-south wing and a new wing that was oddly offset at the southwest corner of the house (see fig. 80). This wing houses a single oval bedroom. The story is that the Blues had this wing built by Italian craftsmen after a trip to Europe. The bedroom's rather florid classical decor is assuredly not in Scheibler's palette of this or any time—although he once did design an oval room, and a classical one at that, at the Steel house.

The Artistic House 87

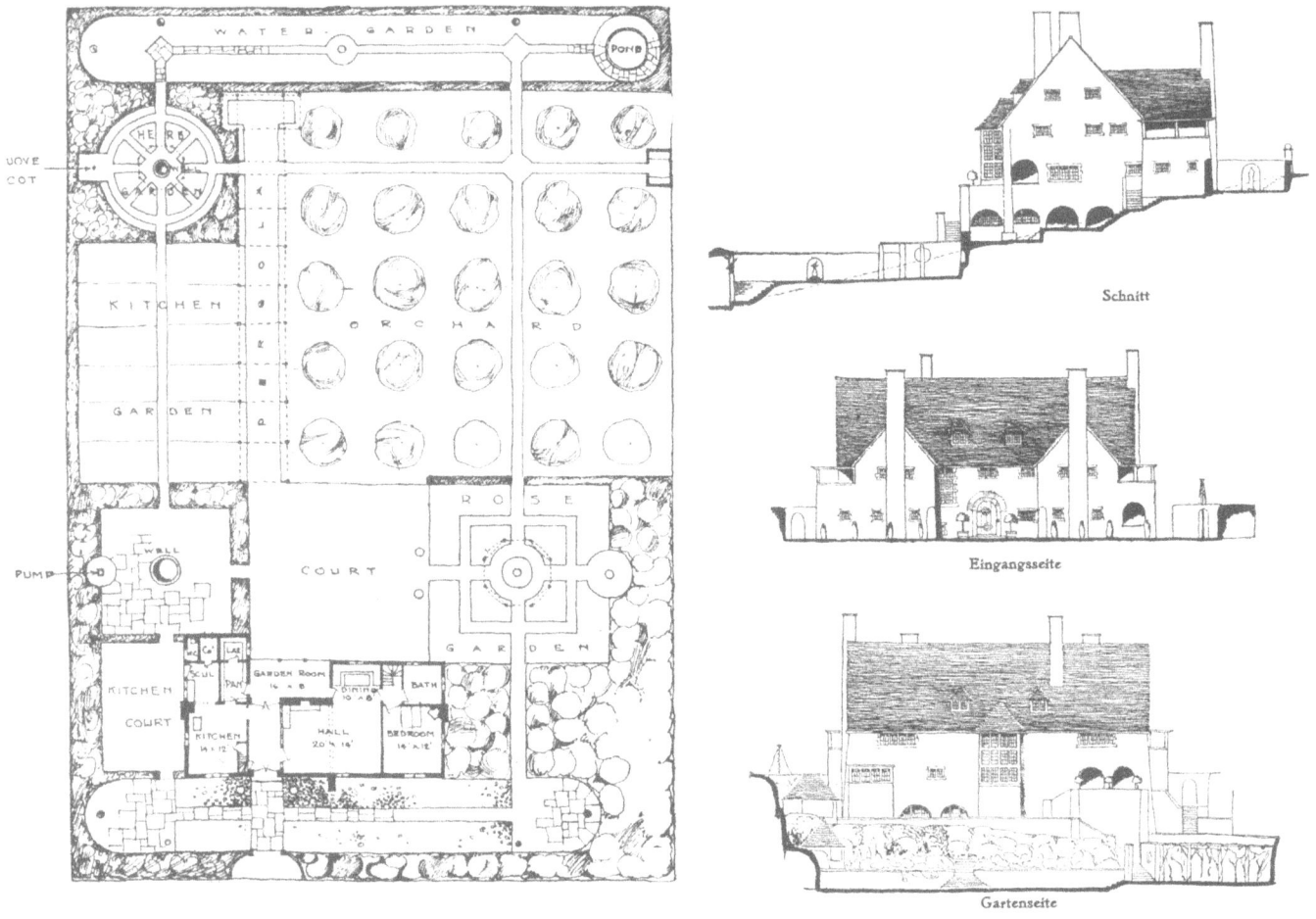

Fig. 81. M. H. Baillie Scott, Springcot, 1903, house and garden plan.

Fig. 82. M. H. Baillie Scott, A house and garden in Switzerland, ca. 1903–1904, elevations.

Whoever designed these additions followed Scheibler's original exterior detailing to the letter and must have returned to the published drawings of Baillie Scott's Springcot as a guide to planning the new work. This time Springcot's garden plan (fig. 81) was apparently the point of reference. This garden was both formal and utilitarian, and its strong rectilinear forms determined the placement of the additions for Mr. and Mrs. Blue. The garage addition corresponds to Springcot's kitchen court and well, and the bedroom wing corresponds to Springcot's rose garden. In this way, the footprint of Baillie Scott's plan for both building and garden was here realized in a building alone. Scheibler must have been responsible for the location and form of these additions, even if the Italian craftsmen held sway in the oval bed-

Fig. 83. Joseph Maria Olbrich, Silber house, 1906–1907, elevations.

room. The additions could have been made as late as 1940 when the Blues purchased additional property behind the house, cleared away an existing home, and planted a formal garden—all in keeping with Baillie Scott's original concept![10] That M. H. Baillie Scott should have had such a compelling influence over the long-term development of a suburban Pittsburgh property is remarkable.

In 1903–1904 Baillie Scott designed a house for a steeply sloping site in Switzerland (fig. 82).[11] The architectural solution placed the entrance toward the high side of the site and dropped the house down the slope, where it issued in descending terraces and gardens. When Olbrich worked with a similarly sloping site for his Silber house of 1906–1907 (fig. 83), he arrived at a quite similar solution.[12] When Scheibler

Fig. 84. Baird house, 1909.

Fig. 85. Baird house, 1909.

Fig. 86. Baird house, 1909, dining room.

was in turn presented with such a site—not at all uncommon in Pittsburgh—for a house for Charles W. Baird in 1909 (figs. 84–85), his solution fell in line in many particulars. Each house has dramatic side and rear elevations as the hillside drops away from it. Each has side and/or rear terraces undercut with low arched openings cut into exposed foundations. Baillie Scott's and Scheibler's houses have inset upper-story porches and first-story archways, and Scheibler's columned pavilion with a half cone roof looks suspiciously like Olbrich's pavilion as seen in partial elevation in published drawings.

Olbrich may have known Baillie Scott's design—

he had borrowed from Baillie Scott before. Scheibler probably knew both sources; but his house is the most informal and asymmetrical of the three and does not really resemble the others. Here Scheibler succeeded in molding a mix of progressive ideas into a more personal composition.

Photographs taken just after the Baird house was completed show how the house and its stone podium were accommodated to the site overlooking Pittsburgh's Oakland district (figs. 84–85). Interior views (figs. 86–88) show the openness of plan and the Arts and Crafts ambiance that Scheibler achieved in this and other houses of the period.[13]

A common feature of the larger country houses designed by Arts and Crafts architects was a differentiation between family living space and service space that was expressed in primary and secondary wings, often arranged as an L.[14] Scheibler used a similar arrangement for two large houses around 1910. In both, he extended the arms of the L in his own manner with a flat-roofed porch at one end and an open archway under a sloping roof at the other.

One of these houses (fig. 89) was designed not for Pittsburgh, but for a Philadelphia suburb. Like Scheibler's other out-of-town clients, Robert J. Scott had Pittsburgh associations. For Scott and Philadelphia, Scheibler designed the largest house of his career and demonstrated his ability to size up a new architectural challenge.

The influence of the Arts and Crafts Movement was felt in Philadelphia perhaps more than in any other American city. Many of the city's early twenti-

Fig. 87. Baird house, 1909, music room.

Fig. 88. Baird house, 1909, living room.

The Artistic House 91

Fig. 89. Scott house, ca. 1910.

eth-century architects used Arts and Crafts building materials and techniques. They resurrected heavy stone construction because of its role in the city's past and its craftsmanlike qualities, utilized neo-Georgian features indigenous to the region, and developed a unique local strain of restrained romantic composition. Scheibler responded to this context with his first major use of stone construction, employing a "Philadelphia schist," quarried near Lancaster, Pennsylvania, that had a highly textured and variegated surface. The Scott house's white wood trim, squarish small-paned windows, and a pent-eave over the entry door have Georgian sensibilities. Its asymmetrical massing and overall sense of expanse and comfort capture the local romantic ideal.

Scheibler brought many ideas from Pittsburgh, however. The tile roof is a familiar Scheibler assemblage of hipped and gabled elements. A flat-roofed sun porch with broadly arched openings is a strong minimalist statement. A prominent window on the facade has art glass with a colorful iris motif, and there are exposed I-beam lintels throughout.

Inside, the passage from the front of the house to the back is a more spacious version of the one at the Ament house; here it leads directly to a frame and glass breakfast room, the first of many polygonal spaces in Scheibler's work, which overlooks the rear garden. A wood-paneled entry hall opens onto a staircase that is the focus point for circulation and natural light. The stair hall is a large two-story cen-

Fig. 90. Rockledge, 1910.

tral space in the English tradition—though it does not function as a living hall as it would have for Baillie Scott. The interior is so spacious that there are continuous circulation patterns in both wings.

Somewhat surprisingly, the interior detailing is understated. The dominant decorative effect comes from the simple contrast of dark wood paneling and white plaster, and even the mantel over the large living room fireplace is but a simple arced board laid flat. Nevertheless, there is the requisite built-in cabinetwork, and interior doors have colorful art-glass panels with occasional floral motifs. The most striking ornament is a Rookwood tile bedroom fireplace with a rose motif.

Meanwhile, back in Pittsburgh, William E. Hamnett, the Wilkinsburg real estate speculator, was purchasing land adjacent to a Frick Park ravine. He named the property Rockledge because of its promontories of natural rock, laid out Briar Cliff Road as a private road through the property, and built a house for himself on the most striking promontory.[15]

Hamnett's house, Rockledge (figs. 90–91), does not share the relaxed sophistication of its Philadelphia counterpart. The front elevation, in particular, is more upright and uptight than the Scott house, and the straightforward sandstone construction, symmetrical fenestration, and gable roof with end chimneys are highly reminiscent of Western Pennsylvania vernacular houses of the early nineteenth century. The design also may have been influenced by Scot-

The Artistic House 93

Fig. 91. Rockledge, 1910. Shown after addition of garden wall.

Fig. 92. Charles Rennie Mackintosh, Windyhill, 1900.

tish vernacular housing by way of Mackintosh—a not totally unnatural synthesis, since many of the early settlers of the Pittsburgh region were from Scotland.

Though they differ somewhat in relative orientation, both Rockledge and Mackintosh's Windyhill (fig. 92) of 1900 are raised on promontories above sequences of planted terraces. Both houses are built of local stone, although Windyhill is stuccoed. Both houses have a dominant wing with an unbroken roofline and a planer elevation, and a secondary wing of more complex massing. The main entrance at Windyhill is located in a projecting block within the crook of the L, while at Rockledge it is located in a recess in the center of the long front elevation. But Windyhill's entry block reappears at Rockledge as a compositional element on a side elevation. Rockledge's open fenestration on either side of the entry, though flush with the facade, recalls the projecting glazed bay on the long elevation at Windyhill.[16]

Inside Rockledge (see fig. 93), the hall passage and stair hall are analogous to those at the Scott house, though the stair hall is an auxiliary space. A projecting glazed sun parlor at the end of the passage corresponds to the Scott house's octagonal breakfast nook. The passage itself was to be defined by screen walls with windows, much like the passage at Baillie Scott's Springcot, but this internal glazing was apparently omitted when the house was built.

Rockledge is remarkably unpretentious for a large house; but its dramatic siting and its natural affinity for its rocky surroundings assure its domination of its environs.

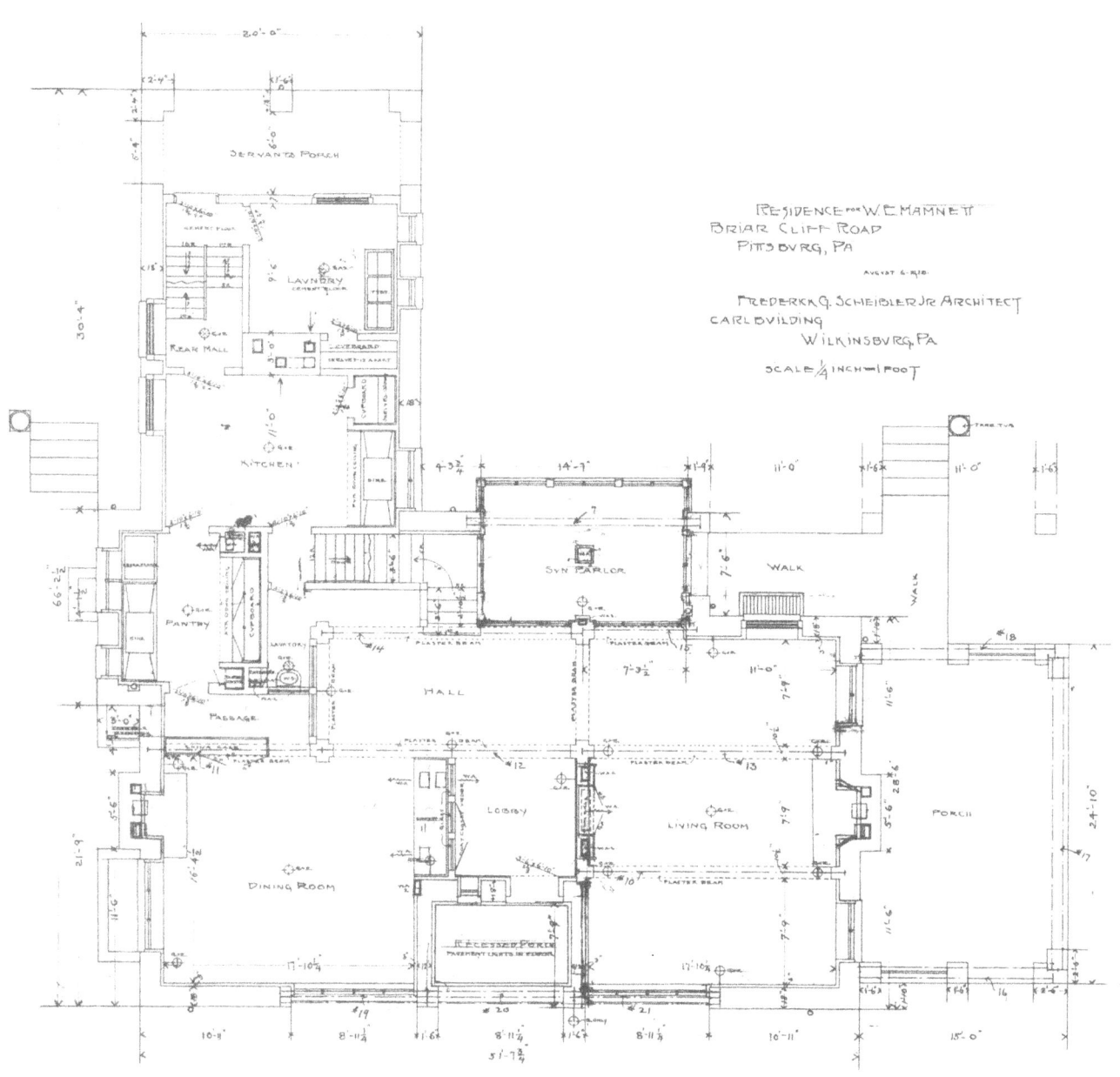

Fig. 93. Rockledge, 1910, first floor plan.

Next Scheibler turned to C. F. A. Voysey (1857–1941)—belatedly in a sense, for Voysey had much influenced both Baillie Scott and Mackintosh years before.[17] Voysey was almost exclusively concerned with small-scale domestic buildings in nonurban settings and believed that it was the architect's task to modify the English rural cottage tradition to meet current domestic needs. He worked out innumerable subtle variations on this theme using a vocabulary of asymmetrical massing, stucco walls, battered wall buttresses, and small casement windows.

"It seems to me," Voysey said, "that to produce any satisfactory work of art we must . . . go to Nature direct for inspiration and guidance. Then we are at once relieved from restrictions of style or period, and can live and work in the present with laws revealing always fresh possibilities."[18] Relieved from restrictions, Voysey's architecture depended largely on a principle of elimination. Voysey limited the form of each building to a minimal number of volumes and considered most ornament to be "pernicious." He was thus hailed as an innovator and in later years was credited with a key role in the advent of the so-called International Style.[19]

Scheibler was well acquainted with Voysey's work, as published in books in his library. He would have been attracted by its simplicity and vernacular sensibilities, and he absorbed much of what was chaste in Voysey's manner. But Scheibler was also drawn to unexpected elements of romanticism and complexity in Voysey's work. Voysey was fascinated by the possibilities of the pitched roof and how the meeting of wall and roof could be varied for visual effect. His experimentation resulted in roofs that run down to meet or dip below first-story rooflines, roofs that project to cover or to frame projecting bays, and portions of roofs carried horizontally across facades. Scheibler's affinity for such plastic roof forms was made apparent in projects like Willo'mound and in the Jones and Hellmund houses.

Scheibler's most blatantly Voyseyesque design was his house for Wesley W. Jones, a Wilkinsburg physician, built in 1915 in the East Wilkinsburg Improvement Company's Edgewood Acres subdivision, now part of the Pittsburgh suburb of Forest Hills. The Jones house (fig. 94) is a vertically attenuated version of the Orchard (fig. 95), Voysey's own house in a London suburb.[20] Both houses shared a favored Voysey idiom—the hipped roof with cross gables at each end.[21] And at both houses, as a further refinement, the symmetry of the twin gables is distorted by a long raking extension of one gable to echo a slope in the terrain.

Scheibler negated some of the simplicity that may have originally attracted him to Voysey by opting for red brick rather than Voysey's stucco. His exterior is furthered textured with accents of tile and art glass, exposed I-beams, and diamond-paned windows. The main entry is set within a central recess that is fitted with a built-in porch seat rather like an outdoor inglenook. These choices contributed to the visual appeal of the Jones house and reflected a then-growing tendency toward complexity and elaboration in Scheibler's work.

The Hellmund house (fig. 96) is well rooted in Scheibler's own work, dating way back to the Steel house of 1901. Both the Steel and Hellmund houses have a hip-roofed central block that is extended by a porch to the left and and a porte cochère to the right. But Voysey's influence dictated a critical difference.

Fig. 94. Wesley Jones house, 1915, front elevation.

Fig. 95. C.F.A. Voysey, the Orchard, 1899, garden elevation.

Fig. 96. Hellmund house, 1915.

At the Steel house, the tripartite scheme was explicit, expressed in three distinct masses. At the Hellmund house, it is implicit as the house embraces its exterior spaces to forge a single triangular mass under one roof.

Voysey's 1896 project for a house and studio for A. Sutro (fig. 97) was a possible influence here.[22] In this design, Voysey carried continuous slopes from a high hip roof down to second-story eaves on two sides, and first-story eaves on the other two sides. He reinforced the sense of slope with his signature battered buttresses. These features were closely echoed in two incomplete Scheibler projects—a "road house" or inn for former client Robert L. Matthews, and an unidentified house project—and again at the Hellmund house, where the configuration of sloping roofs encompasses both the porch and the porte cochère.[23] But where there is only a suggestion in Voysey's design, Scheibler folds back the roof over the porch and the porte cochère, and then halfway across the body of the house. The resulting sloping and folding roof planes forcefully unify the elevations of the house, correcting a weakness in Voysey's concept. Scheibler accents the effect by inserting small triangular spandrels, animated with random fragments of colored tile, at points where the roof planes intersect. The tile fragments and concrete interstices achieve the same general effect as art glass with leading.

All of this marvelously disguises the fact that the house itself is a rather smallish cube. The plan is compact but very open on the first floor (fig. 98). The flow of space between the principal rooms is regu-

98 The Artistic House

lated by a screen wall of dark wood and art glass, which partitions off the so-called ladies' room, and by a large freestanding fireplace, which cleverly opens to both the living and dining rooms. Here are open planning devices that were key to the spatial innovations of Baillie Scott and Frank Lloyd Wright, respectively. The house also has an obsession with corners. The main entry, understated and facing to the side, is located in the front right corner of the house. On the interior, every major room is entered at a corner, and all of the fireplaces—save for the large central one—are located in corners. All of this contributes to a sense of movement and complexity as the eye is alternately drawn through rooms and into their recesses.

The stucco exterior is enlivened with concrete

Fig. 97. C. F. A. Voysey, House and studio for A. Sutro, 1896, front elevation.

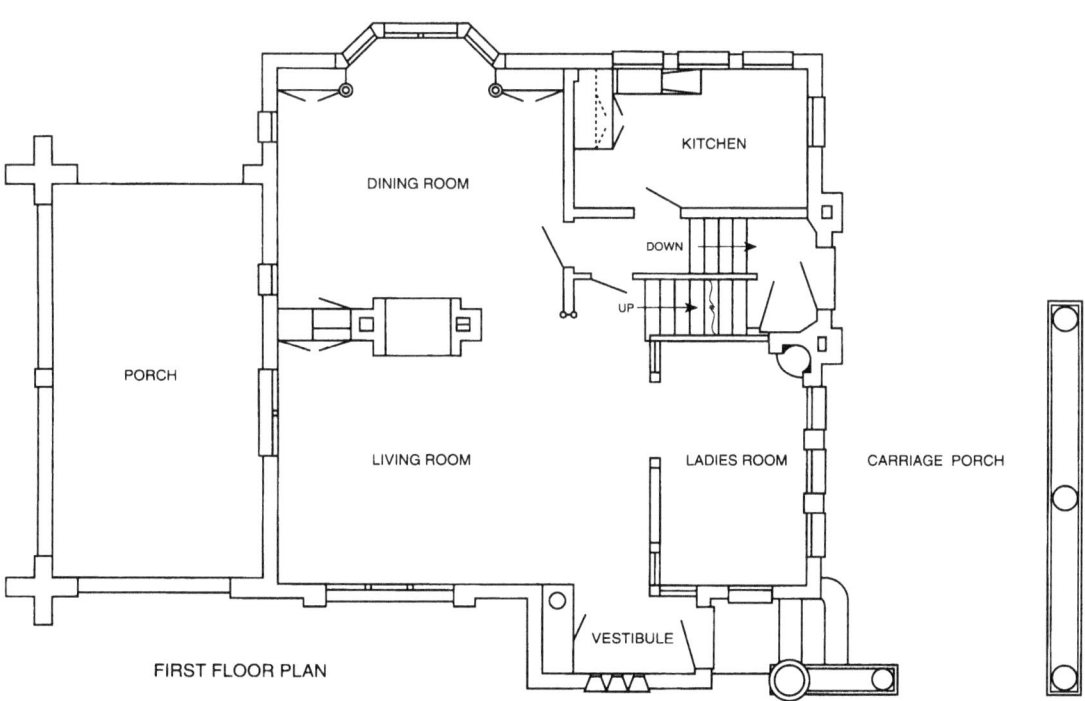

Fig. 98. Hellmund house, 1915, first floor plan (redrawn from blueprint).

The Artistic House 99

balconies and a wide variety of window treatments, ranging from broad window groups with diamond-shaped panes to vertical slits of green glass. A circular art-glass window with a floral motif is a pun on a rose window (they're not roses). The rooms abound with built-in cabinets, fireplaces with inset tiles, and an array of custom-designed lamps ranging from a bejeweled urn to a futuristic recessed ceiling fixture. This abundance of inventive detail turns the house into a jewel box.[24]

The Hellmunds chose Scheibler as their architect because they had lived in the Meado'cots group cottages and because they shared Scheibler's German heritage. A published biographical sketch of Rudolph E. Hellmund offers a rare level of detailed information about a Scheibler client. It states in part:

It was in 1907 that [Hellmund] entered the employ of the Westinghouse Electric & Manufacturing Company, becoming a designer of induction motors; . . . in 1912 he was placed in charge of the design of all current and alternating current railway motors. In this work he attracted the attention of engineers throughout the electrical profession by his inventive genius. . . . [In 1921] he was appointed engineering supervisor of development. In 1926 he was promoted to chief electrical engineer. . . . His prestige as an engineer and inventor has spread not only through the United States, but in the land of his nativity, Germany, and other countries of Europe, by reason of the patents, numbering almost three hundred, taken out in his name here and in foreign lands. . . . His work with the Westinghouse company has taken Mr. Hellmund constantly into other nations . . . At the beautiful Hellmund family home, at No. 7510 Trevanion Avenue, Swissvale, Pennsylvania, Mr. Hellmund devotes much of his leisure time to gardening.[25]

Hellmund was the sort of man to have the inscription *Vincit Omnia Veritas* (Truth Conquers All) painted over his fireplace.

For this practical yet romantic client, Scheibler designed an exemplary artistic house. For their part, the Hellmunds had a love affair with their house, calling it, in an affectionate German diminutive, their *Hauschen*.[26]

A series of houses that followed proceeded naturally out of Scheibler's previous work, but they also share a family resemblance—and a specific vocabulary of battered walls, hip roofs, and segmentally arced window sash—with the Schultz house (fig. 99) in Kenilworth, Illinois, designed by George W. Maher in 1907 and exhibited at the Pittsburgh Architectural Club Exhibition in 1910.[27] Maher, too, had studied Voysey's work, and the battered walls and doorway of the Schultz house were derived from Voysey. Scheibler would have known the Schultz house, at least in a photograph, and it must have elicited a sympathetic response in him.

To the whimsical eye, Scheibler's McLaughlin house (fig. 100) resembles a house of cards with overlapping wall planes leaned into position. The battered walls of Vilsack Row are here rebuilt in white brick and reoriented at the front and rear of a two-story box. The facade is cut away like a template and filled in with broad bands of windows, establishing the solid-void relationships of Vilsack Row. This is a tamer version, to be sure, with the windows and the facade wall operating within the same plane—but the porch still springs out of the void instead of the wall. In his drawings for the Nolan house (fig. 101), Scheibler positioned a second template in front of a near reprise of the McLaughlin house facade to create an open arcadelike porch and porte cochère.

Fig. 99. George W. Maher, Schultz house, 1907.

Fig. 100. McLaughlin house, 1915.

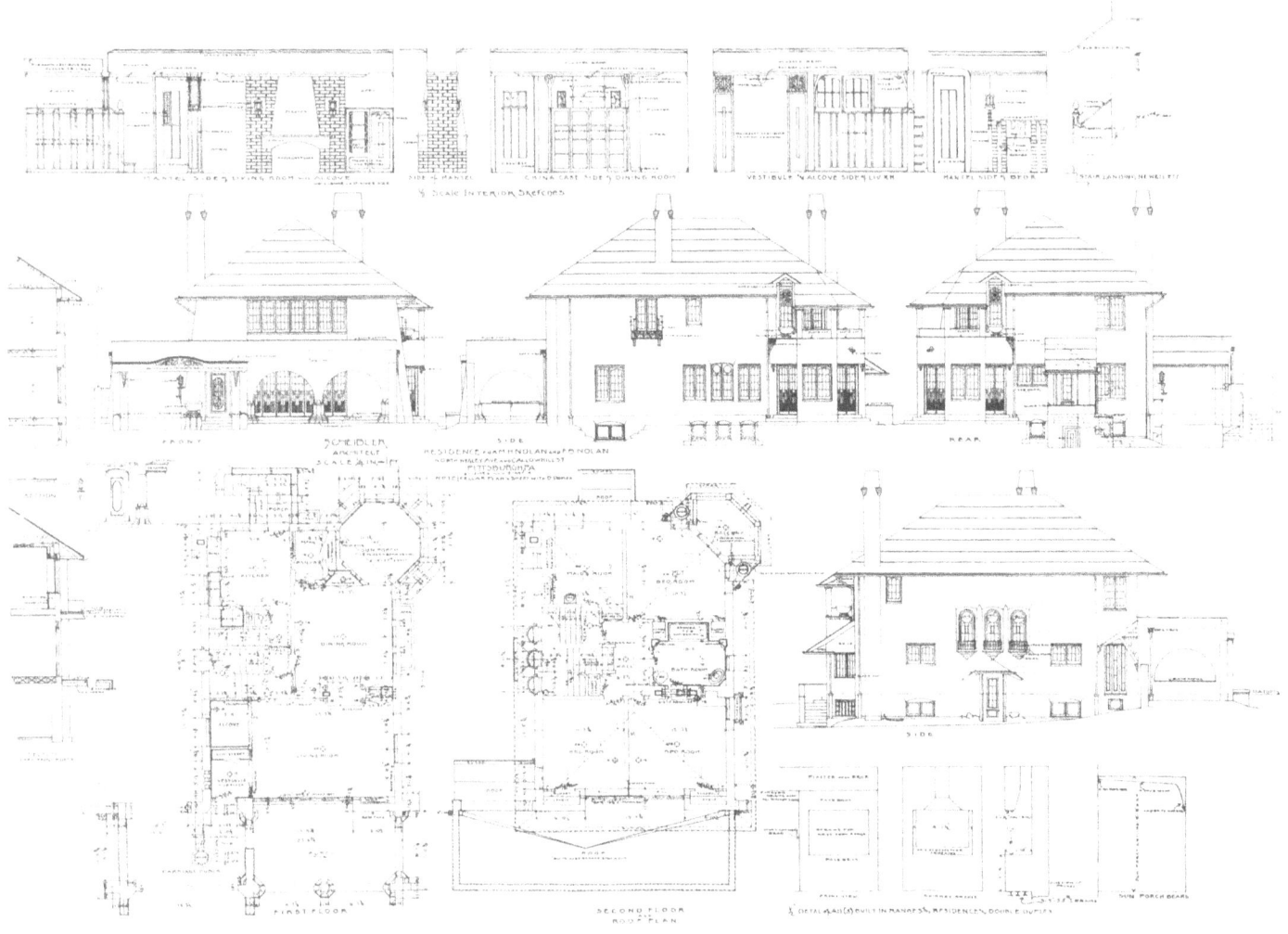

Fig. 101. Nolan house, 1919, elevations and plans.

The potential severity of these treatments is softened by fine detailing. At the McLaughlin house, the front porch has rounded columns with vertically ribbed caps, the entries are framed by surrounds of concentric brick arches, and there is a shallow arced window bay on a side elevation. The Nolan house design called for a polygonal rear sun porch, a metalwork and tile exterior balcony, and an elaborate interior featuring freestanding posts with cutout caps that have their source in Mackintosh. Both house designs have windows with grids of art glass.

At the Wach house (fig. 102) in Swissvale, circa 1920, the horizontal facade, hip roof, window forms, and particularly the planter at the sills of the second-story windows recall Maher's Schultz house once again, more literally than before.[28] But the house's simple boxlike form is unaccountably sober and the detailing is less extensive, larger in scale, and less integral to the design than before. It seems as if the house, built on a large terraced lot in an otherwise dense neighborhood, was designed to be seen from a distance. Two key elements provide focal points from street level: a battered and angled buttress, which accents a front corner and originally pointed to an open inset porch, now enclosed; and an extraordinary not-so-sober front porch, which is centered on the facade. With its three-sided plan, the porch is another variation on a polygonal theme; but here the two angled sides are openwork wood screens with distorted neo-Gothic motifs. These trefoils and pendants recall the work of California architect Bernard Maybeck, but were anomalies for Scheibler.

The 1919 Nolan commission was Scheibler's first major postwar project, but it remained only a case of what might have been. Scheibler initially drew up plans for three side-by-side buildings—a house and two double duplexes. When construction began, however, one double duplex was omitted. And when the Nolan house and the remaining double duplex were completed, they approximated Scheibler's draw-

Fig. 102. Wach house, ca. 1920. Shown with alterations.

ings in both plan and massing, but were simplified to such an extent that they no longer looked like Scheibler's designs. In fact, when builders' contracts for the project were announced, the architect was listed as A. R. Douglass.[29]

The story can be partially reconstructed from court records. Scheibler and the Nolans signed a contract in June 1919. Scheibler subsequently showed little restraint in the design, and when the bids were first let in October, they came in at the staggering figure of $122,621.06, even excluding many items. This was a much higher figure than the clients had anticipated; in fact they later claimed to have made an informal agreement with the architect that the project would not cost more than $50,000. The Nolans dismissed Scheibler after allowing him to supervise the laying of foundations. They then went on to hire Douglass, with whom they had worked before, and acquainted him with Scheibler's plans in a quest for a cheaper version of the design.

Scheibler sued.[30] He denied any agreement about the projected cost, claimed that he had been dismissed without just cause, and alleged that the Nolans and their new architect had improperly used his plans and specifications. The numbers are a little complex, but simply put, Scheibler sued for $7357.26 (6 percent of the projected project cost as bid). Years later, in 1933, he was awarded approximately half that amount, plus interest, by the court. The original contract was held valid and Scheibler officially won, but his design was ruined and withal it must have been a sobering episode.

8 Charmed Territory

AFTER THE ACHIEVEMENTS OF Highland Towers and Vilsack Row, Scheibler's use of a very rich decorative palette seems reactionary, but his projects of the early twenties were more elaborate than anything that came before. Eva Harter blamed this on the influence of her husband, Frank, who apparently encouraged Scheibler to indulge in what she called "doodads." An impulse toward romantic elaboration was, however, a not unnatural by-product of the artistic house philosophy. As Baillie Scott rather histrionically put it:

The natural reaction from the dry mechanical routine of modern life leads to a demand for Romance in every form. In the form of fiction it supplies a retreat, an escape for the mind to an enchanted realm where thrilling deeds may be done without danger, and beautiful habitations enjoyed without expense. In the treatment of the house a more real and permanent haven may be secured. Here at least we may say there shall be no ugliness. On crossing this threshold we pass into charmed territory, where everything we possess shall be in harmony.[1]

In their favor, most of Scheibler's buildings from the early twenties were little dependent upon specific sources and are masterful on their own terms. Here Scheibler emerges fully as a maker of artistic environments. The first intimation of things to come came with the high and almost medieval roof of the Pyle house (fig. 103) in 1919.[2] Thereafter, between 1920 and 1925, Scheibler produced three extraordinary

Fig. 103. Pyle house, 1919.

houses and two multiunit projects in his most effusive domestic manner, before wavering.³

The first such project was a house for William D. Johnston, president of the American Lumber and Supply Company, and his wife Clara E. Johnston. The Johnstons owned three Highland Park building lots. Undecided about how much of the property to retain and develop, they eventually commissioned three designs for differently sized sites.⁴ Scheibler sketched the first two designs on a single sheet of paper. The smaller of the two was suggestive of two overlapping hip-roofed pavilions. The larger design (fig. 104) consisted of a broad central block with battered walls and a hip roof—echoes once again of Ma-

Fig. 104. Johnston house, ca. 1920, sketches.

Fig. 105. Johnston house, 1921–1922, front elevation.

her's Schultz house—extended with subsidiary masses and ultimately by a huge integral garage. A unique feature was an oval forecourt formed by a low wall and a concave indentation in the center of the facade.[5] The house that the Johnstons finally built in 1921–1922, the smallest of the three designs, was another hip-roofed pavilion.

Of all of his houses, the Johnston house (fig. 105) expresses most fully the range of Scheibler's domestic manner. With its simple cubelike massing, self-effacing stucco, and crisp detailing, it is a lineal descendent of the modest early houses. Echoes of Scheibler's classical past also come to the surface. Apparent symmetry and strong compositional centrality convey a sense of classical order. Side elevations feature tripartite neo-Palladian windows. Given a full southern exposure, set further back from the street than its neighbors, and raised on a slight hill (artificially produced by grading of the site), the house masquerades as a pint-sized Palladian villa on a Mediterranean hilltop.[6] A freestanding garage is equipped with living quarters and its own neo-Palladian window and plays the role of a dignified outbuilding in service to its villa.

Scheibler's classical sensibilities are not in full control, however. Columns that frame the entry look Secessionist in their caps of vertical ribs and checkerboard tile inserts. These support a roof shared with an

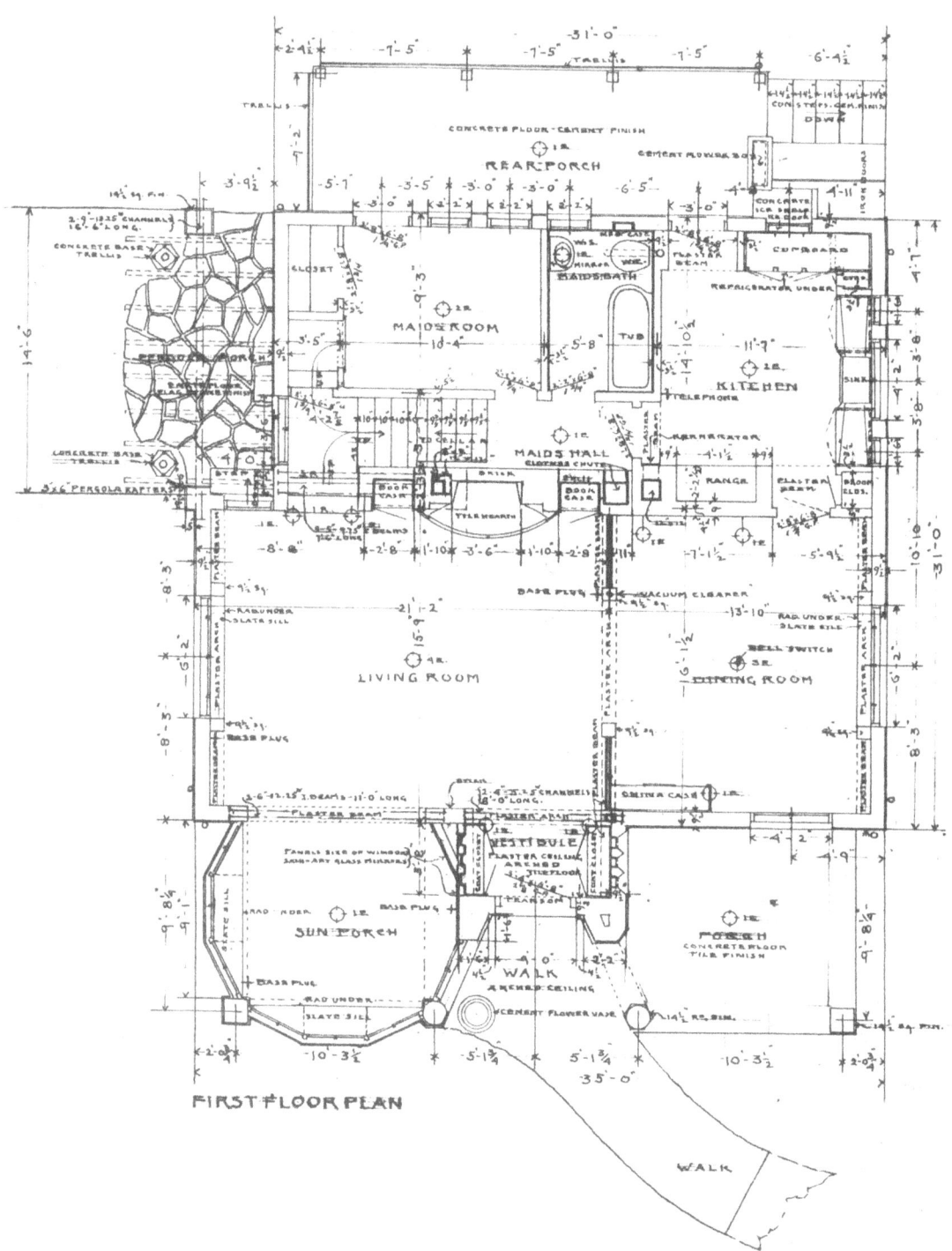

Fig. 106. Johnston house, 1921–1922, first floor plan.

open porch to the right and an enclosed sun porch to the left. The sun porch, a seemingly insubstantial construction of wood and glass, is a particularly subtle use of the polygonal form. It is a free element within the grid of the facade, where it disrupts the apparent symmetry, and it casually unbalances both the massing and the plan of the house.[7] It also functions like a sundial as the sun tracks daily across the southern sky, giving growth to vines in the art-glass windows, motifs reminiscent of the designs of California architects Greene and Greene.[8]

Classical organization breaks down almost entirely inside (see fig. 106). The entry opens onto the living room, where the expectation of a central hall plan is immediately contradicted by a major cross axis extending across the width of the house. This axis links living and dining rooms of unequal size, anchored by arched windows on the side walls and an archway between the two rooms. The living room fireplace, a key focal point, is placed just off-axis from the entry. Centrality reappears only on the second floor where rooms radiate from a central hall. The house is actually quite small, but includes a sun porch, living room, dining room, kitchen, maid's room, three bedrooms, three full bathrooms, and a sleeping porch in its compact plan.[9]

Mahogany cabinets in the entry hall, screen-wall room dividers with art-glass panels, a fireplace surround of Moravian tiles, built-in light fixtures, and other fine details demonstrate Scheibler's growing penchant for rich interior treatments, completing the house's multifaceted personality.

When Scheibler designed a near reprise of this house (fig. 107) for Frank and Eva Harter in Ventnor City, New Jersey, in 1929, he was presented with a very different site, just one lot removed from the Atlantic Ocean. Scheibler responded to the virtues of the site by adding a side entry and bay window facing the ocean, and a historic photograph shows the house in splendid isolation with boardwalk and ocean in the middle distance. But the small dimensions of the lot dictated the placement of the house just behind the sidewalk and forced the incorporation of the garage into a somewhat awkward rear wing; and Scheibler's gestures toward the ocean were ultimately nullified when a house was built on the adjacent lot, permanently blocking the view. These constricted site conditions, the peculiar choice of brown brick as the primary building material, and some simplification of the detailing render the house a less well-conceived object than its antecedent.

Frank Harter was a Russian Jewish immigrant, a dapper man, musical, with a keen artistic sense, who traveled extensively in Europe.[10] He earned his livelihood in Pittsburgh as a builder-developer and a liquor importer.[11] Scheibler's long relationship with the Harters resulted in numerous commissions during the 1920s. These included a Pittsburgh house in the Squirrel Hill district, two summer houses at the New Jersey shore, a house at Conneaut Lake, Pennsylvania, and a couple of proposed houses in Switzerland, though the last may have amounted to little more than daydreams.

When the Harters commissioned their Pittsburgh house (figs. 108–109) in 1922, Scheibler was able to indulge himself and his clients. Unfortunately, they all outdid themselves. A garage was built first, to try out a mortaring technique, and when materials were

Fig. 107. Harter house (Ventnor City, N.J.), ca. 1929.

Fig. 108. Harter house (Pittsburgh), 1922–1924. Shown under construction.

stolen from the building site, the Harters moved into rooms over the garage. Construction of the house was a long process with substantial cost overruns. Both stone and stonemasons were brought from the Philadelphia area at considerable expense, some inferior flooring had to be removed and replaced at Scheibler's insistence, and all the decorative "doo-dads" added up quickly. The Harters finally moved into the house, but soon developed severe cash flow problems. (Prohibition obviously curtailed Harter's liquor importing business, although there are persistent rumors, denied by the family, that Harter was a bootlegger.) The Harters were forced to sell the house early in 1925, and over the next few years sold off many of their other properties, forswore a couple of multifamily projects they had commissioned from Scheibler, and retreated to Europe for a while.

Unlike its neighbors, the Harter house is deeply set back from the street on an oversized lot and is visually screened by a freestanding wall.[12] The house is built into the slope of a hill and acts like a retaining wall and barrier, *forcing* the driveway to curve dramatically around it. It is Scheibler's first western Pennsylvania building to be sheathed in the Philadelphia schist that he had first used at the Scott house. The gray stone walls taken together resemble a weathered boulder. The memorable roofs are massed like mushroom caps and covered with pseudo-thatch wood shingling, somewhat in the manner of moss. If the Johnston house is a white villa on a southern hilltop, the Harter house is a den in a northern forest. This is an *organic* architecture more literal than Frank Lloyd Wright's.

The roofing, of course, harkened back to English vernacular practice. (Voysey occasionally specified

Fig. 109. Harter house (Pittsburgh), 1922–1924.

real thatch.) As for the American version, Scheibler owned a book, published in 1909, in which the prominent architect and writer Aymer Embury II wrote:

One of the most interesting things which has lately been developed is a method of shingling roofs to produce the softness of a thatched roof. Sharp and angular lines are hard to disassociate from new buildings, and it is softness of outline and color which gives to old work its particular charm. Many architects have therefore resorted to all sorts of devices to get the peculiar quality of old work in new houses, and of these, the curving of the shingle roofs is as helpful a one as has yet been found.[13]

In Pittsburgh, the pseudo-thatch roof has become popularly equated with Scheibler, but he neither introduced it locally nor used it frequently.[14] For Scheibler it was only a passing fancy, valued as much for its plasticity as for its antiquated charm. He called for "thatch" in only three known commissions, and only this one was built.[15]

The Harter house is essentially rectangular in plan (see fig. 110), but it is rounded off by bowed bays on three sides and extended by an entry porch and a porte cochère, both with their own mounds of "thatch." The massing is asymmetrical, and the porch is emphatically off-center, swung around a bowed bay housing the internal stairway. The main entry is centered on the facade, however, and the symmetrical centrally organized plan inside is of the sort that one

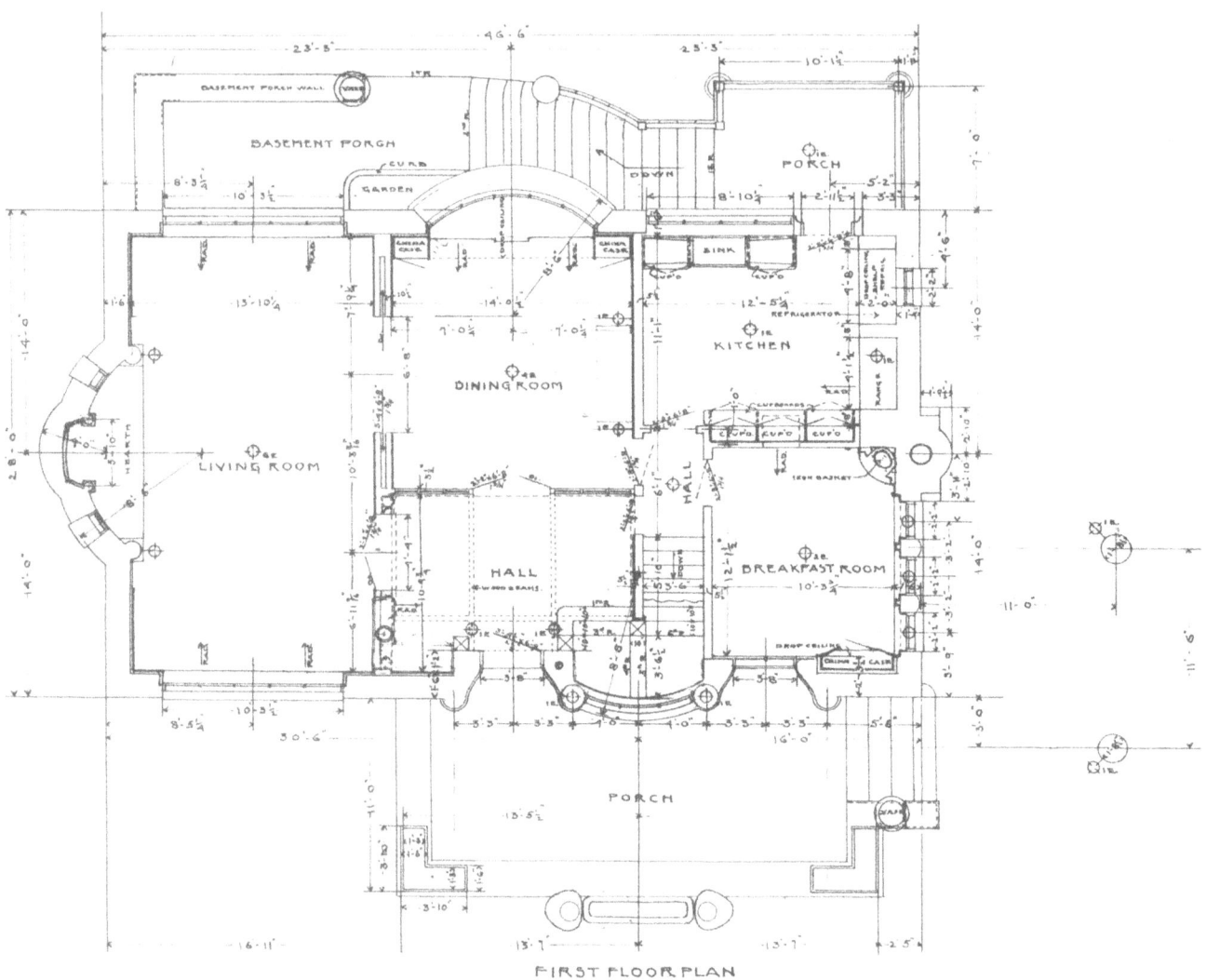

Fig. 110. Harter house (Pittsburgh), 1922–1924, first floor plan.

Fig. 111. Harter house (Pittsburgh), 1922–1924, living room.

expects to find at the Johnston house but doesn't. A three-bay system generates both the first-and second-floor plans, and the stairway, so important to the exterior design, is but an interruption in the plan. Again, Scheibler has unpredictably paired elevations and plans.

The living room is dominated by a huge apselike fireplace (fig. 111) which projects as an independent volume beyond the end wall of the house. The ceiling-height surround is comprised of a series of stone columns and arches, and envelops inset lamps, windows, and mirrors in addition to the hearth itself. This whole thing seems much too large, but not out of keeping: it evokes the whole house within the house.

Throughout the house there is an extraordinary array of built-in cabinets and lamps, tiled fireplaces, and art glass. The entry hall and dining room share a window-wall of double doors and six large art-glass panels with hollyhocks. Art glass elsewhere features naturalistic motifs, including birds and spider webs and, in the master bedroom, water lilies that transform dressing mirrors into reflecting pools.[16] An eagle, perched on the newel post of the stair, may have symbolized the adopted nation of an immigrant client, and carved wood panels with squirrels invoke their namesakes in the Squirrel Hill neighborhood.[17]

Eva Harter complained about the lack of wall space for furniture in her rather overdecorated new home; and the Harter house does in fact exaggerate some basic progressive principles. But, between the thatch and the squirrels, it ultimately succeeds as an artistic, expressive, and even playful object.[18]

Before choosing Scheibler to design their own Highland Park house, Allen M. Klages and his wife, Elizabeth, visited a number of the architect's other buildings, including the house of Elizabeth's cousin, William D. Johnston. The Klages were ultimately proud of their house—family memorabilia includes a Christmas card that displays a drawing of the house shortly after its completion—but they may have questioned their choice at times. They reportedly had to prod Scheibler to assure the house's completion and filed suit against him over a disagreement about upstairs flooring.[19]

The Klages house (figs. 112–113) is among the most easily overlooked of Scheibler's important buildings because it is largely obscured by foliage; but with or without foliage, the house lacks the conceptual clarity of the Johnston and Harter houses, and no dominant theme is apparent when it is viewed from the street. Steep roofs dominate, pitching downward until they meet the relieving arches of the first-story windows and projecting outward over a broad recessed porch. The porch is framed by low canted walls, like recumbent consoles, that visually carry the downward thrust of the roofs safely to the ground. Floor-length windows line the cavity of the porch, and there is no apparent entry. It is only as one begins to move around the building that sizable stone walls emerge and begin to interpret the ambiguous forms of the facade. The house is actually composed of a rectilinear and steeply gabled forward section, a cross-gabled rear section, and a projecting polygonal tower on the east side.

This tower (fig. 113) contains the missing main entrance on its lower level, and above it a glazed sewing room behind a shallow concrete balcony. Despite its status as entry, however, the tower appears as an appendage, peripheral to the exterior as a whole and certainly to the facade. As it turns out, it is also peripheral to the plan. The entry leads into a small hall that issues in the main stair, but all circulation from the entry is oblique, and the main rooms of the house are swung around in an entirely different orientation.

Unlike the Johnston and Harter houses, there is no sudden sense of surprise upon entry because no expectation of the plan has been developed. Nevertheless, it seems peculiar that one must execute a 135-degree turn to proceed from the entry into the primary living spaces of the house. Only then does the axial disposition of the living and dining rooms make clear a similarity to the Johnston house.[20] The plan is somewhat more formal here, however, as the living room fireplace and some doorways establish minor axes.

The house's elaborate decorative program (see fig.

Fig. 112. Klages house, 1922–1923, front elevation.

Fig. 113. Klages house, 1922–1923, detail.

Charmed Territory 115

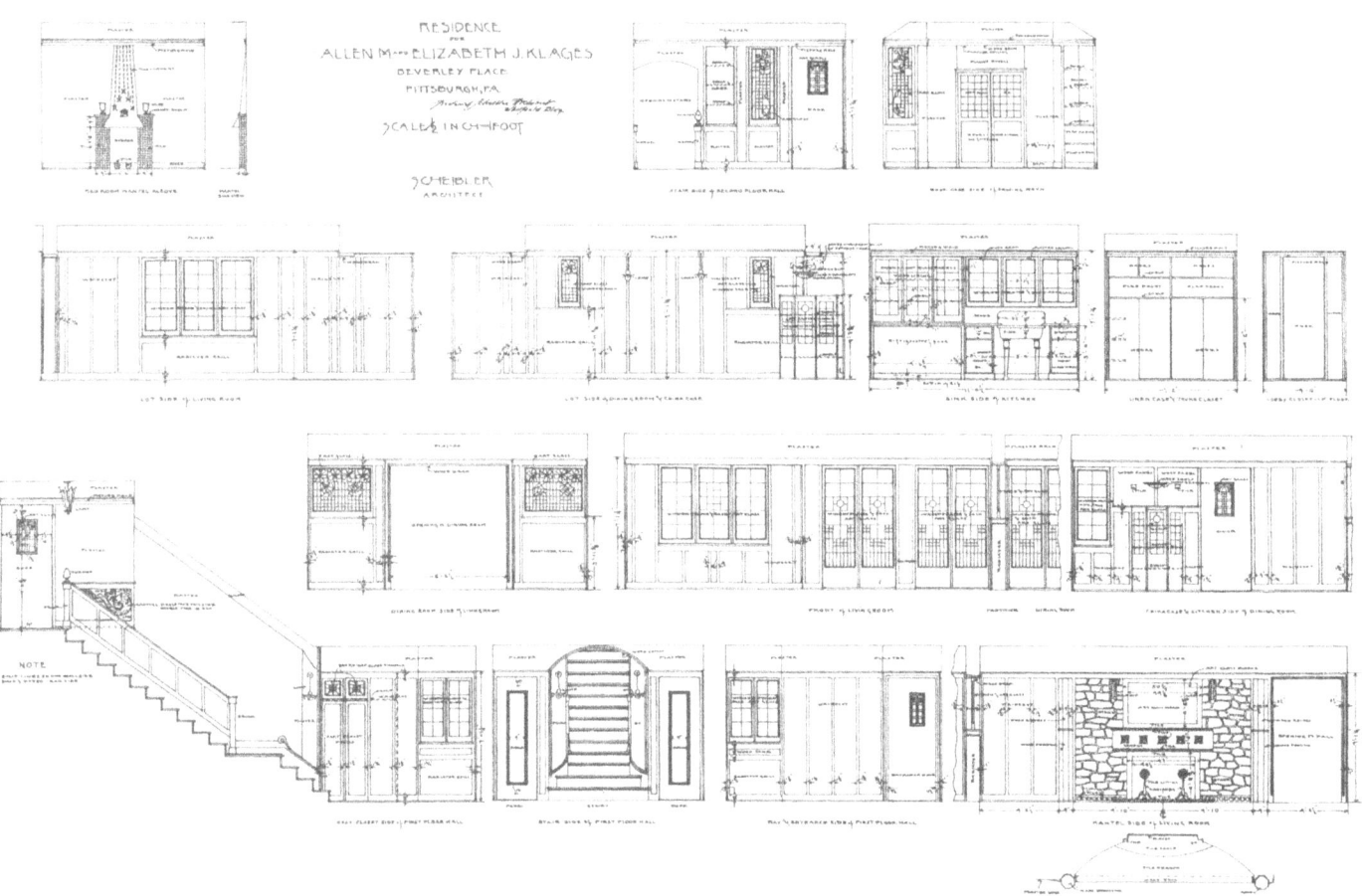

Fig. 114. Klages house, 1922–1923, interior elevations.

114) is second only to that of the Harter house. Dormers with art-glass parrots are among the few features that are clearly visible from the street. The tall windows that line the porch recess have grids of art glass. Inside, the living and dining rooms are paneled in dark wood, and screen-wall room dividers consist of art-glass panels with flower and spider web motifs surmounting radiators masked by grilles. The living room is focused on a large stone and tile fireplace (fig. 115) with an overmantel of opaque art glass that depicts a sailing ship. The ship and other decorative motifs were chosen for Mr. Klages, who reportedly loved travel, birds, and the sea.

The iconography of travel and nature lops easily over into the iconography of European fairy tales. A carved wooden dragon lives at the top of the stair, and perchance the fair maiden's only hope of escape from a solitary life of sewing in the tower room is to let down her hair from the balcony in the hope that a brave knight will climb to her rescue.[21]

Fig. 115. Klages house, 1922–1923, living room.

The closure of the facade by both design and foliage, the indirect entry, and flights of fancy in the detailing make this house, more than any other, a private inner world. One who crosses this threshold truly enters into charmed territory.

Scheibler never designed a typical Pittsburgh duplex, that is, a two-story building with one residential unit on each floor; but he did design a number of double duplexes that accommodate four units, two per floor. At Parkstone Dwellings (fig. 116) in Pittsburgh's Point Breeze neighborhood, the four units are expressed in the unusual and somewhat mannerist device of four side-by-side entry doors approached by four separate walkways. One or two entries was much more common for this building type, but the four discreet entries indeed make these units *dwellings*, private beyond the front stoop. As in previous projects, Scheibler was striving to have it both ways, introduc-

Fig. 116. Parkstone Dwellings, 1922.

ing elements expressive of the home in a multifamily dwelling. But the impact of the four doorways is compositional as well as emotional. The doorways stretch the concept of a compositional center to the limit and ultimately defer to the dominant masses of the outer portions of the building, where polygonal bays give way to large cubes. The differentiated massing is then reined in by a broad high roof and a tall central chimney that forcefully unify the building. The chimney, poised in an unlikely position over entries and stair halls, is first and foremost a compositional device; but it does carry flues that veer over to meet it from the living room fireplaces.

All four units share one basic plan that is flopped from side to side and adjusted slightly on the second floor within a C-shaped footprint. The living rooms open into the polygonal bays and focus on fireplaces along the stair halls. Bedrooms radiate from a so-called telephone lobby toward the rear and are arranged along a central rear court.

Parkstone Dwellings displays blatantly romantic and even exotic qualities. One of Scheibler's drawings shows that the front garden was carefully planned on a diagonal grid, projected outward from the polygonal bays, which determined the placement of plantings and other landscape features. But over-

118 Charmed Territory

laid on this grid is a romantic layout of walkways, and the garden as a whole is strongly oriental in feeling. The roof that assures unity is actually made up of multiple folds with peaks and valleys, like origami. The walls are richly textured schist, and leaded-glass windows add a textural overlay. Naturalistic motifs are rampant. Concrete mushroom piers are planted before each entry—mushrooms more naturalistic in placement but more stylized in form than those at the Old Heidelberg. There is a twining-rose motif in the art glass of the entry doors, and a fully sculpted seagull is randomly perched at the southeast corner of the facade.

The interior is extensively paneled with Laguna mahogany, and each living room has a colorful wall panel of opaque art glass with exotic scenes of mountains and towers.[22] The living room fireplaces are massive stone constructions which, as at the Harter house, echo the exterior on the interior. Large inset tiles depict panthers and kingfishers (see fig. 117).[23] And then there are the oriental carpets.

The image of colorful oriental carpets permanently hung over exterior balconies has intrigued passersby for decades. What appear to be rugs, however, are actually tilework spandrel treatments between the upper and lower stories of the polygonal bays, roughly analogous to the tile spandrels at Highland Towers in both their deployment and their source in fabric design. They provide a great display of Moravian tiles. Presumably requested by the client, who owned a large collection of oriental rugs, the tiles were reportedly arranged and assembled by Scheibler himself.[24]

Parkstone Dwellings was the first of at least four commissions that Scheibler received from Harry Rubins and his sister, Rose Rubins. The Rubins were

Fig. 117. Parkstone Dwellings, 1922, fireplace detail.

both employed by the Wilkinsburg Real Estate Company, but had their own real estate interests as well, and they commissioned both personal and speculative projects from Scheibler. Only ten years after it was built, Harry Rubins lost the Parkstone Dwellings when it was sold at a sheriff's sale. But he demonstrated his love for this memorable building by having Scheibler recreate some aspects of the interior—including the stone fireplace with the kingfisher tiles—at another site.

The Woodlands was one of two multiunit projects commissioned by Frank Harter for prominent sites in Shadyside that never made it off of Scheibler's draw-

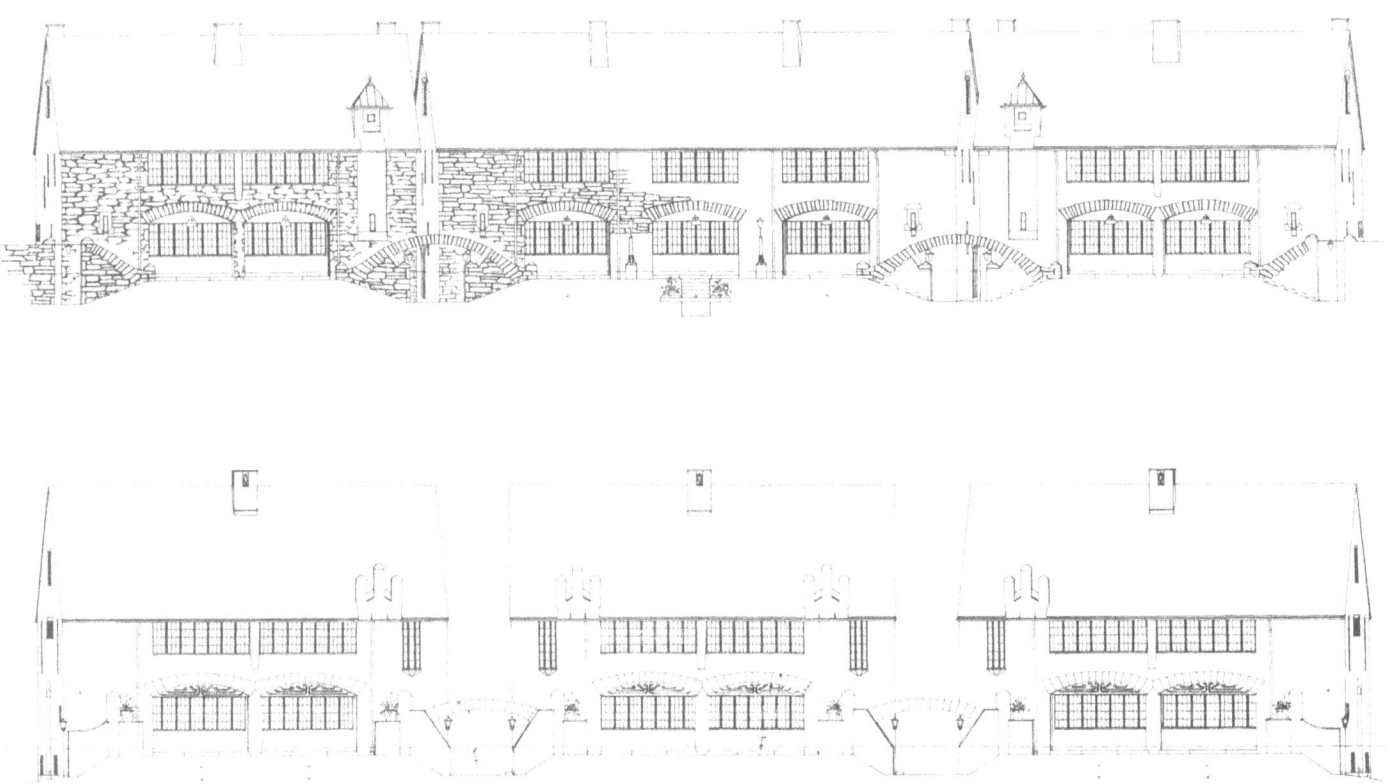

Fig. 118. The Woodlands, 1925, front elevations. Two versions.

ing board. The drawings include two different designs for three groups of semidetached houses (fig. 118). One version called for seven units grouped two-three-two; but the alternate six-unit version was probably the more likely candidate for construction. Both versions incorporated archways that spanned passages between the separate buildings and literally linked the entire group.[25] Both versions featured broad window groups under relieving arches and deeply recessed porches like those at the Klages house. And both versions called for a rich texture of stonework, art glass, and tile, inside and out.

The Woodlands was analogous to Scheibler's group cottages of ten to fifteen years before. But these are group cottages that have lost the audacity of youth and have gone soft. Not only, for instance, are the roofs not flat, but their broad sloping planes are broken by the awkward and arbitrary devices of false dormers with pointy hats in one design and unintelligible trident-shaped thingamajigs in the other. The Woodlands was presumably designed to Frank Harter's liking and was in keeping with the richly detailed projects that came before. But this retreat into charmed territory was lacking in harmony. And in its wake, Scheibler seemingly began to have second thoughts about what he was doing.

9   Up-to-Date and Familiar

FOLLOWING THE EXTRAVAGANCES of the early 1920s, Scheibler's work turned away from elaboration and idiosyncratic architectural concepts toward increasing simplification and a more common denominator of contemporary design. The impulse toward simplification waxed and waned in Scheibler's work, and its reemergence in the late 1920s seems not unnatural, in the wake of such romantic excesses. The growing normalization of Scheibler's work was new, however—heretofore only his very earliest projects could claim to have met any contemporary standard of normalcy. This tendency was made evident, to a greater or lesser degree, in all of Scheibler's subsequent work, to the end that the products of this phase of his career have literally disappeared into the landscape.

Scheibler was not alone in losing his progressive sense of direction. Historical styles were widely resurgent by the 1920s, and many of the progressives ultimately turned back to more conventional sources: Olbrich to the Renaissance Revival, Voysey to the Gothic, Baillie Scott to various medieval modes. With the single exception of Frank Lloyd Wright, the major progressives failed to consistently develop their most important ideas. In fact, Scheibler distinguished himself in this crowd by turning not so much to the historical past but to a more banal present, and he never totally gave up his individualistic detailing.

Most of the progressive European movements were never widely accepted, and interest in the one that was—the English Arts and Crafts Movement—was fading as early as 1910.[1] The Arts and Crafts Movement is often said to have ended with the failure of the American furniture and publishing empire of Gustav Stickley in 1916 and the subsequent onset of World War I, which dispatched many a progressive notion. The 1920s was an age of instant gratification and materialism, a mindset diametrically opposed to the handcrafts aesthetic, and machine-age Art Deco and Art Moderne assumed the banner of newness. Eventually, of course, the European modernists won the day; men like Adolph Loos, who repudiated all ornament, and Walter Gropius and Le Corbusier, who denied any need for links to the past and associations with tradition.

The change in Scheibler's work during the 1920s and 1930s may have grown out of his self-directed evolution. More likely, it was an inevitable result of the increasingly difficult job of obtaining commissions. His later work was a less distinctive architecture; but it was not without achievement. There were unexpected experiments along the way, and a whole body of work was done for a major new client.

Scheibler's first domestic project of this period was the only one to flirt with traditional architectural styling. Albert Q. Starr, whose house was sited deep within its Squirrel Hill lot, commissioned two houses for the street front of his property in 1927. The two new buildings were sited to flank the preexisting driveway and frame a common central space. Ultimately, Starr demolished the original house and kept one of the new houses for himself. The Starr houses (fig. 119) are planer red brick masses with successive cross-gabled wings that step down the sloped grade of the site. The forward sections are broken by inset porches with angled and peaked corner piers. Ornamentation was limited to broad bands of tile along selected cornices and diamond-shaped panes in the leaded-glass windows, none of which was carried out.[2] The tall thin gable ends, the peaked porch piers, and the diamond-shaped panes all suggest the Gothic. Inside, a round entrance hall opens directly from the porch and controls all passage into the surrounding spaces and the second floor. One of a series of circular and oval spaces found in Scheibler's work, it is the only one to establish a radial spatial scheme.

The Kinter and Frease houses, Scheibler's large-budget houses of the late 1920s, were built in the desirable residential suburbs of Greentree and Churchill, where deed restrictions set minimum costs for new house construction. The Kinter house recalls the

Fig. 119. Starr houses, ca. 1927, side elevation.

Fig. 120. Frease house, 1928.

Scott house of 1910, the largest of Scheibler's early houses, in the broad disposition of its massing and the hip-roofed pavilion that projects from its facade. The Frease house (fig. 120) is similar in composition, but its lot demanded a higher minimum cost, so for their extra money the clients got stone rather than brick and more rooms. The stone construction is aptly emphasized by stone relieving arches and a massive stone block lintel over the main entry.

These houses are all picturesque to a degree, but there is little to distinguish them from other houses of their time and place. They fit all too comfortably within their communities.

Considerably more modest but more appealing are a pair of identical speculative houses designed for Rose Rubins (fig. 121) at the eastern edge of Pittsburgh's Frick Park in about 1929.[3] Each house is a gabled box, common and undistinguished save for a few details that reveal Scheibler's hand and suggest that distinctive ornamentation was still possible—at least for a familiar client. A few windows have art glass with familiar bird motifs, and a large colorful tile is prominently situated above the front door.[4] Most significantly, a polygonal two-story bay with a spandrel treatment of small brownish red tiles is almost a caricature of the bays and "oriental carpets" at the

Parkstone Dwellings, which had been designed for Rubins's brother some years before.

One final multiunit domestic structure shows Scheibler come sort of full circle. In 1930 Fred C. McCafferty sold Scheibler his mail-order house in the North Hills. Shortly thereafter he commissioned a group of four row houses in the town of Turtle Creek.[5] Scheibler's first row house design after fifteen years shares much of the simplicity of his earlier row house projects, but lacks their aggressiveness. There are no receding planes or bands of glazing, just planer white-brick surfaces and—until recently—leaded-glass windows. The roof, far from flat, is hipped and causes the units to read almost as one. Here Scheibler placed multiple units within the simple white hip-roofed box that he might have used for a small house years before.

Scheibler also received commercial commissions during the 1920s and 1930s, his first in many years. A commission circa 1926 from Daniel L. Dillinger for the Penn store and office building in Wilkinsburg went unrealized, probably because of Dillinger's death in 1927.[6] A larger and more important project for Rose Rubins (fig. 122) involved alterations and additions to an existing complex of commercial and residential spaces, which had already grown by accretion to face two Wilkinsburg streets.[7] Scheibler unified this awkward L-shaped whole with severe planes of white brick relieved by occasional tile medallions and art glass. The primary (Wood Street) facade is recessed on its upper stories, but the side walls project forward like the flanges of one of Scheibler's I-beams. Fragile art-glass pavilions once nestled in the corner recesses of this facade just above the first story, their romantic aura and programmatic uselessness in ironic

Fig. 121. Rubins houses, ca. 1929.

Fig. 122. Rubins store and apartment building, ca. 1935?. Shown after one of the art-glass pavilions was removed.

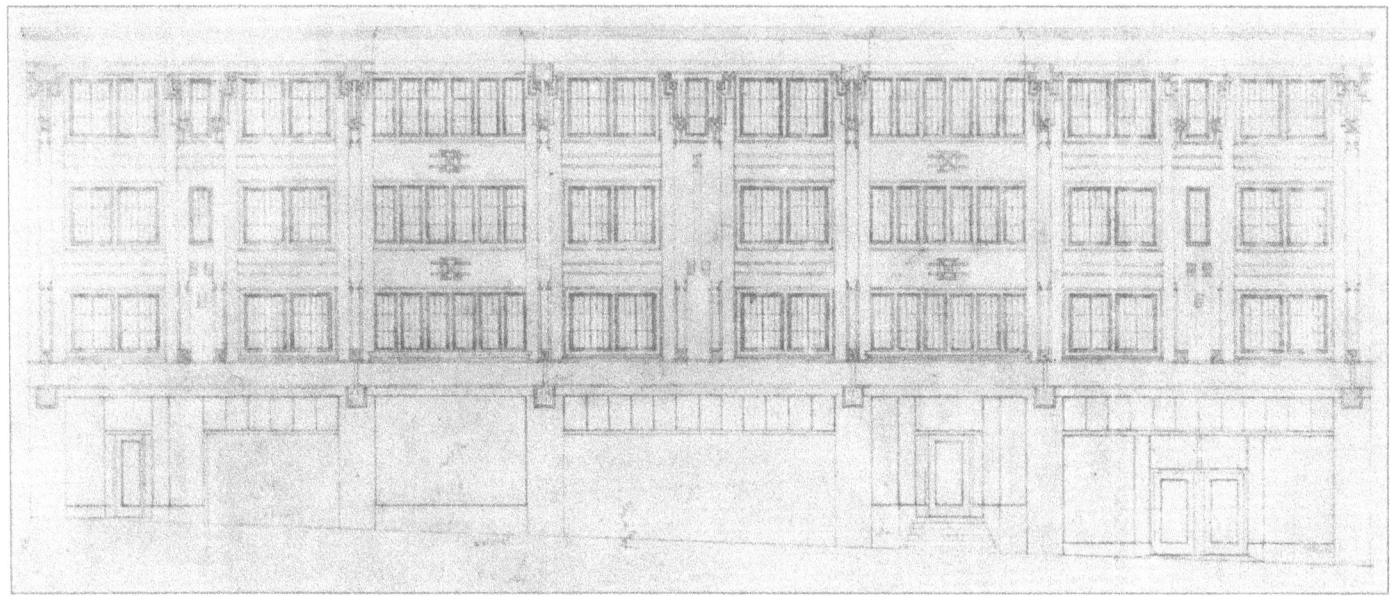

Fig. 123. Unidentified store and office building, ca. 1939?, front elevation.

contrast to the building's overall functional austerity, crystallizing a dichotomy inherent in Scheibler's work. Unfortunately, these pavilions have been lost in recent years, the storefronts rebuilt, and Scheibler's building—which was always an unlikely interruption of the streetscape—has been rendered quite ungainly.

Very different but equally surprising are the elevations of the largest commercial design of Scheibler's career: a four-story brick store and office building (fig. 123) that could have occupied the greater part of a block front had it progressed beyond a single sheet of unlabeled drawings. The configuration of first-story display windows and upper-story office windows is common enough. But the building is extensively detailed with brick and tile, as if the modest tile medallions that Scheibler used for the Rubins project and his Democrat Messenger Building had been allowed to grow wild and cascade over the building's cornice and facades. The result was very similar to the heavily decorated rectilinear work of lesser Prairie School architects.[8]

Robert H. Robinson, a businessman in Monongahela, a Washington County town south of Pittsburgh, almost singlehandedly kept Scheibler's career alive in the depressed 1930s. In 1924, Robinson was part of a group of local businessmen that formed the Monongahela Publishing Company and immediately purchased the local newspaper: the *Daily Republican*. Robinson soon took control of the company as president, and sons John and William were also installed in positions of authority. The three men went on to create a modest newspaper empire in southwestern Pennsylvania under the name of R. H. Robinson and Associates, purchasing the *Democrat Messenger* newspaper of Waynesburg in 1929, and acquiring the Notes Publishing and Printing Company of Canonsburg, publishers of the *Daily Notes* newspaper, in 1934.

Robinson may have come to know Scheibler through his brother, who lived and operated a retail shoe business in Wilkinsburg.[9] As a director of the First National Bank of Monongahela City, Robert H. Robinson was apparently responsible for a 1930 Scheibler commission to convert a bank-owned property into an apartment building. As publishing entrepreneurs, the Robinsons commissioned two newspaper printing plant and office facilities from Scheibler: a 1935 project for the Notes Publishing and Printing Company, and, more important, a 1939 commission for the Democrat Messenger Building.

Externally, the Democrat Messenger Building (fig. 124) is Scheibler's most functionalist design; it's just a white brick box with a flat roof and groups of metal casement windows. The severe elevations are enlivened only by a Moravian tile entry surround and decorative tile medallions. The internal requirements led to some ingenious planning, however. Shipping facilities were located on the ground floor (which is exposed at the rear elevation); the printing plant was placed at the rear of the first floor; and offices were located in the front portion of the first floor and on the

Fig. 124. Democrat Messenger newspaper plant and office building, 1939.

Up-to-Date and Familiar

second floor. In order to provide direct access to both the offices and the printing plant from the front entry, the entry hallway was planned as an internal street, paved with multicolored slate and lined with both doorways and windows. Shortly before it reaches the printing plant, the hallway branches to either side in open stairways that turn at landings to parallel the hallway as they rise. At the second floor, a long hall provides access to most offices, while another passage doubles back through the stair hall as a kind of bridge giving access to offices in the front portion of the floor. The building, therefore, is largely accessed from its center, with a bit of spatial drama.[10]

As the Democrat Messenger Building was going up, the Robinsons hatched a plan that yielded their architect a final day in the spotlight. The country was experiencing a significant housing shortage after a long period of depression. In the Monongahela Valley, as elsewhere, the demand for affordable modern housing far exceeded the supply. Public and private efforts to solve the crisis included programs to stimulate the conventional building industry, mortgage assistance, public housing developments, and experimental projects such as prefabricated houses. The convergence of the Robinsons' newspaper interests and the housing crisis set the stage for the Model Home (fig. 125).[11]

Exhibition houses became staple fare for the public trade shows of the house building industry during this period. But the specific inspiration for the Model Home may have come from a display of demonstration houses that was a major attraction of the 1939 New York World's Fair.[12] The aggressively futuristic fair billed itself, with the somewhat forced optimism of the day, as the World of Tomorrow, and the building industry was appropriately represented by the Homes of Tomorrow. The model home concept apparently struck a responsive chord with the Robinsons—Robert H. Robinson had considerable experience in real estate—and in the summer of 1939 they decided to sponsor the construction of a model home in Monongahela as a public-spirited promotion for their community, for the local building industry, and—not incidentally—for the local newspaper.

On September 22, 1939, *Daily Republican* subscribers were treated to the following front-page headline and announcement:

Daily Republican to Sponsor Model Dwelling
How would you like to visit a home of tomorrow—a dream home, you might say—where you could see the latest in home construction methods and furnishings?
Well, the opportunity will soon be afforded you.
Having long recognized that Monongahela is a City of Homes in a highly industrialized river valley, and also being cognizant of the acute shortage of modern homes in this area, The Daily Republican has decided to sponsor an undertaking that promises both to enhance the community's age-old reputation and to stimulate building, to the end that the housing shortage here will be relieved.
The project will be the erection of a modern, fireproof home incorporating the latest and most up-to-date methods of construction....

In future issues of the paper, the *Daily Republican* enthusiastically embraced its dual role as newsmaker and news reporter, and it ran numerous articles to fan interest in the Model Home project. (Understandably, the beginnings of World War II actually dominated the headlines during this period.) Photographs of the house site appeared on September 25, and a laudatory article about architect Scheibler, largely quoted from the *Pittsburgh Sunday Sun-Telegraph* article of five years before, was published on September

Fig. 125. Daily Republican Model Home, 1939.

28. In October, a series of eight articles detailed construction progress and the use of specific building products. The article for October 21, 1939, discussed "an entirely new type [of sand-finished] brick . . . developed by the Monongahela Clay Manufacturing Company . . . for the Daily Republican–sponsored model home" to be manufactured under the trade name "Vel-V-Tone." This type of tapestry brick was said to have been "long-envisioned" by the architect. Though it is nowhere clearly stated in the newspaper promotions, it is believed that building products and perhaps even labor were donated by suppliers and contractors in return for publicity.

The grand announcement came on May 17, 1940: the "Home of Tomorrow" would open to the public on the following day. This issue of the *Daily Republican* devoted sixteen pages of articles to the Model Home and numerous additional pages to advertisements from participating firms. The firms were formally acknowledged in a lengthy list, and a construction chronology gave a step-by-step account of the project. Individual articles focused on architect Scheibler and the house's every detail from lumber to landscaping to linens.

Finally, between May 18 and June 1, the newspaper reported on fifteen days of public visitation at the

Model Home. Herbert and Rose Seger, of the nearby town of Donora, were probably among the many visitors, for they later commissioned Scheibler to design a house for their Craven Hills property south of Monongahela. Scheibler drew up two sets of plans for the Segers, one version clearly modeled after the Model Home, but neither was built.

As promised, the Model Home incorporated up-to-date materials and methods of construction such as steel joists, concrete floor slabs, and linoleum flooring; new products such as "Vel-V-Tone" brick and "Lustraglass"; and the latest in mechanical systems. It displayed strong geometric massing and unusual detailing. The focal point was a polygonal stair tower that projected from the center of the facade with overlapping brickwork joints, a large panel of glass blocks, and a copper roof. This tower was flanked by the main entry and a window, both of which featured L-shaped surrounds of Moravian tile. The porch was framed with large exposed I-beams. Scheibler's use of his "Vel-V-Tone" tapestry brick, varicolored roof slates, decorative tiles, copper, and glass block achieved a highly polychromatic effect, showing the house to be a distant descendant of Highland Towers.

The Model Home was far from average for its time. On the other hand, it was not highly adventuresome in either styling or plan and was far removed from achievements at the forefront of modern architecture (where, for example, white was now the unofficial official color). It is not at all convincing as a futuristic Home of Tomorrow. Scheibler himself had been a more aggressively modern designer twenty-five years before. Of course, the Homes of Tomorrow at the 1939 New York World's Fair were not revolutionary either, and most of them were very traditional in their styling. Many if not most of the houses actually built in the world of tomorrow have been similarly traditional. It seems that a consistent key to selling houses (and perhaps newspapers as well) is to be simultaneously up-to-date and familiar. In this respect, Scheibler struck the appropriate chord.

Recent discoveries indicate that Scheibler had a more extensive late practice than previously supposed, and the bottom didn't really fall out of his career until he was nearing retirement age, when all architects were suffering from the ill effects of economic depression. But the fact remains that 80 percent of Scheibler's work was completed in the first twenty-five years of his fifty years of practice. Why, once converted—at least in part—to a more common and acceptable mode of design in the late 1920s, did Scheibler fail to capitalize on it and maximize his career?

The difficulty in finding clients was real. Scheibler suffered from self-imposed professional isolation resulting from a failure to call attention to himself and to articulate and promote his ideas. Whereas he published and exhibited early in his career, he did not do so in his later years. His geographical isolation in the North Hills suburbs gradually separated him from his natural clientele. And through no fault of his own, many of his faithful clients stopped building.

He may have lost conviction in his work and was too principled to press on. If the Model Home smacked of compromise, a 1931 commission to design a high-rise apartment building for the Vilsack family revealed a different aspect of Scheibler's dilemma. An enormous project for the Depression years, this was easily the single largest commission of Scheibler's career and required design on a previously unexplored scale. Scheibler reportedly commenced to draw plans for the building, but after great delay professed himself unsatisfied with his work, tore up his drawings, and renounced the commission. A Scheibler high-rise can only be imagined, and he truly faced a difficult task in adapting his preferred manner of design for a large apartment building. Scheibler's talents—as well as his opportunities—lay primarily in small-scale design. But this episode suggests that Scheibler's convictions may have hindered his career.[13]

Finally, personal problems took their toll. The evidence is all hearsay, but those who knew Scheibler after about 1920 note his indifference to both his finances and his personal appearance, remark on his womanizing tendencies, and speculate about alcoholism. One report holds that Scheibler often failed to appear at a job site and kept workmen idle, so the client proceeded to pick Scheibler up and take him to breakfast to assure his presence on the job. Some have said that Scheibler was "never the same" after the death of his son in 1911 and the subsequent loss of his wife and family. A final blow was the progressive blindness that afflicted him for at least the last ten years of his life.

Scheibler was not alone in many of these afflictions. Nearly all of the progressives worked alone in various degrees of isolation and failed to adequately sell and perpetuate their ideas by way of publicity or disciples. Voysey, in particular, suffered from self-imposed isolation, and his career gradually shriveled away when he refused to adjust his ideals to the demands of his few prospective clients. Mackintosh, who originally reveled in his challenge to the establishment, grew bitter after years of rejection and turned to drink out of frustration and the stress of his perfectionist manner.

Scheibler's only recorded comment on the decline of his career was his regret "that [he] didn't take on a young man who could keep these things going."[14]

10 A Place Among Progressives

SCHEIBLER WAS A TALENTED architectural form giver. His buildings took shape as simple volumes, commonly comprised of one or two basic building blocks. He favored elemental geometric forms like the cube and basic roof types like the gable and the hip roof. But he turned gables, broke up rooflines, used subsidiary forms to extend basic volumes, and added more complex forms such as polygons to set up complicated overall geometries. He experimented with unexpected forms such as flat roofs.

He explored dynamic contrasts of solids and voids by juxtaposing solid masses with incidents of fenestration that opened up and were in turn framed by those masses. He was a master of surface and line and brought flat surfaces to life with linear detail—a sense of Scheibler's pen is never far from his work. He designed buildings in the round as finely crafted objects.

His work displayed the rigor of controlling mechanisms such as symmetry and axiality and compensatory mechanisms such as the balance of parts. He utilized grids to systematically subdivide and discipline everything from leaded glass windows to entire facades. Yet he was willing and able to introduce elements of complexity and contradiction—mismatching elevations and floor plans, skewing apparent symmetry, and playing rhythmic games with doorways, windows, and porches.

He introduced extraordinary variety. His fenestration, for instance, ranged broadly in both form and placement—from broad expanses of ribbon windows to long vertical slits of green art glass; from windows asymmetrically afloat in a plane to those abruptly jammed under the overhanging eaves of a high roof. Fireplaces nested in corners under pointy hoods, stood free, straddling multiple rooms, or engulfed entire walls with heavy stone construction.

Scheibler was an accomplished space planner. His plans were extremely compact. His spaces were interdependent, but had clearly defined roles. He used continuous circulation patterns and multiple points of entry and exit to keep hallways to a minimum. He carefully separated living spaces from service spaces and skillfully accounted for the presence of maids and their activities even in small houses. Unusually shaped or double-height spaces and dramatic staircases showed his willingness to experiment with internal spatial effects. More often, external spaces simply extended his floor plans and carried them out-of-doors.

He consistently used open planning devices such

as broad openings between rooms, partial partitions, screen walls with internal windows, and panels of art glass to bring light into his interiors and to create a sense of spaciousness, that, while sometimes deceptive, was always welcome. Open planning had economic advantages: it required fewer interior walls and doors and accommodated lower ceilings. But it was clearly an aesthetic choice as well: it created and maximized visual axes while providing opportunities for ornamental treatments.

Scheibler was an inspired decorator. With a few key exceptions, he ornamented his buildings inside and out. This ornamentation was sometimes extensive, but never showy. It was romantic and often playful, but never hackneyed. Shear and Schmertz said of Scheibler's ornamentation: "Whimsical it may be . . . but its freshness and strong departure from the rules of the day must be conceded."[1]

He tended to spot ornament, rather than subscribe to any overall treatment, and related it to structural elements such as spandrels or columns. Scheibler himself said: "One must use ornament to emphasize construction. For a long time, years ago, I tried to discover why farmhouses and French cathedrals were beautiful. It's a matter of relationships. Simple relationships. And the relationship of the ornament to the structure is one of the most important of these."[2] This concept was made apparent in Scheibler's use of the exposed steel I-beam. As a lintel over a door or window, or as a beam supporting a porch roof, the I-beam was a structural device; but one with a distinctive visual quality that could be manipulated for dramatic effects.

His other favorite decorative tools, art glass and tile, were for beautification, but they too served their larger architectural settings. Art glass substituted for clear glass in windows and cabinet doors and acted as an agent of light and continuous space in room dividers. Tile, freer by nature, was nonetheless used primarily in the architectural setting of a spandrel, a fireplace, or a doorway. Scheibler exploited these materials for their linear definition and color, and he experimented with mural painting and tile fragments embedded in concrete for similar effects. In these and other media, Scheibler favored natural motifs like flowers and birds that abetted his other means of integrating architecture and nature.

Scheibler demonstrated a keen interest in construction techniques and materials. With little reason or opportunity to break new ground in his modest practice, Scheibler nevertheless utilized some very contemporary building techniques including pseudo–curtain walls and concrete frames. Scheibler favored traditional building materials like stucco, brick, and stone; but he also employed blatantly modern materials like concrete, sheet glass, steel, and aluminum boldly and without apology. He used smooth expanses of stucco and brick to unify and cloak construction. But he also gave expression to structure by exposing framing members such as reinforced concrete columns and steel I-beams, a practice that departed from the general rules of the day. That Scheibler laid claim to a number of more prosaic innovations in building products and equipment further suggests an inquiring mind. He devised a new type of brick for his Model Home project, and aluminum casements and even open-front toilet seats "entered the local scene at his urging," according to Shear and Schmertz.[3]

Scheibler designed total environments, never

stopping at the mere appearance of the external envelope or the detailing of a single prominent room. Scheibler's outlook was essentially suburban, and he carefully sited his buildings amid natural—but not too natural—surroundings. Though hindered by the limitations of the available lots, he employed artfully contrived gardens or yards as key elements of many designs. He used sun rooms, projecting bays, loggias, balconies, verandas, and porches to maximize the interchange between indoors and out by capturing fresh air, sunlight, and views. Inside, wood trim and fireplaces were integral to their varied settings; and though he never designed freestanding furniture, Scheibler often provided built-in custom furnishings, including window seats, cabinets, and light fixtures.

Scheibler displayed photographs of Highland Towers and Vilsack Row in his office, and he must have rightly considered them his best work. These two projects, and many others besides, amply demonstrate both his distinctive architectural vocabulary and his mastery of key architectural principles.

Much of Scheibler's work was essentially conservative, rooted in vernacular precedents and infused with traditional domestic values. But he was also willing to experiment with new ideas. His practice of exposing I-beams can be traced to Viollet-le-Duc, whose theories regarding structural expression provided important underpinnings for the development of modern architecture. His minimalist buildings were nearly unprecedented and are especially significant in light of later developments. Scheibler did not, however, aspire to the sort of universal architectural language sought by the modernism of the Bauhaus. He was not, strictly speaking, a pioneer of modern architecture, because he was not a leader either by personality or professional influence. And to call him a prophet is to miss the point that his architecture was very much a product of its time. But Scheibler was deeply involved in a reformative and innovative movement that strove to bring architecture into harmony with modern life without discarding the sensibilities of the past. He was a full member of the company of progressive architects.

Scheibler's true peers were lesser-known regional American architects like Wilson Eyre in Philadelphia, George Maher in Chicago, and California's Irving Gill and Bernard Maybeck. These men were not of the status of a Mackintosh or a Wright and were not followers of any one progressive movement, but they practiced a sort of progressive eclecticism coupled with individuality.

Wilson Eyre (1858–1944) is best remembered for his early work in the Shingle Style, but he also had an enduring interest in the English Arts and Crafts Movement and showed strong individuality in his urban work.[4] George Maher (1864–1926) is commonly considered to be a Prairie School architect, but he also turned consciously to Europe for inspiration. His myriad progressive sources resulted in a body of distinctive work, though his design skills were often found lacking.[5] Bernard Maybeck (1862–1956) was more influenced by traditional European architecture than by other progressives, but he parlayed an interest in structure, indigenous materials, and the craft of building into an architecture of individualism bordering on the eccentric.[6] Irving Gill (1870–1936) had a strong interest in progressive European developments and shared the European interest in lost-cost mass housing. Also influenced by southern California's indigenous Mission Style, he made startling advances in simplification.[7]

Like Eyre and Maher, Scheibler's work had considerable interest, but lacked the consistency of purpose and form that characterized the work of Gill and Maybeck. Scheibler was less influential than Eyre, but a better designer than Maher. With Maybeck, he shared a capacity for evoking delight and affirming the human spirit. He sometimes equaled Gill's level of abstraction and did it first.

Scheibler might have ranked with the best but for the constraints of his geographic and professional isolation and his own personal limitations. But perhaps the key constraint was his lack of a strong regional vernacular to build upon. Mackintosh's best work could only have been done in Scotland. Wright and the Prairie School managed to tap the distinctive character of the American Midwest. Gill's work grew directly out of Southern California, and Maybeck's out of the Pacific Northwest. Scheibler found no such natural point of departure on which to hang his innovative tendencies and build a body of work. Thus his heavy and somewhat flighty foreign dependence, a dependence that limited the regional meaning of his architecture. Scheibler's German heritage led him first to Germanic work, and his sympathy for simplicity to the English. Neither source constituted a wholly appropriate intellectual tradition from which to build in Pittsburgh. Scheibler's buildings were often a startling presence in the Pittsburgh landscape. Perhaps only the exposed I-beam was fully assimilated in the Steel City.

This was not all bad, however. There was and is something to be said for being a startling presence in the landscape, especially in early twentieth-century Pittsburgh. Scheibler's buildings were undeniably different. They were light-hearted and often light-colored in a city of sober, dark, and dirty architecture. They were meticulously designed and finely crafted. They were lovingly conceived. Through them, Scheibler claims his place among progressives.

Appendixes
Notes
Selected Bibliography
Index

# Appendix 1
Catalogue of the Works of Fredrick G. Scheibler, Jr.

Each catalogue entry represents an architectural commission received by Frederick G. Scheibler, Jr. Entries consist of headings, general notes, and reference notes.

Each heading consists of a catalogue number, date, project identification, status note, and location. Catalogue numbers are assigned chronologically. Dates are those of the design, not construction. Project identifications are organized in a building name/building type/client format, and echo as nearly as practicable those found in Scheibler's office records. Each identification is followed by a bracketed indication of the project's current status (for example, extant, not built, demolished). Locations given are the current addresses of a building or site.

Heading data not obtainable from Scheibler's own records was obtained or extrapolated from other primary sources, including atlases and plat books, building permits, city directories, deeds, and water company records.

General notes, which may follow the headings, include clarifications and cross-references. Projects that are documented *only* through a handwritten inventory of Scheibler's office materials, made by James D. Van Trump while these materials were in private hands, are noted accordingly. This inventory overlaps with but differs considerably from more recent inventories of archival records, since many items were lost in the interim. Projects for which Scheibler's participation is undocumented by any primary sources are marked as attributions. Properties that have been altered beyond recognition in whole or part are noted as substantially altered.

Reference notes include listings of extant archival records and citations of published and unpublished sources.

Listings of archival records indicate the record type and the repository. The Frederick G. Scheibler, Jr., Collection at the Carnegie Mellon University Architecture Archives is the primary public repository for archival records. This collection consists of more than 350 drawings, blueprints, renderings, and watercolor cartoons for art glass and tilework, as well as approximately one linear foot of photographs, specifications, other written records, and ephemera. Most of these records were obtained from Scheibler's office and given to the University by Pittsburgh architect Thomas Sutton in 1966. The Archives retains a copy of the Van Trump inventory and a computer inventory of the current collection. All identified items in the collection are cited here. Items cited from other repositories are limited to those of historic character or special informational significance. Photographs resulting from historic sites surveys, for example, are not cited. Privately owned archival materials are cited only if they provide key documentation for a project. Items that record more than one project are cited under each relevant project.

Reference citations are limited to those that provide important documentation or individual treatment of a project. Additional mentions of a given project may be found in the more general sources listed in the Selected Bibliography.

Abbreviations

CMUAA	Carnegie Mellon University Architecture Archives
JVT	James D. Van Trump inventory
PHLF	Pittsburgh History and Landmarks Foundation
SLMM	Spruance Library, Mercer Museum, Doylestown, Pennsylvania

1   1897
Cottage for Frederick G. Scheibler, Jr. [demolished]
7405 Washington Street, Swissvale, Pa.
Two versions.

drawings, photograph of rendering [CMUAA]

2   1901
House for Edward A. Kitzmiller [extant]
2526 Braddock Avenue, Swissvale, Pa.
By Raisig and Scheibler.

drawings [CMUAA]

3   1901
Longfellow School competition entry for the Swissvale Borough School District [not built]
Monroe Street and McClure Avenue, Swissvale, Pa.
The invitation to compete was extended to Raisig and Scheibler, but the entry was submitted by Scheibler alone. Scheibler did not win the competition.

Swissvale Borough School Board, Minute Book (June 1899–August 1907), 46–47. [Woodland Hills School District]

4   1901
House for Robert L. Matthews [not built]
3622 Fleming Avenue, Pittsburgh
Same design as cat. 5.

drawings [CMUAA]

5   ca. 1901
House for Joseph W. Steel [destroyed]
214 North Main Street, Greensburg, Pa.
Same design as cat. 4.

photographs [CMUAA]

Pittsburgh Architectural Club, *Catalogue of the Third Exhibition* (Pittsburgh, 1905), List of Exhibits.

City of Greensburg: A History (Greensburg, Pa.: Greensburg Sesquicentennial Corporation, 1949), n.p.

The Greater Greensburg Profile (Greensburg, Pa., 1962), 382.

6   ca. 1901?
House for Paul H. Chapin [not built]
182 Gordon Street, Edgewood, Pa.
Recorded by JVT.

7   ca. 1901
House for Kitty (Mrs. W. J.) Allston [extant]
1425 Coal Street, Wilkinsburg, Pa.

specifications [CMUAA]

8   ca. 1901
Colonial apartment building for the United Real Estate and Construction Company [extant]
300 Craft Avenue, Pittsburgh
This building is part of a complex of five apartment buildings built by company president William G. Price, Jr. in late 1901 and early 1902. Four of the buildings were of related design (one has been destroyed by fire). The fifth is presumably the Scheibler project. Substantially altered.

specifications [CMUAA]

9   ca. 1902?
House for Frank M. Barnes [not built?]
McKeesport, Pa.

specifications [CMUAA]

10   ca. 1902
House for Thomas M. Donehoo [not built]
1305 Singer Place, Wilkinsburg, Pa.
Recorded by JVT.

11   ca. 1902?
Apartment building for Benjamin S. Johns [not built]
3328 Ward Street, Pittsburgh

drawing [CMUAA]

12   ca. 1902?
Store and apartment building for William E. Hamnett [not built]
Penn Avenue, Wilkinsburg, Pa.

specifications [CMUAA]

13   ca. 1902

House for Emma C. Forssen [demolished?]
2053 Monongahela Avenue, Swissvale, Pa.
Recorded by JVT.

14   1902

Store building for Robert L. Matthews [extant]
1740 Eckert Street, Pittsburgh
In previous studies of Scheibler's work, this building is identified as a hotel in Woods Run, and dated prior to 1900. It actually corresponds with Matthews' commission for a "department store building" as documented by specifications and recorded in the City of Allegheny building permit docket on July 13, 1903. The design is dated November 1902 by JVT. Formerly 33 McClure Avenue. Substantially altered.

specifications, photograph [CMUAA]

15   ca. 1903

Store building for William E. Hamnett [extant]
712 Wood Street, Wilkinsburg, Pa.
This was the Heck Bros. men's furnishings store for many years. Substantially altered.

specifications [CMUAA]

Souvenir Book: Silver Anniversary 1887–1912 (Wilkinsburg, Pa., 1912), 38.

16   1903

Apartment building for Robinson and Bruckman [extant]
226 East End Avenue, Pittsburgh
Recorded by JVT. The building permit was issued in the name of W. J. Brown, who briefly boarded at Bruckman's residence.

17   ca. 1903?

Apartment building for Frank Johnston [not built]
426 Biddle Avenue, Wilkinsburg, Pa.
Specifications incorrectly name the client as F. E. Johnson.

specifications [CMUAA]

18   ca. 1904

Store building for Harry I. Neamann [demolished]
7213–7215 Hamilton Avenue, Pittsburgh

specifications [CMUAA]

Uptown: Greater Pittsburgh's Classic Section / East End: The World's Most Beautiful Suburb (Pittsburgh: Pittsburgh Board of Trade, 1907), 116.

19   1904

Syria, Kismet, and Nelda apartment buildings for Robinson, Bruckman and McClelland, Inc. [extant]
7530, 7534, 7540 Bennett Street, Pittsburgh
Recorded by JVT.

photographs [CMUAA]

Hamilton Realty Company, Minute Book (1902–1938), 9. [private]

20   1904

Arden apartment building for Robinson and Bruckman [extant]
7710 Waverly Street, Pittsburgh
JVT plausibly names Robinson and Bruckman as the client, but the building permit was issued in the name of George A. Knorr, who actually owned the property and lived next door.

art-glass cartoon [CMUAA]; photograph [PHLF]

21   ca. 1904?

Three houses for James S. Crawford [not built]
400–404 South Braddock Avenue, Pittsburgh
Recorded by JVT.

22   ca. 1904?

House for James Harrington [not built]
2116 Collingwood Avenue, Swissvale, Pa.
Recorded by JVT.

23   1904

Hawkins School competition entry and school building for the Swissvale Borough School District [extant]
South Braddock and Vernon Avenues, Swissvale, Pa.
Scheibler won the competition. Later renamed Milligan School. Later converted into housing.

drawings, photostat of rendering [CMUAA]

Construction 1:25 (June 24, 1905), 5.

Pittsburgh Architectural Club, *Catalogue of the Third*

Exhibition (Pittsburgh, 1905), List of Exhibits.

Swissvale Borough School Board, Minute Book (June 1899–August 1907), 193, 194, 198, 206, 207, 210. [Woodland Hills School District]

The Twentieth Anniversary of Swissvale Borough (Allegheny County Fireman's Association, 1918), 36.

Golden Progress [50th Anniversary Booklet] (Swissvale, Pa.: 1948), 56.

Swissvale Diamond Jubilee [75th Anniversary Booklet] (Swissvale, Pa.: 1973), 38.

24   ca. 1904

Five houses for David B. Little and George H. Pfeil [extant]
7309, 7313, 7317, 7321, 7325 Whipple Street, Swissvale, Pa.
JVT recorded one of two related projects, citing location as near Maxwelton Street [now Monroe Street]; see cat. 25. Formerly Alice Avenue.

25   1905

Seven houses for David B. Little and George H. Pfeil [extant]
7304, 7308, 7312, 7316, 7320, 7324, 7328 Whipple Street, Swissvale, Pa.
Formerly Alice Avenue. For related project see cat. 24.

Construction 1:18 (May 6, 1905), 5; 1:21 (May 27, 1905), 6; 2:1 (July 8, 1905), 5.

26   1905

Old Heidelberg apartment building for Robinson and Bruckman [extant]
405–421 South Braddock Avenue, Pittsburgh
For related projects see cats. 46, 49, 54.

drawings, art-glass cartoons, tile cartoon, postcard, photographs [CMUAA]

Construction 1:4 (January 28, 1905), 22; 1:18 (May 6, 1905), 5; 1:22 (June 3, 1905), 8; 1:24 (June 17, 1905), 5.

Pittsburgh Architectural Club, *Catalogue of the Third Exhibition* (Pittsburgh, 1905), List of Exhibits.

[Advertisement for Standard Sanitary Manufacturing Company. Source unknown.]

American Architect and Building News 91:1619 (January 5, 1907), 20, plate 3.

Architecture 15:3 (March 15, 1907), plate 21.

Hans Berger, "Das Wohnung in Amerika," *Der Architekt* 14 (1908), 27, 30.

[Advertisement.] *The Shield* (1909).

Pittsburgh Architectural Club, *Catalogue of the Fifth Exhibition* (Pittsburgh, 1910), List of Exhibits; plate.

The Brickbuilder 20:1 (January 1911), 19.

Western Architect 17:6 (June 1911), plate 6.

Carole Rifkind, *Field Guide to American Architecture* (New York: New American Library, Inc., 1980), 88.

Historic American Building Survey, PA-431.

National Register of Historic Places.

27   ca. 1905

Apartment building for Joseph Wahlstrom [not built]
7410 Irvine Avenue, Swissvale, Pa.
Construction 1:18 (May 6, 1905), 5.

28   1905

Interior alterations to Deniston School for the Swissvale Borough School District [destroyed]
Monroe Street and McClure Avenue, Swissvale, Pa.
Previously Longfellow School.

Swissvale Borough School Board, Minute Book (June 1899 – August 1907), 235, 238, 240, 243, 249. [Woodland Hills School District]

29   1905

Wall, fence, and changes to tower at McKelvy School for Swissvale Borough School District [wall extant; fence destroyed; changes to tower not built?]
South Braddock and Westmoreland Avenues, Swissvale, Pa.

Swissvale Borough School Board, Minute Book (June 1899–August 1907), 236, 238, 240–41, 249. [Woodland Hills School District]

The Twentieth Anniversary of Swissvale Borough (Allegheny County Fireman's Association, 1918), 38.

Golden Progress [50th Anniversary Booklet] (Swissvale, Pa.: 1948), 60.

30   1905

House for Ralph E. Miller [extant]
7506 Trevanion Avenue, Swissvale, Pa.

drawings, art-glass cartoons, specifications [CMUAA]

31   1905

Store and apartment building [not built?]
Swissvale, Pa.

Construction 2:15 (October 14, 1905), 341.

32   ca. 1906?

House for William K. Gamble [extant]
Fourteenth Street near Oak Street, Oakmont, Pa.
Substantially altered.

specifications [CMUAA]

33   ca. 1906

Store and apartment building for Dr. Adolph L. Lewin [not built]
3534 Penn Avenue, Pittsburgh

Construction 3:1 (January 6, 1906), 5.

34   ca. 1906

Two houses for Daniel L. Dillinger [not built?]
1010, 1012 Chislett Street, Pittsburgh

Dillinger obtained a building permit for this project and Scheibler received the commission, according to specifications. The resulting buildings are problematic, however, for they do not resemble any of Scheibler's other work.

specifications [CMUAA]

35   1906

Apartment building [not built]
Lang Avenue, Pittsburgh

Construction 3:12 (March 24, 1906), 270.

36   1906

Linwood apartment building for Daniel L. Dillinger [extant]
6801 McPherson Boulevard, Pittsburgh

specifications, photographs [CMUAA]

Construction 3:12 (March 24, 1906), 270.

Pittsburgh Architectural Club, *Catalogue of the Fifth Exhibition* (Pittsburgh, 1910), List of Exhibits; plate.

37   1906

Whitehall apartment building for Harry D. Hasson [extant]
201 East End Avenue, Pittsburgh

specifications, photograph [CMUAA]

Construction 3:12 (March 24, 1906), 270.

38   1906

Apartment building for Mary M. (Mrs. J. H.) Coleman [extant]
936 Mellon Street, Pittsburgh

drawings [CMUAA]

39   1907

Wilkins School for the Swissvale Borough School District [destroyed]
Charleston, South Braddock and Milton Avenues, Swissvale, Pa.
The present building at this site is a replacement structure.

drawings, photostat of rendering [CMUAA]

Construction 2:19 (November 11, 1905), 438; 2:25 (December 23, 1905), 581; 3:1 (January 6, 1906), 5.

Swissvale Borough School Board, Minute Book (June 1899–August 1907), 151, 198, 268, 332, 336. [Woodland Hills School District]

The Twentieth Anniversary of Swissvale Borough (Allegheny County Fireman's Association, 1918), 36.

40   1907

House for Joseph Wright [extant]
653 Bank Street, Bridgeville, Pa.

drawings [CMUAA]

41   1907

Twenty row houses for Jesse F. Robinson [extant]
7908–7930, 7909–7923 Inglenook Place, Pittsburgh
A Robinson and Bruckman project. Formerly Topeka Street. Exterior design similar to cat. 42.

specifications [CMUAA]

Hamilton Realty Company, Minute Book (1902–1938), 22. [private]

42   ca. 1907
House for Howard B. Kappel [extant]
301 West Swissvale Avenue, Edgewood, Pa.
Attribution. Exterior design similar to cat. 41.

43   1907
Remodeling of house into store building for William E. Hamnett [not built]
1001–1003 Penn Avenue, Wilkinsburg, Pa.

drawings, specifications [CMUAA]

44   1907
House for Silas M. Ament [extant]
1204 Hulton Avenue, Oakmont, Pa.
For related projects see cats. 79, 144.

drawings [CMUAA]

Donald Miller, "Eclectic Charm in Oakmont," *Pittsburgh Post-Gazette*, September 3, 1987, 15.

45   1907
Wilkinsburg Natatorium for the Wilkinsburg Natatorium Company [not built]
735 Ross Avenue, Wilkinsburg, Pa.

drawings, specifications [CMUAA]

Pittsburgh Architectural Club, *Catalogue of the Fifth Exhibition* (Pittsburgh, 1910), List of Exhibits.

Wilkinsburg Gazette, November 1, 1962, 13.

46   1908
Four cottage additions to Old Heidelberg apartment building for Fred Bruckman [extant]
401–403 South Braddock Avenue and 7612–7614 Waverly Street, Pittsburgh
For related projects see cats. 26, 49, 54.

drawings, postcard [CMUAA]

Pittsburgh Architectural Club, *Catalogue of the Fifth Exhibition* (Pittsburgh, 1910), List of Exhibits; plate.

Historic American Building Survey, PA-431.

National Register of Historic Places.

47   1908
Minnetonka Building store and apartment building for Edward C. Wefing [extant]
5421–5431 Walnut Street, Pittsburgh

drawings, specifications, photographs [CMUAA]

48   1908
Two houses for Fred Bruckman [not built]
South Braddock Avenue, Pittsburgh
Recorded by JVT. Not clear if related to cats. 26, 46, 49, 54.

49   1908
Cottage addition to Old Heidelberg apartment building for Sam Dempster [extant]
423 South Braddock Avenue, Pittsburgh
For related projects see cats. 26, 46, 54.

drawings [CMUAA]

Pittsburgh Architectural Club, *Catalogue of the Fifth Exhibition* (Pittsburgh, 1910), List of Exhibits; plate.

Historic American Building Survey, PA-431.

National Register of Historic Places.

50   ca. 1908
House for Walter O. Phillips [extant]
19 Richey Avenue, Pittsburgh
Recorded by JVT.

photographs [CMUAA]

51   1909
Two houses for William M. Ebberts [extant]
117, 119 LaCrosse Street, Edgewood, Pa.
For related project see cat. 63.

drawing [CMUAA]

52   1909
Twelve row houses for the Hamilton Realty Company [extant]
6928–6950 Bennett Street, Pittsburgh
Attribution. A Robinson and Bruckman project. Same design as cat. 53.

Hamilton Realty Company, Minute Book (1902–1938), 28. [private]

53   1909
Eight row houses for Jesse F. Robinson and Anna Wingerson [extant]

7900–7906, 7901–7907 Inglenook Place, Pittsburgh
Attribution. A Robinson and Bruckman project. Formerly Topeka Street. Same design as cat. 52.

54   1909
House for William C. Hoffman [extant]
425 South Braddock Avenue, Pittsburgh
For related projects see cats. 26, 46, 49.

postcard [CMUAA]

Pittsburgh Architectural Club, *Catalogue of the Fifth Exhibition* (Pittsburgh, 1910), plate.

National Register of Historic Places.

55   1909
House for John G. Kaiser [demolished]
7238 McPherson Boulevard, Pittsburgh
Recorded by JVT.

56   ca. 1909
House for Laura E. Vogeley [extant]
1328 Singer Place, Wilkinsburg, Pa.
Recorded by JVT. Later converted into duplex.

57   1909
House and garage for Dr. James M. McNall [house extant; garage demolished]
1306 Penn Avenue, Wilkinsburg, Pa.
Recorded by JVT.

58   ca. 1909?
Inn for Catherine P. (Mrs. R. L.) Matthews [not built]
Three Degree Road and First Street, Ross Township, Allegheny County, Pa.

drawings [CMUAA]

59   1909
House and garage for Charles W. Baird [extant]
1090 Devon Road, Pittsburgh

drawings, specifications, photographs [CMUAA]

60   1909
Five row houses for Daniel L. Dillinger [demolished]
6363–6371 Aurelia Street, Pittsburgh
Same design as cats. 65, 66, 67.

specifications, photographs [CMUAA]; photographs [PHLF]

61   ca. 1909
House for William M. Ebberts [extant]
143 Gordon Street, Edgewood, Pa.
Attribution. Same design as cats. 63, 64.

62   ca. 1909?
Six row houses for John N. Straub [not built]
100–104 Oakview Avenue, Edgewood, Pa.

specifications [CMUAA]

63   1910
Two houses for William M. Ebberts [extant]
115, 121 LaCrosse Street, Edgewood, Pa.
Same design as cats. 61, 64. For related project see cat. 51.

drawings [CMUAA]

64   ca. 1910?
House for William M. Ebberts [extant]
129 LaCrosse Street, Edgewood, Pa.
Attribution. Same design as cats. 61, 63.

65   1910
Twelve row houses for Joseph and Anna Wingerson, Jacob and Guy Adams, and Jesse F. Robinson [extant]
7902–7924 Hamilton Avenue, Pittsburgh
Attribution. A Robinson and Bruckman project. Same design as cats. 60, 66, 67.

66   ca. 1910
Eight row houses for Daniel L. Dillinger [extant]
425–435 Biddle Avenue and 204–206 West Street, Wilkinsburg, Pa.
Same design as cats. 60, 65, 67.

specifications [CMUAA]

67   ca. 1910
Two row houses and garage for Robert P. McDowell [extant]
525–527 Holmes Street, Wilkinsburg, Pa.
JVT recorded one of two similar projects; see cat. 76. Same design as cats. 60, 65, 66.

68   ca. 1910
House and garage for Robert J. Scott [extant]
366 Penn Road, Wynnewood, Pa. [near Philadelphia]

specifications [CMUAA]

Pittsburgh Architectural Club, *Catalogue of the Seventh Exhibition* (Pittsburgh, 1912), List of Exhibits.

69   1910
Rockledge: house for William E. Hamnett [extant]
579 Briar Cliff Road, Pittsburgh
The complementary garage and garden wall were later additions by other architects.

drawings, photographs [CMUAA]

Pittsburgh Architectural Club, *Catalogue of the Seventh Exhibition* (Pittsburgh: 1912), List of Exhibits.

70   1910–1911
Hamilton Cottages: nineteen group cottages for Hamilton Realty Company [twenty-one cottages built; extant]
5629–5669 Beacon Street, Pittsburgh
A Robinson and Bruckman project. Design similar to cat. 75.

drawings, specifications, photograph of rendering, photographs, survey maps [CMUAA]

Hamilton Realty Company, Minute Book (1902–1938), 33–38. [private]

Pittsburgh Architectural Club, *Catalogue of the Seventh Exhibition* (Pittsburgh, 1912), List of Exhibits.

71   1910
House for Robert E. Cluhey [extant]
5819 Northumberland Street, Pittsburgh
Recorded by JVT.

72   ca. 1910
Apartment building with office for Ella D. Wetherall [extant]
501 Hill Street, Wilkinsburg, Pa.

specifications [CMUAA]

73   ca. 1910?
House for Joseph D'Ambrosio [not built]
Shetland Avenue, Pittsburgh

specifications [CMUAA]

74   ca. 1910?
House for Elder W. Marshall [not built]
621 Pennsylvania Avenue, Oakmont, Pa.
Recorded by JVT.

75   1911
Five cottages for Jesse F. Robinson [extant]
5671–5679 Beacon Street, Pittsburgh
Attribution. A Robinson and Bruckman project. Design similar to cat. 70.

76   ca. 1911
Two row houses and garage for Robert P. McDowell [extant]
521–523 Holmes Street, Wilkinsburg, Pa.
JVT recorded one of two similar projects; see cat. 67.

77   ca. 1911?
Cottages [not built?]
Oakmont, Pa.

Pittsburgh Architectural Club, *Catalogue of the Seventh Exhibition* (Pittsburgh, 1912), List of Exhibits.

78   1911
Willo'mound: eighteen group cottages for Thorniley Realty Company [not built]
5000–5026 Friendship Avenue, Pittsburgh

rendering, specifications [CMUAA]

Pittsburgh Architectural Club, *Catalogue of the Seventh Exhibition* (Pittsburgh, 1912), List of Exhibits.

79   ca. 1911
Alterations to Ament house for W. K. Dunlap [extant]
1204 Hulton Avenue, Oakmont, Pa.
Attribution based on penciled notes on Scheibler's drawings for cat. 44. For related projects see cats. 44, 144.

80   1912
Two houses for Dwight B. Foster [extant]
6243 Monitor Street and 2916 Shady Avenue, Pittsburgh
Attribution.

81   1912
Four houses for Albert Q. Starr [extant]
5670, 5674, 5702, 5706 Beacon Street, Pittsburgh
Attribution.

82   1912
Meado'cots: twenty group cottages for Mary Doran [sixteen cottages built; extant]
425–447 Rosedale Street and 7817–1823 Madiera Street, Pittsburgh

specifications, photographs, photograph of measured drawing [CMUAA]

83   ca. 1913?
Three row houses for Robert P. McDowell [demolished]
404–408 Ross Avenue, Wilkinsburg, Pa.
Recorded by JVT. According to the W.P.A. Property Survey (1937), two of the houses shared a single semi-circular bay window, so that each had a quarter-round wedge-like extension of its living room.

84   1913–1914
Highland Towers apartment building and two garages for Daniel L. Dillinger [extant]
340 South Highland Avenue, Pittsburgh

drawings, specifications, correspondence, brochure, photographs, plates [CMUAA]

"Highland Towers, 340–342 South Highland Avenue, Pittsburgh" (advertising brochure), n.d.

Pittsburgh Architectural Club, *Catalogue of the Ninth Exhibition* (Pittsburgh, 1914), List of Exhibits; plate.

Bulletin Index (March 20, 1915), 13; (April 17, 1915), 16.

Aymer Embury, "Impressions of Three Cities: III Pittsburgh," *Architecture* 31:4 (April 1915), 106.

National Register of Historic Places.

85   1913
Three row houses for W. Hugh Johnston [extant]
420–422 East End Avenue, Pittsburgh

specifications, photograph [CMUAA]

86   1913
Vilsack Row: eighteen row houses for the Vilsack Estate [extant]
1659–1693 Jancey Street, Pittsburgh
Same design as cat. 87.

specifications, photographs [CMUAA]

87   1914
Six row houses for William V. and Albert A. Kreuer [extant]
7124–7134 Churchland Street, Pittsburgh
Formerly Agnew Street. Same design as cat. 86.

specifications [CMUAA]

88   1914
Nineteen row houses for the Hamilton Realty Company [extant]
1330–1366 Singer Place, Wilkinsburg, Pa.
A Robinson and Bruckman project.

drawing [CMUAA]

Hamilton Realty Company, Minute Book (1902–1938), 59–61. [private]

89   1914
Double house for Daniel L. Dillinger [extant]
728–730 East End Avenue, Pittsburgh
For related project see cat. 113.

specifications, photograph [CMUAA]

90   1914
House for Eleanor Mae (Mrs. C. M.) Logue [not built]
5529–5531 Beacon Street, Pittsburgh

drawings, specifications [CMUAA]

91   ca. 1914?
Store and apartment building [not built?]

drawing [CMUAA]

92   ca. 1914?
Remodeling of house, garage for Caroline A. White [extant]
6035–6037 St. Marie Street, Pittsburgh
Specifications name the client as a Mr. Johnson, but Caroline A. White owned the property.

specifications [CMUAA]

93   1915
House [not built?]
The sketch that documents this project is scrawled with the notes "Freehold RE" and "Crawley," but no association with an actual client or site has been possible.

sketch [private]

94   1915
House for Dr. Wesley W. Jones [extant]
1831 Ardmore Boulevard, Forest Hills, Pa.

drawing, specifications, photograph [CMUAA]

95   1915
Lincoln Highway Marker and Street Sign Post competition entry for the Art Commission of the City of Pittsburgh [not built]
"Lincoln Highway," Pittsburgh
Scheibler did not win the competition.

list of competitors [CMUAA]

96   1915
House for Louis T. Frederick [extant]
132 Braddock Road, Forest Hills, Pa.

drawing [CMUAA]

97   1915
House and garage for Thomas McLaughlin [extant]
5844 Marlborough Avenue, Pittsburgh

specifications [CMUAA]

98   ca. 1915?
House and garage [not built]

drawings [CMUAA]

99   1915
House and garage for Rudolph E. Hellmund [extant]
7510 Trevanion Avenue, Swissvale, Pa.

drawing, specifications, photographs [CMUAA]

Frank C. Harper, *Pittsburgh of Today: Its Resources and People* (New York: American Historical Society, 1931–1932), 4:588–89.

Anna Marie Defino Certo, "Swissvale Has Community Pride," *Carnegie Magazine* 44 (February 1970), 78.

100   1916
Double duplex for William Robinson [extant]
1308 Singer Place, Wilkinsburg, Pa.

drawings [CMUAA]

101   1916
House with office for Dr. Enoch L. Jones [extant]
100 East James Street, Munhall, Pa.
Drawing and specifications cite location as Homestead.

drawing, specifications [CMUAA]

102   1916
House for J. Lee Barnes [extant]
584 Briar Cliff Road, Pittsburgh

drawing, specifications, photographs [CMUAA]

103   1917
House for John C. Myers [not built]
1351 Cordova Road, Pittsburgh

Builders Bulletin 1:24 (February 10, 1917), 3; 1:28 (March 10, 1917), 2; 1:36 (May 5, 1917), 3; 1:37 (May 12, 1917), 3; 1:38 (May 19, 1917), 2; 1:39 (May 26, 1917), 3.

104   1917
House and garage for Albert J. Best [not built]
1357-1359 Cordova Road, Pittsburgh

specifications [CMUAA]

Builders Bulletin 1:36 (May 5, 1917), 3; 1:37 (May 12, 1917), 3; 1:38 (May 19, 1917), 2; 1:39 (May 26, 1917), 3.

105   1917
House for Lawrence C. Letzkus [not built]
1349 Cordova Road, Pittsburgh

Builders Bulletin 1:36 (May 5, 1917), 3; 1:37 (May 12, 1917), 3; 1:38 (May 19, 1917), 2; 1:39 (May 26, 1917), 3.

106   1919
House, two double duplexes, and three garages for Mark H. and Fannie B. Nolan [not built]
1400, 1402-1408 North Negley Avenue, Pittsburgh
Scheibler supervised the laying of foundations for the house and one double duplex before he was dismissed from the job.

drawings [CMUAA]

Builders Bulletin 4:13 (November 29, 1919), 5.

107   1919
House for Dr. William T. Pyle [extant]
7328 Schoyer Avenue, Swissvale, Pa.
Substantially altered.

drawing, photographs [CMUAA]

108   ca. 1920
House for Stephen Wach [extant]
1810 Hanover Street, Swissvale, Pa.
Attribution confirmed by Arpad Wach. Substantially altered.

109   ca. 1920?
House with garage for William D. Johnston [not built]
Jackson Street, Pittsburgh
Two versions. For subsequent project see cat. 110.

sketches [CMUAA]

110   1921–1922
House and garage for Clara E. Johnston [extant]
6349 Jackson Street, Pittsburgh
Design similar to cat. 132. For preliminary projects see cat. 109.

drawings, specifications, photograph [CMUAA]

111   ca. 1921
House for Frank K. Harter [not built]
Pennsylvania Route 18, Summit Township, Crawford County, Pa.
Recorded by JVT, which cites location as Conneaut Lake, opposite Exposition Park, and describes house as frame and cement [or stucco] with a [pseudo-]thatch roof.

112   1922–1923
House with garage for Rudolph E. Hellmund and Hedwig Borgman [extant]
7508 Trevanion Avenue, Swissvale, Pa.
Drawings and specifications name Hellmund as the client, but Hedwig Borgman, Hellmund's widowed mother-in-law, actually owned the property.

drawings, specifications, survey maps, survey notes [CMUAA]

Historic American Building Survey, PA-626.

113   1922
Garage for Harry D. Hasson [extant]
728R East End Avenue, Pittsburgh
For related project see cat. 89.

drawing [CMUAA]

114   1922–1924
House, garage, and wall for Eva R. Harter [extant]
2557 Beechwood Boulevard, Pittsburgh

drawings, specifications, photographs [CMUAA]; drawings, notes and sketches, correspondences [SLMM]

Historic American Building Survey, PA-622.

115   1922
House for Walter Schmidt [not built]
329 Downey Avenue, Modesto, California
Formerly 1929 Downey Street.

drawings [CMUAA]

116   ca. 1922?
House and garage for Jacob A. Harter [not built]
5429 Beacon Street, Pittsburgh

specifications [CMUAA]

117   ca. 1922?
House with garage [not built]

drawings [CMUAA]

118   1922
Parkstone Dwellings: double duplex and two garages for Harry Rubins [extant]
6937–6943 Penn Avenue, Pittsburgh
Interior design similar to cat. 147.

drawings, specifications, photographs [CMUAA]; drawings, tile cartoons, notes and sketches, correspondences [SLMM]

119   1922–1923
House and garage for Allen M. and Elizabeth Klages [extant]
5525 Beverly Place, Pittsburgh

drawings, specifications, bids, expense records, invoice, photographs [CMUAA]; drawings, tile rubbings, notes and sketches, correspondences [SLMM]

Historic American Building Survey, PA-621.

120   1925
The Woodlands: three double houses and three garages for Frank K. Harter [not built]
Fifth Avenue near Woodland Road, Pittsburgh
Two versions.

drawings, specifications [CMUAA]; drawings, notes and sketches [SLMM]

121   ca. 1926
Penn store and office building for Daniel L. Dillinger [not built]
800 Penn Avenue, Wilkinsburg, Pa.

drawings, specifications [CMUAA]

122   1926–1927
Two porch additions to house for Harry S. Wherrett [front porch destroyed?; rear porch extant]
Maryland Route 5, St. Mary's City, Maryland

drawings with specifications, photographs [CMUAA]

123   1926
House and garage for Florie Trondle [extant]
51 Orchard Street, Fair Oaks, Leet Township, Allegheny County, Pa.

drawings, specifications [CMUAA]

124   1926
Double house with garage for Frank K. Harter [not built]
5943–5945 Fifth Avenue, Pittsburgh

drawings, specifications [CMUAA]

125   1927
Two houses with garages for Albert Q. Starr [extant]
1715–1717 Denniston Street, Pittsburgh

drawings, specifications [CMUAA]; notes and sketches, correspondences [SLMM]

126   1927
House and Garage for Eva R. Harter [extant]
107 South Knight Avenue, Margate City, New Jersey

specifications, photographs [CMUAA]

127   1928
Interior design for apartment for Harry S. Wherrett [demolished]
Apartment 4-C, Park Mansions, 5023 Frew Street, Pittsburgh

drawing [CMUAA]; drawings, notes and sketches, correspondence [SLMM]

128   ca. 1928?
House for Harry Dorfman [not built]
Beacon Street, Pittsburgh
Recorded by JVT.

129   1928
House with garage for George L. and Jessie M. Kinter [extant]
1139 Greenridge Lane, Greentree, Pa.

drawing, specifications [CMUAA]

130   1928
House and garage for Jennie D. Frease [extant]
66 Churchill Road, Churchill, Pa.

drawings, specifications, photographs [CMUAA]; drawings, notes and sketches, correspondences [SLMM]

131   ca. 1929
Two houses for Rose Rubins [extant]
7521 Graymore Road and 7520 Rockshale Road, Pittsburgh
Attribution.

132   ca. 1929
House with garage for Frank K. and Eva R. Harter [extant]
109 South Washington Avenue, Ventnor City, New Jersey
Attribution confirmed by Earl Harter. Design similar to cat. 110.

photograph [CMUAA]

133   1930
Remodeling of lodge building into apartment building for the First National Bank of Monongahela City [extant]
500 West Main Street, Monongahela, Pa.
A Robert H. Robinson project.

specifications [CMUAA]

Daily Republican (Monongahela, Pa.), June 18, 1930, 1.

134   ca. 1931
Alterations to house for Frederick and Blanche Scheibler [destroyed]
2891 Talley Cavey Road, Talley Cavey, Hampton Township, Allegheny County, Pa.
Attribution. Location is also variously cited as Wildwood and Allison Park.

photograph [CMUAA]

135   1931
Four row houses for Fred C. McCafferty [extant]
545–551 James Street, Turtle Creek, Pa.
Attribution.

136   ca. 1931?
Vilsack Arms apartment building for the Vilsack Family [not built]
5216 Liberty Avenue, Pittsburgh
Attribution by George Bailey.

137   ca. 1935?
Alterations and additions to store and apartment building for Rose Rubins [extant]
714–718 Wood Street and 708–710 South Avenue, Wilkinsburg, Pa.
Attribution. Formerly the Snively Arcade Building. Substantially altered.

photographs [PHLF]

138   1936
Publishing plant, garage, and remodeling of hotel into office building for Notes Publishing and Printing Company [extant]
23 North Central Avenue, Canonsburg, Pa.
A Robert H. Robinson project. Substantially altered.

drawings, specifications [CMUAA]

139   1939
Newspaper plant and office building for the Democrat Messenger [extant]
32 Church Street, Waynesburg, Pa.
A Robert H. Robinson project.

drawings, specifications, photographs [CMUAA]

Daily Republican (Monongahela, Pa.), February 16, 1940, 1; September 17, 1946, 3:1.

Observer-Reporter (Washington / Waynesburg, Pa.), March 15, 1986, 1.

140   1939
Addition to school [not built?]

drawing [CMUAA]

141   1939
School [not built?]

drawing [CMUAA]

142   1939
Model Home with garage for the Daily Republican [extant]
522 Fourth Street, Monongahela, Pa.
The project was sponsored by Robert H. Robinson's Daily Republican newspaper, but drawings and specifications name the client as Robinson's son John Robinson, who eventually lived in the house.

drawings, specifications [CMUAA]

Daily Republican (Monongahela, Pa.), *from 1939:* September 22, 1, 5, 10; September 25, 1; September 28, 1, 7; October 4, 1; October 11, 1, 8; October 18, 1; October 19, 1, 2; October 20, 1, 3; October 21, 1; October 24, 1, 2; October 26, 1, 3; November 15, 1, 3; December 1, 1, 6; *from 1940:* February 3, 1; February 13, 1; May 17, 1:1, 10; 3:1–6; 4:1–8; May 18, 1; May 20, 1, 7; May 21, 1, 7; May 22, 1, 7; May 23, 1; May 25, 1; May 29, 1; May 31, 1; June 1, 1.

Martin Aurand, "Monongahela's Model Home," *Monongahela Valley-Review* 3 (September 1987), 4.

143   ca. 1939?
Store and office building [not built?]

drawing [CMUAA]

144   ca. 1940?
Additions to Ament house for Charles F. and Marie S. Blue [extant]
1204 Hulton Avenue, Oakmont, Pa.
Attribution. For related projects see cats. 44, 79.

blueprint [private]

145   1942
House with garage for Rose and Herbert Seger [not built]
1348 Wickerham Drive, Carroll Township, Washington County, Pa.
Two versions.

drawings, specifications [CMUAA]

146   1948
House with garage for William C. Teach [not built]
3855 Anderson Avenue, Gibsonia, Pa.

drawings, specifications [CMUAA]

147   ?
Alterations to house for Harry Rubins [extant]
1619 Beechwood Boulevard, Pittsburgh
Attribution. Interior design similar to cat. 118.

148   ?
Alterations to house for Daniel L. Dillinger [demolished]
353 North Main Street, Greensburg, Pa.
Recorded by JVT.

149   ?
House for Thomas B. Moreland [not built?]
Recorded by JVT.

150   ?
House for O. H. Kreider [not built?]
Thornburg, Pa.
Recorded by JVT.

151   ?
Apartment building for Frank K. Harter [not built]
New Jersey
Attribution by Earl Harter.

152   ?
Houses for Frank K. Harter [not built]
Switzerland
Attribution by Earl Harter.

Misattributions:

Apartment building
736 North Avenue, Wilkinsburg, Pa.

Double house
365–367 Spahr Street, Pittsburgh

Garage
44 Biddle Street, Pittsburgh
Commonly confused with cat. 113.

Henius House
1315 Cordova Road, Pittsburgh
Commonly confused with cat. 104. Actually designed by Kiehnel and Elliott.

Builders Bulletin 2:7 (October 13, 1917), 4.

House
5864 Marlborough Street, Pittsburgh

House
1442 Murray Avenue, Pittsburgh

Row houses
5927–5937 Alder Street, Pittsburgh

Row houses
1147–1155 King Avenue, Pittsburgh
Attribution by Shear and Schmertz. No other evidence links to Scheibler.

Row houses
368–382 McKee Place, Pittsburgh

Row houses
5509–5513 Phillips Street, Pittsburgh

Appendix 11
Scheibler's Library

Partial list compiled from the holdings of Gillian H. Belnap, Mildred Kilham, and Thomas Sutton.

Academy Architecture and Architectural Review 30 (December 1906).

Architektur von Olbrich. Vols. 1–2. Berlin: Ernst Wasmuth, 1901–1908.

Beuhlmann, J. Die Architekturdes Klassichen Altertums und die Renaissance. Vols. 1–3. Stuttgart: Paul Neff, 1904.

Bond, Francis. Gothic Architecture in England. London: B. T. Batsford, 1905.

Dekorative Kunst, July 1905.

Embury, Aymer, II. One Hundred Country Houses: Modern American Examples. New York: Century, 1909.

Holme, Charles. Modern British Domestic Architecture and Decoration. London: The Studio, 1901.

Lyongrun, Arnold. Vorbilder für Kunstverglasungen im Style der Neuzeit. Berlin and New York: B. Hessing, 1900. [Miscellaneous plates.]

Moderne Bauformen: Monatshefte für Architektur und Raumkunst 4 (1905); 8 (1909); 9 (1910).

Modern Surface Ornament. New York: J. Sabin and Sons, 1877.

Muthesius, Hermann. Das Moderne Landhaus und seine innere Ausstattung. 2d ed. Munich: F. Bruckmann, 1905.

Rouam, J., ed. Fantaisies Décoratives par Habert-Dys. Paris: Librairie de l'Art, 1886.

Schnorr, Julius et al., eds. Gewerbehalle Organ für den Fortschritt in allen Zweigen der Kunstindustrie. Stuttgart: J. Engelhorn, 1873.

Scott, H. H. Baillie. Hauser und Garten. Berlin: Ernst Wasmuth, 1912.

Sparrow, W. S., ed. The British Home of Today. New York: A. C. Armstrong and Son, 1904.

Sparrow, W. S., ed. The Modern Home. London: Hodder and Stoughton, n.d.

The Studio Year Book of Decorative Art. London: Studio, 1906, 1908.

Weaver, Lawrence. Houses and Gardens by E. L. Luytens. London: Country Life, 1913.

Wright, Frank Lloyd. Ausgefuhrte Bauten. Berlin: Ernst Wasmuth, 1911.

Notes

Introduction

1. See the exhibit catalog, *Modern Architecture: International Exhibition* (New York: Museum of Modern Art, 1932).

2. Penelope Redd, "Scheibler Anticipated Modern Architecture," *Pittsburgh Sunday Sun-Telegraph*, September 23, 1934, 4:7.

3. John Knox Shear and Robert W. Schmertz, "A Pittsburgh Original," *Charette* 28 (September 1948): 4–5.

4. See *Charette* 28 (December 1948): 3, where Scheibler's sudden discovery is compared to the discovery of John Kane, the great Pittsburgh primitive artist.

5. John Knox Shear, "Pittsburgh Rediscovers an Architect Pioneer," *Architectural Record* 106 (July 1949): 98–100.

6. James D. Van Trump, "Frederick G. Scheibler, Jr.: A Prophet of Modern Architecture in Pittsburgh," *Charette* 42 (October 1962): 11–15.

7. Montgomery Schuyler, "The Building of Pittsburgh," *Architectural Record* 30:3 (September 1911): 206–82.

8. Quoted in Ian Latham, *Joseph Maria Olbrich* (London: Academy Editions, 1980), p. 40.

9. Wiegfried Wichmann, "The Lily and Iris as European Picture Motifs in the Nineteenth and Early Twentieth Centuries," *World Cultures and Modern Art: The Encounter of 19th and 20th Century European Art and Music with Asia, Africa, Oceania, Afro-and Indo-America* (Munich: F. Bruckmann, 1972), pp. 108–12. Many of these motifs had been previously adopted by European impressionists.

10. Peter Selz, "Art Nouveau: Art and Design at the Turn of the Century," *Art in a Turbulent Era* (Ann Arbor, Mich.: UMI Research Press), p. 12.

11. Aspects of de Bobula's work appear also to have been influenced by the Floreale, a progressive Italian movement.

12. *Construction* 1:21 (May 27, 1905): 13. The article was reprinted as John T. Comes, "The Pittsburgh Architectural Club Exhibition 1905," *House and Garden* 8:2 (August 1905): 83–89. Renderings of de Bobula's projects were published in Pittsburgh Architectural Club, *Catalogue of the Third Exhibition* (Pittsburgh: 1905).

13. At least two other de Bobula projects may be traceable to designs by Viennese architect Otto Wagner.

14. Gillian H. Belnap, "The Apartment Buildings of Frederick G. Scheibler, Jr., with a Catalogue of All His Multiple Residences," Ph.D. diss., University of Pittsburgh, 1985 (Ann Arbor, Mich.: University Microfilms International, 1986), p. 218.

15. Scheibler is mentioned briefly in one general history of American architecture and one scholarly essay: John Burchard and Albert Bush-Brown, *The Architecture of America: A Social and Cultural History* (Boston: Little, Brown, 1961), p. 233; R. J. Clark, "Stylistic Interplay between Central Europe and America: Architecture and Painting from 1860 to 1914," in *The Shaping of Art and Architecture in Nineteenth Century America* (New York: Metropolitan Museum of Art, 1972), pp. 71, 78.

Chapter 1. Man and Architect

1. An understanding of Scheibler is impoverished by minimal biographical data and by a total lack of personal writings and insights from colleagues. Excepting a published biographical sketch in 1908 and the Shear and Schmertz interview in 1948, no biographical information was compiled on Scheibler during his lifetime. All else that is known has been assembled from primary sources and the reminiscences of family members and other acquaintances. John Newton Boucher, *A Century and a Half of Pittsburgh and Her People* (New York: Lewis Publishing Company, 1908): 4:7; and Shear and Schmertz, "A Pittsburgh Original," pp. 4–5.

2. Shear and Schmertz, "A Pittsburgh Original," p. 5.

3. The house still stands at 3305 Dawson (formerly Bouquet) Street. Scheibler may also have closely watched the concurrent construction of Henry Hobson

Richardson's Allegheny County Courthouse and Jail which would have been highly visible from Central High School's hilltop location.

4. Scheibler himself told of his apprenticeship to Moser, and his presence in the office was also noted by Henry Kropff in Tall McKee, "Charette Vignette [Henry Kropff]," *Charette* 29 (April 1949): 15. The associations with the Thalman and the Longfellow, Alden and Harlow offices were reported by Scheibler's brother Will in an interview with James D. Van Trump of uncertain date.

5. Thalman made this claim in an advertisement in the 1896 Pittsburgh city directory.

6. Among Scheibler's earliest extant drawings is a series of the classical orders, carefully drawn as if they were an academic exercise. These postdate his apprenticeship period, however.

7. Scheibler shared a downtown Pittsburgh office with architect John L. Beatty in 1899, according to the city directory for that year. The exact nature of this arrangement is unclear. During his years in Wilkinsburg he had offices in the First National Bank Building, the Milligan and Miller Building, and the Carl Building.

8. Interview with George Raisig, November 1988.

9. Scheibler's election to office in the Pittsburgh Architectural Club was reported in *Construction* 1:24 (June 17, 1905): 13. Scheibler was also a member of the Architectural League of America, an organization of affiliated architectural clubs. He applied for membership in the Pittsburgh Chapter of the American Institute of Architects in 1907, but his application was not approved until more than a year later. He did not actively participate in chapter affairs, but remained a member until 1916 when his membership was terminated for nonpayment of dues. He was never a member of the national A.I.A. organization. Pittsburgh Chapter, American Institute of Architects, Minute Books (1908–1916).

10. Two exhibited projects remain unidentified: "Store and Apartment Building, Pittsburgh" (probably the Minnetonka Building) in Pittsburgh Architectural Club, *Catalogue of the Fifth Exhibition* (Pittsburgh: 1910): List of Exhibits; and "Residence, Pittsburgh" in Pittsburgh Architectural Club, *Catalogue of the Seventh Exhibition* (Pittsburgh: 1912): List of Exhibits. The last such exhibition was held in 1916.

11. Letter from Mildred Scheibler Kilham to Gillian H. Belnap, 1976.

12. Scheibler's office was variously located in the Lloyd Building, the East End Savings and Trust Company Building, and the Whitfield Building during his years in East Liberty.

13. Scheibler does not appear in city directories between 1912 and 1917. Earl Harter, son of Frank and Eva Harter, says that Scheibler lived with the Harter family during this period. The Harters lived at a number of different addresses during the 1910s. Interview with Earl Harter, June 1989.

14. All four names are on White's 1955 will. Scheibler may have continued to work on White's house into the 1930s. Interview with Judge Henry X. O'Brien, White's lawyer, November 1986.

15. There are curious parallels here with the personal life of Frank Lloyd Wright. Both Scheibler and Wright were musically inclined and had volatile temperaments that led to financial and family problems. Both developed reputations as womanizers and were separated from their wives and children.

16. The landlord and grantor was Fred C. McCafferty, who commissioned a row house project from Scheibler at approximately this time.

17. Belnap, "The Apartment Buildings of Frederick G. Scheibler, Jr., p. 218.

18. Scheibler's clients had much in common with the early clients of Frank Lloyd Wright in these respects. As a group, however, Scheibler's clients probably had a somewhat lower economic status. A number of Wright's clients were inventors; Scheibler's included Rudolph Hellmund, who held many patents in electrical engineering, and Stephen Wach, who reportedly had a hand in the invention of the automotive self-starter. See Leonard K. Eaton, *Two Chicago Architects and Their Clients* (Cambridge, Mass.: MIT Press, 1969), pp. 32–41.

19. Scheibler also prepared typed specifications to accompany his working drawings. Many of the examples that survive were reused or adapted for use with other projects and include pencil notations that document multiple projects.

20. Only two of the renderings survive as original watercolors.

21. For Mercer and the Moravian Tile and Pottery Works see Cleota Reed, *Henry Chapman Mercer and the Moravian Pottery and Tile Works* (Philadelphia: University of Pennsylvania Press, 1987), pp. 55, 103–10. Scheibler

and Frank Harter reportedly went on occasional fishing expeditions with Mercer in eastern Pennsylvania.

22. Shear and Schmertz, "A Pittsburgh Original," pp. 4–5.

23. Ibid., p. 4.

24. Letter from Mary Pyle Fleck to James D. Van Trump, January 1970.

25. C. F. A. Voysey, as told in *Studio* 11:51 (June 1897): 25.

26. Shear and Schmertz, "A Pittsburgh Original," p. 5.

27. According to Scheibler, Kato (who was born in Japan and died in New York City) was the son of the then postmaster-general of Japan (ibid., p. 5). He studied painting in Denver with Henry Read and was awarded the Hallgarten Prize at the National Academy of Design in 1920 for his "Portrait of a Young Woman" (Belnap, "The Apartment Buildings of Frederick G. Scheibler, Jr.," p. 37). His presence in Pittsburgh and the reasons for his acquaintance with Scheibler are not documented.

Chapter 2. Half and Half

1. Quoted in Shear and Schmertz, "A Pittsburgh Original," p. 4.

2. Scheibler's earliest residential works, the Scheibler cottage, the Kitzmiller house, and Matthews/Steel house, recall the tentative beginnings of Frank Lloyd Wright. These houses occupy essentially the same positions in Scheibler's career as Wright's early Shingle Style home and so-called bootlegged houses do in his career. See Grant Carpenter Manson, *Frank Lloyd Wright to 1910: The First Golden Age* (New York: Van Nostrand Reinhold, 1958), pp. 42–60.

3. Allegheny was annexed to Pittsburgh in 1907 and became Pittsburgh's North Side.

4. Both the Steel house, and Frank Lloyd Wright's 1891 Blossom house, have an affinity with McKim, Mead and White's 1885–1886 H. C. A. Taylor house, a pivotal building in the development of American neoclassical domestic architecture. Scheibler's elevations are closely related to the Taylor house, and his plan is remarkably similar to Wright's. See Belnap, "The Apartment Buildings of Frederick G. Scheibler, Jr.," p. 30; and Henry-Russell Hitchcock, "Frank Lloyd Wright and the 'Academic Tradition' of the Early Eighteen-Nineties," *Journal of the Warburg and Courtland Institutes* 7 (January–June 1944): 46–63; rpt. in *Nineteenth and Twentieth Century Architecture*, Garland Library of the History of Art no. 11 (New York: Garland Publishing, 1987), pp. 127–50.

5. A document representing Saint Paul's Evangelical Lutheran Church (807 Ross Avenue, Wilkinsburg) was reported found among Scheibler's now lost office records. This building was apparently designed by Milligan and Miller in 1900. Perhaps Scheibler was involved in the project in some capacity.

6. Swissvale Borough School Board, Minute Book (June 1899–August 1907): pp. 46–47, 193–194.

7. This building represents Matthews's commission for a so-called department store building, but he actually operated it as a hotel, accommodating his longstanding hotel business previously located in a building next door. The design seems more appropriate for a store building than for a hotel.

8. Suggested in Belnap, "The Apartment Buildings of Frederick G. Scheibler, Jr.," pp. 33–34.

9. For a time, Scheibler even owned twenty shares of Hamilton Realty Company stock.

10. Baillie Scott used similar bold floral motifs with heart-shaped leaves in a number of projects including the library at The Garth and the music room at the Reiss house in Mannheim (both circa 1900). These projects were published in a number of sources by 1904. The transoms have all been removed.

11. The Olbrich art-glass design was borrowed from the Ganss house as published in *Architektur Von Olbrich* (Berlin: Ernst Wasmuth, 1901–1914), I:73. The exposed I-beam is found in a small number of Olbrich designs. The unconventional Philadelphia architect Frank Furness had used exposed I-beams in projects of the 1870s and 1880s, and Henry Hornbostel used exposed iron and steel in buildings at Carnegie Tech in Pittsburgh starting in 1905. The only established use for I-beam lintels, however, was in rough finish elevations or in warehouses.

12. The source is a window designed by Oscar Paterson published in Charles Holme, *Modern British Domestic Architecture and Decoration* (London: Studio, 1901), p. 145. The lunette is now lost.

Chapter 3. Old Heidelberg

1. The following discussion of the Old Heidelberg apartment building is significantly indebted to Belnap,

"The Apartment Buildings of Frederick G. Scheibler, Jr."

2. *Construction* 1:22 (June 3, 1905): 8.

3. This description was belatedly published in ibid.

4. Van Trump, "Frederick G. Scheibler, Jr.," p. 12.

5. The walls are brick beneath the stucco. One early discussion was incorrect in postulating that the building was reinforced concrete. *The American Architect and Building News* 91:1619 (January 5, 1907): 20.

6. Claude Bragdon provided an American perspective in Claude Bragdon, "Plastered Houses," *Architectural Review* 11 (1904): 21–22.

7. M. H. Baillie Scott, *Houses and Gardens* (London: George Newnes, Ltd., 1906), p. 6.

8. Hans Berger, "Das Wohnung in Amerika," *Der Architekt* 14 (1908): 27; and an advertisement for the Standard Sanitary Manufacturing Company, whose products were installed in the building, source unknown.

9. *American Architect and Building News* 91:1619 (January 5, 1907): 20.

10. For the Viennese Secession, see Franco Bosi and Ezio Godoli, *Vienna 1900: Architecture and Design* (New York: Rizzoli, 1986). For Olbrich, see Robert Judson Clark, "J. M. Olbrich 1867–1908," *Architectural Design* 37:12 (December 1967): 565–72; and a reprint of Olbrich's portfolio published as *Architecture / Joseph Maria Olbrich* (New York: Rizzoli, 1988).

11. Olbrich gradually conceived an almost obsessive desire to create total environments and dictate art and life (*Gesamtkunst*) that was more despotic than democratic.

12. Clark, "J. M. Olbrich 1867–1908," p. 566.

13. Olbrich was influenced by Englishman M. H. Baillie Scott in particular. Olbrich house has an inglenook borrowed from from Baillie Scott and this and other Darmstadt houses have two-story halls in the Baillie Scott manner (Clark, "J. M. Olbrich 1867–1908," pp. 567–68). Olbrich was also influenced by the simple whitewashed vernacular houses in the Mediterranean villages of Italy.

14. *Architektur von Olbrich*, 1:75. This correpondence was first noted in R. J. Clark, "Stylistic Interplay between Central Europe and America," p. 71.

15. *Architektur von Olbrich*, 2:48.

16. Ibid., 2:10.

17. Ibid., 1:85.

18. Ibid., 2:9.

19. Holme, *Modern British Domestic Architecture and Decoration*, pp. 161, 113, 115.

20. Arnold Lyongrun, *Vorbilder für Kunstverglasungen im Style der Neuzeit* (Berlin and New York: B. Hessing, 1900). A few plates from this publication were found among Scheibler's books.

21. Holme, *Modern British Domestic Architecture and Decoration*, pp. 107, 109.

22. Sculptural reliefs in plaster, concrete, or stone also appeared in the work of M. H. Baillie Scott, Wilson Eyre, and Frank Lloyd Wright. Claude Bragdon ("Plastered Houses," p. 22) specifically recommended cast-plaster reliefs. Scheibler eventually tried out Olbrich's more organic technique on a drawing for an unidentified house where a surface treatment of foliage on the front porch is lightly suggested by Scheibler's pen and pencil. Scheibler also devised a species of custom-designed lighting fixtures that emerged from the corners of cabinets and fireplaces like plant growth.

23. Belnap, "The Apartment Buildings of Frederick G. Scheibler, Jr.," p. 115.

24. Robinson and Bruckman sold the original Old Heidelberg property to Sam Dempster on April 1, 1908, but remained involved with the subsequent additions at both ends of the building.

25. Only Carlton Strong's Bellefield Dwellings (1902–1904) could rival the Old Heidelberg in architectural interest among Pittsburgh's handful of notable apartment buildings of the day. Bellefield Dwellings was large and urbane and up-to-date in every respect; but it too reassured its tenants with domestically scaled towers and a name suggestive of domestic privacy.

26. Secessionist influence is little evident along the East Coast, but can occasionally be found in the American Midwest. A number of Chicago architects experimented with Secessionist motifs. There was Scheibler and de Bobula in Pittsburgh. And there was H. Jordon MacKenzie in New Orleans, among whose houses are direct adaptations of Olbrich's Bahr, Olbrich, and Habich houses, designed between 1905 and 1910. Michael D. Eversmeyer, "H. Jordon MacKenzie" (unpublished paper), n.d.

27. The Old Heidelberg was displayed at the Pittsburgh Architectural Club exhibits in 1905 and 1910 and published in the following: *American Architect and Building News* 91:1619 (January 5, 1907): 20, plate 3; *Architecture* 15:3 (March 15, 1907), plate 21; Hans Berger, "Das Wohnung in Amerika," *Der Architekt* 14 (1908): 27, 30; *Brickbuilder* 20:1 (January 1911): 19; and *Western Architect* 17:6 (June 1911): plate 6.

28. Belnap, "The Apartment Buildings of Frederick G. Scheibler, Jr.," p. 112.

Chapter 4. The New Manner

1. *Construction* 3:12 (March 24, 1906): 270. A third apartment building on Lang Avenue was announced at the same time, but never built.

2. Dillinger's sister, Eliza L., married an Albert A. Hasson. See Belnap, "The Apartment Buildings of Frederick G. Scheibler, Jr.," pp. 122–23. Dillinger briefly owned the Whitehall in 1908.

3. One parallel for the doorway is Olbrich's Deiters house. The source for the parrot design was Lyongrun. Scheibler used parrots again at the Klages house.

4. The following discussion of the Coleman apartment building is significantly indebted to Belnap, "The Apartment Buildings of Frederick G. Scheibler, Jr."

5. See Thomas Howarth, *Charles Rennie Mackintosh and the Modern Movement* (London: Routledge and Kegan Paul, 1977). Mackintosh and McNair each married one of the MacDonald sisters.

6. Quoted in ibid., p. 287.

7. Even Mackintosh's revolutionary entry in the famous 1901 *Haus Eines Kunstfreundes* (house for an art lover) competition, though acknowledged and lauded in some parts, was much less copied than a more conservative entry in the same competition by Baillie Scott.

8. This design was published in Hermann Muthesius, "Die Glasgower Kunstbewegung: Charles Mackintosh und Margaret MacDonald-Mackintosh," *Dekorative Kunst*, March 1902, p. 211.

9. One feature, the flat projecting roof over Scheibler's third-floor porch, is taken from another Mackintosh project, the Martyr's Public School of 1905.

10. The light fixtures may have been modeled after more elaborate ones at Mackintosh's Willow Tea Rooms. See "Ein Mackintosh—Teehaus in Glasgow," *Dekorative Kunst*, April 1905, p. 257–75.

11. This feature also shares a family resemblance with Louis Sullivan's Schlesinger and Mayer (later Carson Pirie Scott) department store of 1903–1904 in Chicago.

12. The rose motif appeared often in Mackintosh's work, most pervasively in the large house Windyhill (1900), where it was used in wall decoration, lighting fixtures, and furniture. Windyhill was thoroughly illustrated in Muthesius, "Die Glasgower Kunstbewegung: Charles Mackintosh und Margaret MacDonald-Mackintosh," pp. 193–203. Scheibler reused the motif in art glass at his Wetherall apartment building.

13. The fireplace surrounds are derived from Mackintosh's Hill house as published in Wilhelm Michel, "Zur Asthetik der Illustration," *Deutsche Kunst und Dekoration* 15 (1904): 362–68. Hill house was exhibited at the Pittsburgh Architectural Club exhibition of 1907.

14. Swissvale Borough School Board Minute Book, (June 1899–August 1907), p. 198.

15. Scheibler was seemingly on retainer with the school district between the Hawkins School and Wilkins School projects, for he received two minor commissions from the district during this time.

16. The source is a exhibition booth for the Glasgow School of Art. Mackintosh apparently derived this detail from one of his so-called tree motifs. Muthesius, "Die Glasgower Kunstbewegung: Charles Mackintosh und Margaret MacDonald-Mackintosh," p. 214. When Scheibler received another school commission very late in his career, he designed a straightforward contemporary building with none of the progressive associations of his early work, save for a reprise of this circular namestone.

17. The closest parallel is to Olbrich's Glückert house.

Chapter 5. Group Cottages

1. See Peter Davey, *Arts and Crafts Architecture: The Search for Earthly Paradise* (London: The Architectural Press, 1980); James D. Kornwolf, *M. H. Baillie Scott and the Arts and Crafts Movement* (Baltimore: Johns Hopkins Press, 1972); and Margaret Richardson, *The Craft Architects* (New York: Rizzoli, 1983).

2. The closest American counterpart early in the century was the southern California bungalow court. As it appeared after about 1909, the bungalow court consisted of a centrally planned group of houses sharing planted open space. A "speculator's dream," it also served the purpose of providing healthful housing for people of low or moderate income. See Robert Winter, *The California Bungalow* (Los Angeles: Hennessey and Ingalls, 1980), pp. 58–67.

3. This was roughly the period of the sobering Pittsburgh Survey, the findings of which were publicized in 1908–1909.

4. De Bobula's authorship is documented in *Construction* 2:22 (December 2, 1905): 509.

5. Inglenook Place was originally known as Topeka Street. David Wilkins has suggested that Scheibler may have suggested the new name for the one-block-long

street, as the inglenook was a common element of symbolic importance in Arts and Crafts design.

6. See Robert Venturi, *Complexity and Contradiction in Architecture* (New York: Museum of Modern Art, 1966).

7. *Ausgefürte Bauten und Entwürfte von Frank Lloyd Wright* (Berlin: Ernst Wasmuth, 1910), plate 40.

8. Five cottages were erected on an adjacent lot while the later part of Hamilton Cottages was being built. Commissioned in the name of Jesse F. Robinson, they were never considered part of Hamilton Cottages.

9. The very deep blocks in this part of Squirrel Hill allow for this arrangement in an otherwise dense urban context.

10. *Cot* is an Anglo-Saxon word for a simple house.

11. See M. H. Baillie Scott, "The Cheap Cottage," *Studio* 51 (March 1914): 133–39.

12. Meado'cots has fallen on hard times and is perhaps the most endangered of Scheibler's major works.

13. Dillinger commissioned this project, but Harry D. Hasson was again deeply involved. Hasson was listed as the builder on the building permit and purchased half of the double house with his wife Clara in 1921. Scheibler designed a garage for the Hassons at this address in 1922. Inside, a panel inset with oriental art glass acts as a room divider on the first floor of each unit, an arrangement found at Highland Towers and thus familiar to both Dillinger and Hasson.

14. Versions of this entrance arrangement can occasionally be found in turn-of-the-century architecture. Some Parker and Unwin houses, such as Whirriestone, have an entry recessed behind a lowered arch; workers' rowhouses in Wilmerding, Pennsylvania, built by the Westinghouse Air Brake Company, have paired entries under low arches. Such examples lack the clarity, emphasis, and level of abstraction of Vilsack Row, however.

15. The living room fireplaces resemble those at Highland Towers.

16. A six-unit reprise was built in the same year for William V. and Albert A. Kreuer. This is the derivative project of the two, however, and lacks the visual impact of Vilsack Row.

17. Esther McCoy remarks that Lewis Courts displayed Gill's ability to build good houses at a price that would allow the client to rent it for a nominal sum, while displaying a reverence for the individual that was "never equalled in the field of minimum housing." Esther McCoy, *Five California Architects* (New York: Reinhold Publishing Corporation, 1960), p. 85.

18. E. M. Roorbach, "The Garden Apartments of California," *Architectural Record* 34 (December 1913): 520–30.

19. Shear, "Pittsburgh Rediscovers an Architect Pioneer," 99.

20. This aesthetic is eloquently represented in the Pittsburgh region by the work of Tasso Katselas. Katselas knows Scheibler's work, and even used the arched entries of Vilsack Row in his Niagara Square townhouses of 1985. But the Katselas house of 1962, which has a considerable kinship with Vilsack Row, was clearly inspired by the Maisons Jaoul.

21. Unfortunately, Scheibler's daring vision has not been sufficiently understood, and Vilsack Row has suffered substantially from alterations. The porches were so unnerving that they have all been rebuilt or given new supports.

22. Interview with Elizabeth Doran Myers, March 1989.

23. Barry Parker, "True Economy in Architecture," *The Art of Building a Home: A Collection of Lectures and Illustrations* (London, New York, and Bombay: Longmans, Green, 1901); rpt. in Dean Hawkes, editor, *Modern Country Houses in England: The Arts and Crafts Architecture of Barry Parker* (Cambridge: Cambridge University Press, 1986), p. 71.

24. Many of the Robinson and Bruckman properties were still owned by the Bruckman family until recently.

25. Van Trump, "Frederick G. Scheibler, Jr.," p. 14.

Chapter 6. Highland Towers

1. The following discussion of Highland Towers is indebted in part to Belnap, "The Apartment Buildings of Frederick G. Scheibler, Jr."

2. "Highland Towers, 340–342 South Highland Avenue, Pittsburgh, Pa." (advertising brochure), n.d., n.p.

3. One important tenant was Harry S. Wherrett, president of the Pittsburgh Plate Glass Company. When Wherrett moved to Park Mansions, Pittsburgh's first cooperative apartment building, he asked Scheibler to design the interior of his new apartment. Scheibler's design was presumably executed, but apartments at Park Mansions are continually susceptible to tenant redesign, so Scheibler's interior ultimately met its fate.

4. Like Tasso Katselas, Arthur Lubetz is an important contemporary Pittsburgh architect with a respect for Scheibler. His architecture is one of simple materials and incisive geometry. His suburban Fort Couch Tower office

building of 1986 is a recapitulation of the compositional themes of Highland Towers.

5. Extensive advertisements for Fiske and Company Inc., New York, "sole manufacturers of tapestry brick," appeared in the Pittsburgh Architectural Club, *Catalogue of the Fifth Exhibition* (Pittsburgh, 1910), pp. 133–38, and *Catalogue of the Sixth Exhibition* (Pittsburgh, 1911), pp. 126–29.

6. Quoted from the forward of a promotional pamphlet for the brick industry entitled "Suggestions in Artistic Brickwork," 1910; rpt. as Louis H. Sullivan, "Artistic Brick," *The Prairie School Review* 4:2 (second quarter 1967): 26. Sullivan used tapestry brick for all but one of his small midwestern bank buildings designed between 1907 and 1919. See Lauren S. Weingarden, *Louis H. Sullivan: The Banks* (Cambridge, Mass.: The MIT Press, 1987), 10–12. Frank Lloyd Wright made a similar statement about his so-called textile block system: "A building for the first time may be lightly fabricated, complete, of mono-material—literally woven into a pattern or design as was the oriental rug." Frank Lloyd Wright, "In the Cause of Architecture IV," *Architectural Record* 62 (October 1927): 319. For a provocative discussion of Wright's architecture in this vein see Kenneth Frampton, "The Text-Tile Tectonic: The Origin and Evolution of Wright's Woven Architecture," in *Frank Lloyd Wright: A Primer on Architectural Principles*, ed. Robert McCarter (New York: Princeton Architectural Press, pp. 124–49.

7. Julius Meier-Graefe, "Peter Behrens—Dusseldorf," *Dekorative Kunst*, July 1905, p. 420. This issue of *Dekorative Kunst* was part of Scheibler's library.

8. "Ein Mackintosh—Teehaus in Glasgow," pp. 257–75.

9. The probable source for the fireplaces was an obscure advertisement for "Gipsy Fires" by Joshua W. Taylor, Ltd., in *Academy Architecture and Architectural Review* 30 (December 1906): xviii.

10. One of the art-glass panels was displayed at a Pittsburgh Architectural Club exhibition by its maker, the Rudy Bros. Co., and published in Pittsburgh Architectural Club, *Catalogue of the Ninth Exhibition* (Pittsburgh, 1914), list of exhibits; plate.

11. Letter from Mildred Kilham to James D. Van Trump, 1962. This occasion, of course, would have been prior to the breakup of the family in about 1911.

12. *Ausgefürte Bauten und Entwürfte von Frank Lloyd Wright*. All of Scheibler's Wrightian sources were represented in this portfolio. For one of the earliest and best studies of Wright, see Henry-Russell Hitchcock, *In the Nature of Materials* (New York: Duell, Sloan and Pearce, 1942; rpt. New York: Da Capo Press, 1973).

13. See Frank Lloyd Wright, *A Testament* (New York: Horizon Press, 1957), pp. 84, 204–05; and Brendan Gill, *Many Masks: A Life of Frank Lloyd Wright* (New York: G. P. Putnam's Sons, 1987), pp. 178–83, 209.

14. Belnap, "The Apartment Buildings of Frederick G. Scheibler, Jr.," p. 217.

15. The Highland Towers design was not formally published, but a photograph of the building was included without caption or comment in Aymer Embury, "Impressions of Three Cities: III Pittsburgh," *Architecture* 31:4 (April 1915): 106.

Chapter 7. The Artistic House

1. Apart from Scheibler, Kiehnel and Elliott was the only Pittsburgh architectural firm of the era to complete a substantial body of work in a manner influenced by international progressive movements. This work, executed between about 1909 and 1916, included both Prairie School and European elements, but appears tentative beside the bold inventions of Scheibler and de Bobula. The firm eventually abandoned both its progressive manner and Pittsburgh, and moved on to greater renown in Florida and the Spanish Colonial style.

2. The exception was the Gamble house, the closest thing to a grand country house that Scheibler ever designed, and his only house to feature half-timbering in the full-blown English manner. At first glance it appears to be a conventional Tudor Revival period house, but Scheibler's hand is apparent in the Flemish bond brickwork of the first story and the hipped and gabled roof forms. The house underwent extensive alterations by architect Theodore Eicholz in 1927, and since there are no drawings or early photographs of the house, it is difficult to assess Scheibler's work. *Charette* 7:1 (January 1927), 20.

3. Claude Bragdon wrote in 1904: "Half-timber work as constructed nowadays is never anything but a sham—the imitation of an abandoned method of construction. . . . However, when the half-timber work is confined to an occasional gable . . . no serious objection can be raised against it, for the effect is charming." Bragdon also specifically approved of half-timbering modified as a simple sequences of vertical timbers (see Bragdon, "Plastered

Houses," p. 122). Many of the Prairie School architects also used half-timbering in this manner.

4. The pastoral motifs at the Miller house were borrowed from a design by T. S. Brydon published in the *Studio Yearbook of Decorative Art* (London: Studio, 1906), p. 158. Two of the windows with transoms meet at a corner like at the earlier Kitzmiller house. One transom was reused at Scheibler's Hoffman house.

5. Scheibler used this configuration of freestanding houses again at the Starr houses on Beacon Street.

6. See Kornwolf, *M. H. Baillie Scott*.

7. Hermann Muthesius, *Das Englische Haus* (Berlin: Ernst Wasmuth, 1904), 1:177, as quoted in Kornwolf, *M. H. Baillie Scott*, p. 324.

8. Baillie Scott, *Houses and Gardens*, plates following p. 110. Scheibler could have seen the copy that is at Pittsburgh's Carnegie Library. He owned a later edition of the book published in Berlin by Ernst Wasmuth in 1912.

9. See Kornwolf, *M. H. Baillie Scott*, pp. 255–58. There are also similarities to both Voysey and the American Shingle Style.

10. A blueprint dated 1940 shows the landscape plan for the new garden and an additional freestanding garage, which could also be Scheibler's. The Blues may deserve credit for the external consonance of the property, but they understood little of Scheibler's interiors and detailing. Victorian fireplaces, the enclosure of the garden porch, and a profusion of wrought iron seemingly also date from the Blue period. Hand-penciled notes on Scheibler's drawings for Ament indicate that Scheibler also designed alterations for the owner at the time, W. K. Dunlap, between 1911 and 1919.

11. Baillie Scott, *Houses and Gardens*, pp. 121–27.

12. *Architektur von Olbrich*, 3:78–79.

13. In Scheibler's drawings, the living room fireplace appears in an arch of Rookwood tile with scattered ornamental tiles, a brass hood, and an inglenook arrangement of flanking seats. This design may be derived from the drawing room of Baillie Scott's White house. The fireplace was much simplified as built.

14. This traditional British form is represented in the work of Voysey (Broadleys), Baillie Scott (Blackwell), Parker and Unwin (Homestead), and Mackintosh (Windyhill and Hill House).

15. The remainder of the property was divided into building lots, and Scheibler designed one of the subsequent houses, the J. Lee Barnes house. There is no evidence that Scheibler designed the beehivelike stone gateposts at either end of Briar Cliff Road, but he could have. The garage and the garden wall at Rockledge were later additions by other architects (interview with A. H. Lindsay, December 1991).

16. Views of Windyhill were published in Hermann Muthesius, *Das Moderne Landhaus und seine innere Ausstatung*, 2d ed. (Munich: F. Bruckmann, 1905), pp. 170-71; and Muthesius, "Die Glasgower Kunstbewegung: Charles R. Mackintosh und Margaret MacDonald-Mackintosh," pp. 193–203. The former book was represented in Scheibler's library.

17. See Duncan Simpson, *C. F. A. Voysey: An Architect of Individuality* (New York: Whitney Library of Design, 1981); and David Gebhard, *Charles F. A. Voysey, Architect* (Los Angeles: Hennessey and Ingalls, 1975).

18. "An Interview with Mr. Charles F. Annesley Voysey, Architect and Designer," *Studio* 1:6 (September 1893): 234.

19. Voysey's approach to design was so rooted in tradition that he could not understand why he should be credited as a innovator and refused to accept any responsibility for the development of modern ideas.

20. The Jones house is also closely related to Baillie Scott's Elmwood Cottages. Both the Orchard and Elmwood Cottages were published in 1901 in Holme, *Modern British Domestic Architecture and Decoration*, pp. 60, 181–93, again represented in Scheibler's library.

21. This tripartite form became a rather popular model for early twentieth-century American houses in a rare instance of broad absorption of an Arts and Crafts concept.

22. House and Studio at Studland Bay, Swanage, Dorset, for A. Sutro (1896). Scheibler was familiar with at least a key elevation for this project as published in Muthesius, *Das Moderne Landhaus und seine innere Ausstattung*, p. 146.

23. The Matthews inn project, commissioned under the name of Mrs. Matthews about 1909, marked the removal of the Matthews's business from their previously commissioned Scheibler-designed building to a site in the outer suburbs north of Pittsburgh. In the circa 1915 house project, Scheibler carried the controlling effect of the triangular massing scheme to a garage as well. His pencil extended the angled line of the house's sloping roof to the ground, and then projected it upward at the same angle to

establish the slope of the garage roof and the distance between the two buildings.

24. Unfortunately, some of the decorative features described here have been stripped from the house in recent years.

25. Frank C. Harper, *Pittsburgh of Today: Its Resources and People* (New York: American Historical Society, Inc., 1931–1932), 4:588–89.

26. Interview with Doris Hellmund, October 1991. The Hellmund house was the second of three Scheibler houses that line a block of Trevanion Avenue. The Miller house of 1905 was the first, and a house that Hellmund built with his mother-in-law in 1922–1923 was the third.

27. The Schultz house was published in Pittsburgh Architectural Club, *Catalogue of the Fifth Exhibition* (Pittsburgh: 1910), plate; and had been previously published in *Western Architect*.

28. In a May 1987 interview, Arpad Wach, son of client Stephen Wach, confirmed Scheibler's authorship of this house.

29. *Builders Bulletin* 4:13 (November 29, 1919): 5.

30. *Frederick Scheibler vs. M. H. Nolan and Fannie B. Nolan*, No. 647, Court of Common Pleas, Allegheny County, Pennsylvania (January Term 1925). The award was made in 1933. Unfortunately, the testimony is missing from the court record, and the Nolans' appeal of the award has been untraceable.

Chapter 8. Charmed Territory

1. M. H. Baillie Scott, "A Small County House," *Studio*, December 1897, p. 170.

2. Scheibler was forced to use stucco at the Pyle house when the white brick that he originally specified proved unavailable. Letter from Mary Pyle Fleck to James D. Van Trump, January 1970. The house has since been covered with permastone.

3. The following discussions of the Johnston, Harter, and Klages houses are indebted to David Andrew Golden, "The 1920's Single Family Houses of Frederick G. Scheibler, Jr.," Master's thesis, Carnegie Mellon University, 1988.

4. The first two designs were commissioned in the name of William D. Johnston; the third in the name of Clara E. Johnston.

5. This arrangement is reminiscent of the entry courts in some domestic designs of Englishman Sir Edwin Lutyens.

6. This was the fruit, it seems, of a Mediterranean seed initially planted by Olbrich.

7. Golden notes and speculates on a symbolic meaning to the sequence of square, triangle, and circle represented by the porch, the entry, and the sunporch in plan ("The 1920's Single Family Houses of Frederick G. Scheibler, Jr.," pp. 50–51).

8. See, for example, the art glass in Greene and Greene's Gamble and Blacker houses.

9. The sleeping porch was a space designed for sleeping in the summertime, an innovation of bungalow design that reached its apotheosis in the California houses of Greene and Greene. Scheibler's version is extensively glazed.

10. Information concerning the Harters is derived from a series of interviews with their son Earl Harter conducted in 1988–1991, an interview with George Bailey in June 1987, and interviews with later owners of the Harter house conducted by Gary Cirrincione in 1976. The Harter family's ties with Scheibler were wide-ranging. Frank Harter's uncle, Jacob Harter, also commissioned a house from Scheibler. The Harters' daughter Miriam operated a club called the Casbah in Scheibler's Minnetonka Building. And the Harter family reaquired the Harter house in 1964 and purchased Scheibler's Parkstone Dwellings in 1970.

11. Harter was known to design his own liquor labels. The chimneys of the Scheibler's Harter house resemble whiskey bottles (and are emphatically phallic at the same time).

12. A single drawing for the wall, dated January 1924, shows a lavish design with wood gates, lighting fixtures, and inset decorative tile. The basic wall of concrete and stone construction was built, but it was never completed in full.

13. Aymer Embury II, *One Hundred Country Houses, Modern American Examples* (New York: Century Co., 1909), p. 198. Scheibler never indulged in other popular aging devices like rubble brick walls and artfully sagging roofs.

14. Edward J. Weber designed an English country house with a pseudo-thatched roof that was published in the Pittsburgh Architectural Club, *Catalogue of the Ninth Exhibition* (Pittsburgh: 1914); and another house with a pseudo-thatched roof was designed by Kiehnel and Elliott at 1315 Cordova Road, Pittsburgh, in 1917. This latter house—the Henius House—has often been attributed to Scheibler, but the true architects are identified in a notice in *Builders Bulletin* 2:7 (October 13, 1917): 4.

15. The two unbuilt projects were a summer house for the Harters at Conneaut Lake, Pennsylvania, and a house for Walter Schmidt in Modesto, California. Walter Schmidt, a catcher for the Pittsburgh Pirates baseball club between 1916 and 1925, made his off-season home in Modesto. Schmidt's career statistics were modest, but he had a productive year in 1921 when he hit .282. Schmidt was a salary holdout the next spring, but returned to appear in forty games, hitting .329. With the flush of success—and presumably a boost in salary—Schmidt commissioned a house late in the 1922 season. He presumably took a set of drawings west after the season was over, but the house was never built. The basis of Schmidt's acquaintance with Scheibler is unknown. See David S. Neft and Richard M. Cohen, *The Sports Encyclopedia: Baseball*, 6th ed. (New York: St. Martin's/Marek, 1985), p. 134; and Joseph L. Reichler, editor, *The Baseball Encyclopedia*, 6th ed. (New York: Macmillan, 1985), p. 1370.

16. The idea of combining art glass and mirrored glass was borrowed from Mackintosh. Here the mirror predominates, but elsewhere Scheibler introduced mirrored fragments into predominantly art-glass panels.

17. A large tile in the house called "Woman Dipping Candles" was one of the so-called mosaic tiles that the Moravian Pottery and Tile Works manufactured for the tile flooring of the Pennsylvania state capitol and later offered for public sale. See Reed, *Henry Chapman Mercer and the Moravian Pottery and Tile Works*, pp. 55, 103-110; and Henry C. Mercer, *Guidebook to the Tiled Pavement in the Capitol of Pennsylvania* (Harrisburg, Pa.: 1908).

18. Among the unsubstantiated rumors about the Harter house is the claim that Edgar J. Kaufmann, the Pittsburgh department store tycoon and noted architectural client, rented the house in the mid-1930s for his girlfriend. If so, Scheibler can be added to the list of architects (including Pittsburgher Benno Janssen, Frank Lloyd Wright, and Richard Neutra) whom Kaufmann in some sense patronized. Kaufmann's womanizing is well documented in Leon A. Harris, *Merchant Princes: An Intimate History of Jewish Families Who Built Great Department Stores* (New York: Harper and Row, 1979), pp. 95–101.

19. Interview with Suzanne Klages, Allen Klages's second wife, July 1987.

20. Both of these plans bear a resemblance to Parker and Unwin's Whirriestone, where the living and dining rooms are disposed in an unbalanced axial sequence behind a symmetrical facade. This house also has wings flanking a recessed veranda, an arrangement not unlike the Klages house. It is tempting to name Whirriestone as one of Scheibler's sources, especially since its entry bears a family resemblance to those at Vilsack Row. Whirriestone's overall appearance is quite unlike any of Scheibler's buildings, however, and there is no persuasive evidence that Scheibler knew of it.

21. Golden, "The 1920's Single Family Houses of Frederick G. Scheibler, Jr.," p. 81.

22. The art-glass designs are by William Morris and Company (not *the* William Morris) and taken from *The Studio Year Book of Decorative Art* (London: Studio, 1906), p. 148; and *The Studio Year Book of Decorative Art* (London: Studio, 1908), p. B182.

23. The kingfisher and so-called Indian panther tiles are also mosaic tiles produced by the Moravian Pottery and Tile Works.

24. They are the literal incarnation of Sullivan's and Wright's comments noted above (see chap. 6, n. 6). Balconies hung with carpets also recur in Wright's drawings of his houses.

25. An Olbrich design for workers' housing is a possible source for this arrangement, and similar linkages can be found in the work of Irving Gill. See *Architektur von Olbrich* 3:21; and Gill's Lewis Courts as published in Roorbach, "The Garden Apartments of California," pp. 520–30.

Chapter 9. Up-to-Date and Familiar

1. The Arts and Crafts Movement was never endorsed by official architectural bodies in England or elsewhere, but its principles were widely disseminated and adopted.

2. This manner of tile ornamentation was a departure for Scheibler, but is akin to the Pittsburgh work of Henry Hornbostel, who favored broad bands of geometric terra cotta ornament to bind and unify his large Beaux Arts masses.

3. The two identical houses are placed on lots that face different streets but nearly meet back to back.

4. Scheibler had previously used this tile on a fireplace at the Hellmund house.

5. When McCafferty sold the Turtle Creek property in 1938, Harry Rubins's name appeared on the deed as a witness. Perhaps Rubins was the middleman for the Scheibler-McCafferty acquaintance.

6. A first-floor space labeled "tearoom" on Scheibler's drawing was a final faint echo of Mackintosh, who

designed a number of popular tearooms in Glasgow.

7. Rose Rubins located her own real estate and insurance business in the building.

8. The detailing recalls terra-cotta work by Kiehnel and Elliott at their Greenfield School of 1917–1919.

9. There is apparently no relation between these Robinsons and William and Jesse Robinson.

10. One of Scheibler's preliminary drawings shows a ROBINSON nameplate over the entry where a MESSENGER nameplate was ultimately installed. A 1946 article in the Robinson-owned *Daily Republican* anticipated the addition of another story to the building, but this never happened.

11. The Model Home was built under provisions of the Federal Housing Administration to better acquaint Monongahelans with the agency. *Daily Republican*, September 22, 1939, p. 1.

12. See *Architectural Forum* 71:1 (July 1939): 65–72.

13. Interview with George Bailey, June 1987.

14. Shear and Schmertz, "A Pittsburgh Original," p. 5.

Chapter 10. A Place Among Progressives

1. Shear and Schmertz, "A Pittsburgh Original," p. 4.

2. Quoted in ibid. Baillie Scott once said: "Construction is decoration and decoration construction," but Kornwolf notes that this is almost too facile an integration. See Kornwolf, M. H. *Baillie Scott*, pp. 124.

3. Shear and Schmertz, "A Pittsburgh Original," p. 5. Tapestry brick is also mentioned in this regard, but it is a doubtful claim. See chap. 6, n. 5.

4. See Julian Millard, "The Work of Wilson Eyre," *Architectural Record* 14:4 (October 1903): 279–325; and Betsy Fahlman and Edward Teitelman, "Wilson Eyre: The Philadelphia Domestic Ideal," *Pennsylvania Heritage*, Summer 1982, pp. 23–27.

5. See Harold Allen Brooks, *The Prairie School: Frank Lloyd Wright and his Midwest Contemporaries* (Toronto: University of Toronto Press, 1972), pp. 105–12.

6. See Kenneth H. Cardwell, *Bernard Maybeck: Artisan, Architect, Artist* (Salt Lake City: Peregrine Smith Books, 1977); and Sally B. Woodbridge, *Bernard Maybeck: Visionary Architect* (New York: Abbeville Press, 1992).

7. See McCoy, *Five California Architects*, pp. 59–100; and William H. Jordy, *American Buildings and Their Architects: Progressive and Academic Ideals at the Turn of the Twentieth Century* (Garden City, N.Y.: Doubleday, 1972), pp. 246–74.

Selected Bibliography

Published and unpublished sources on Frederick G. Scheibler, Jr. Entries are listed in chronological order.

Comes, John T. "The Architectural Exhibit." *Construction* 1:21 (May 27, 1905): 6. Rpt. as "The Pittsburgh Architectural Club Exhibition 1905." *House and Garden* 8 (August 1905): 89.

Boucher, John Newton. *A Century and a Half of Pittsburgh and her People.* New York: Lewis Publishing Company, 1908, 4:16.

Redd, Penelope. "Scheibler Anticipated Modern Architecture." *Pittsburgh Sunday Sun-Telegraph*, September 23, 1934, sec. 4, p. 7.

Daily Republican (Monongahela, Pa.), September 28, 1939, pp. 1, 7.

Daily Republican (Monongahela, Pa.), May 17, 1940, sec. 3, p. 3.

Shear, John Knox, and Robert W. Schmertz. "A Pittsburgh Original." *Charette* 28 (September 1948): 4–5.

Charette 28 (December 1948): 3.

McKee, Tally. "Charette Vignette [Henry Kropff]." *Charette* 29 (April 1949): 15.

Shear, John Knox. "Pittsburgh Rediscovers an Architect Pioneer." *Architectural Record* 106 (July 1949): 98–100.

Kidney, Walter. "The Missing Link in Architecture Today." *Charette* 30 (August 1950): 19.

Dickson, Harold E. *A Hundred Pennsylvania Buildings.* State College, Pa.: Bald Eagle Press, 1954. Entry 84.

Obituary. *Pittsburgh Press*, June 17, 1958, p. 27.

Obituary. *Pittsburgh Post-Gazette*, June 18, 1958, p. 25.

Obituary. *Pittsburgh Press*, June 18, 1958, p. 49.

Van Trump, James D. "An Architectural Tour of Pittsburgh." *Charette* 39 (November 1959): 20–21; rpt. Pittsburgh: Pittsburgh Chapter of the A.I.A., 1960. n.p.; and Pittsburgh: Pittsburgh History and Landmarks Foundation, 1965. n.p.

Remington, Fred. "Good Show on Buildings." *Pittsburgh Press*, April 26, 1961, p. 62.

Burchard, John, and Albert Bush-Brown. *The Architecture of America: A Social and Cultural History.* Boston: Little, Brown, 1961, p. 233.

Van Trump, James D. "A Prophet of Modern Architecture in Pittsburgh: Frederick G. Scheibler, Jr." *Charette* 42 (October 1962): 11–15. Rpt. in Van Trump, *Life and Architecture in Pittsburgh.* Pittsburgh: Pittsburgh History and Landmarks Foundation, 1983, pp. 282–90.

Van Trump, James D. "Frederick G. Scheibler, Jr.: A Prophet of Modern Architecture in Pittsburgh." *Carnegie Magazine* 36 (October 1962): 267–70.

Van Trump, James D., and James Cook. *The Architecture of Frederick G. Scheibler, Jr., 1872–1958* (exhibit catalog). Pittsburgh: Carnegie Institute, 1962.

Brem, Ralph. "Architect Scheibler Shown Far Ahead of His Time." *Pittsburgh Press*, October 14, 1962, sec. 3, p. 1.

Ziegler, Arthur P., and James D. Van Trump. *Landmark Architecture of Allegheny County, Pennsylvania.* Pittsburgh: Pittsburgh History and Landmarks Foundation, 1967, pp. 15, 87, 108, 113, 114, 115, 116, 118, 119, 121, 124.

Richman, Irwin. *Pennsylvania's Architecture.* University Park, Pa.: Pennsylvania Historical Association, 1969, p. 52.

Clark, R. J. "Stylistic Interplay between Central Europe and America: Architecture and Painting from 1860 to 1914." In *The Shaping of Art and Architecture in Nineteenth Century America.* New York: Metropolitan Museum of Art, 1972, pp. 71, 78.

Kidney, Walter C. *The Architecture of Choice: Eclecticism in America 1880–1930.* New York: George Braziller, 1974, p. 35, fig. 87.

Van Trump, James D. "Wilkinsburg, A Personal View." *Carnegie Magazine* 48 (June 1974): 251–52.

Wilkins, David G. "The Architecture of Frederick G. Scheibler, Jr.: A Tentative Catalogue." Manuscript, 1975.

Remington, Fred. "Scheibler's Buildings." *Pittsburgh Magazine* 8 (June 1977): 70–75.

Cannell, Gillian C. *Experiencing Architecture: Focus on Pittsburgh.* Pittsburgh: University of Pittsburgh External Studies Program, 1977, 4:16–24.

Wilkins, David G., et al. *Art Nouveau: Works by Tiffany, Mucha, Toulouse-Lautrec, Gallé, Beardsley, Scheibler, and Others.* Pittsburgh: University of Pittsburgh Art Gallery, 1978.

Roper, Matthew. "Stained Glass in Pittsburgh: Styles, Techniques, Innovators." *Carnegie Magazine* 52 (December 1978): 12–13.

Pittsburgh History and Landmarks Foundation and Pennsylvania Historical and Museum Commission. "Allegheny County Survey," 1979–1984.

Jucha, Robert J. "The Anatomy of a Streetcar Suburb: A Development and Architectural History of Pittsburgh's Shadyside District, 1860–1920." Ph.D. diss., George Washington University, 1980; Ann Arbor, Mich.: University Microfilms International, 1984, pp. 305–08.

Kidney, Walter C. *Landmark Architecture: Pittsburgh and Allegheny County.* Pittsburgh: Pittsburgh History and Landmarks Foundation, 1985, pp. 14, 77, 115, 244, 250, 251, 262, 263, 266, 269, 270, 271, 285–86, 340.

Belnap, Gillian H. "The Apartment Buildings of Frederick G. Scheibler, Jr., with a Catalogue of All His Multiple Residences." Ph.D. diss., University of Pittsburgh, 1985; Ann Arbor, Mich.: University Microfilms International, 1986.

Van Trump, James D. "Architectural Ornament." *Greensburg Tribune-Review: Focus*, December 15, 1985, pp. 8–9.

Toker, Franklin. *Pittsburgh: An Urban Portrait.* University Park, Pa.: Pennsylvania State University Press, 1986, pp. 14, 214, 220, 224, 228, 248–49, 260–61, 308.

Kidney, Walter C. *A History of the Pittsburgh Builders Exchange, 1886–1986.* Pittsburgh: Pittsburgh Builders Exchange, 1986, pp. 19–20.

Pittsburgh History and Landmarks Foundation and Pennsylvania Historical and Museum Commission. "The Works of Frederick G. Scheibler, Jr." (survey). 1986–1987.

Kidney, Walter C. "The People's Architect." *In Pittsburgh* 3 (April 15, 1987): 8.

Kidney, Walter C. "Architectural Evolution: How Buildings Reflect Social, Economic Change." *In Pittsburgh* 4 (November 11, 1987): 19.

Kidney, Walter C. *Pittsburgh in Your Pocket: A Guide to Pittsburgh-Area Architecture.* Pittsburgh: Pittsburgh History and Landmarks Foundation, 1988, pp. 26–28.

Lowry, Patricia. "The Scheibler Touch: More Than Just An Environment," and "A Legacy in Five Parts." *Pittsburgh Press Sunday Magazine*, June 5, 1988, pp. 14–25.

Golden, David Andrew. "The 1920's Single Family Houses of Frederick G. Scheibler, Jr.: An Architectural Analysis of Four Examples Built in Pittsburgh's East End." Master of Architecture thesis, Carnegie Mellon University, 1988.

Aurand, Martin. "Frederick G. Scheibler, Jr.: The Wilkinsburg Years." In *Historic Wilkinsburg, 1887–1987: One Hundred Years of Pride* (Wilkinsburg, Pa., 1988), pp. 42–43.

Floyd, Margaret Henderson. *Architecture After Richardson: Regonalism Before Modernism; Longfellow, Alden, and Harlow in Boston and Pittsburgh.* Chicago: University of Chicago Press and the Pittsburgh History and Landmarks Foundation, 1994, pp. 20, 175, 213–14, 439, 463n.55, 482n.4.

Index

Page references for illustrations are *italicized*.
Entries in the Catalogue of Works are indexed by catalog number in **bold** type.

Alden, Frank, 10
Alden and Harlow, 4. *See also* Longfellow, Alden and Harlow
Alladin Company, 13
Allegheny County Courthouse and Jail, 156n3
Allegheny (Pa.), 18, 157n3, **4, 14**
Allston, Kitty, house, **7**
Ament, Silas M., 87; house, 86–87, *87–89*, 92, **44**; additions to house, 87–89, 162n10, **144**; alterations to house, 162n10, **79**
American Architect and Building News, 38
American Institute of Architects, 156n9; Pittsburgh Chapter, 11–12, 156n9
Apartment buildings, 8, 24–51, 70–82. *See also* by project name
Architectural League of America, 156n9
Architectural Record, 3–4, 13, 67
Architecture, 38
Architektur von Olbrich, 32–34
Arden apartment building, 26–27, *27*, **20**
Art Commission, City of Pittsburgh, **95**
Art Deco, 122
Art glass, 8, *8*, 15, 16, 27, 79, *79*, 133, 164n16
Art Moderne, 122
Art Nouveau, 6–7, 31, 53
Artist's country cottage and studio (Charles Rennie Mackintosh), *44*, 45
Arts and Crafts Movement, 6, 10, 16–17, 27, 31, 34–35, 54, 79, 82–83, 91–92, 122, 160n5, 162n21, 164n1
Aurelia Street row houses, 57–60, *58*, *60*
Ausgeführte Bauten und Entwürfte von Frank Lloyd Wright, 80, 161n12

Baillie Scott, M. H., 30, 54, 69, 76, 79, 85, 87, 93, 96, 105, 122, 158n13, 158n22, 159n7, 165n2; works of, 35, 64, 86, *87–88*, *88*, *94*, 157n10, 162n13, 162n14, 162n20; influence on Scheibler of, 27, 35, 41, 63, 76, 87–91, 94, 99, 157n10, 162n13
Baird, Charles W., house, 89–91, *90–91*, 162n13, **59**
Barnes, Frank M., house, **9**
Barnes, J. Lee, house, 162n15, **102**
Bartberger and Dietrich, **9**
Beatty, John L., 156n7
Behrens, Peter, 76; fabric design, *76*

Bellefield Dwellings (Carlton Strong), 158n25
Belnap, Gillian H., 8
Bennett Street row houses, 56–57, *57*, **52**
Best, Albert J., house, **104**
Blacker house (Greene and Greene), 163n8
Blake, Peter, 3
Blaue house (Joseph Maria Olbrich), 33, *33*
Blossom house (Frank Lloyd Wright), 157n4
Blue, Charles F., and Marie S. Blue, 162n10; additions to Ament house, 87–89, 162n10, **144**
Bobula, Titus de. *See* de Bobula, Titus
Borgman, Hedwig, 112
Braddock parochial school (Titus de Bobula), 7, 8, 22
Bragdon, Claude, 158n6, 161n3
Brickbuilder, 38
Bridgeville (Pa.), 40
Brighton Heights (Pgh.), 4
Brown, W. J., 16
Bruckman, Frederick, 15, 25–26, 29; cottage additions to Old Heidelberg apartment building, 36, *36–37*, **46**; houses, **48**. *See also* Robinson and Bruckman
Brydon, T. S., 162n4

California bungalow, 159n2, 163n9
Canonsburg (Pa.), **138**
Carl Building, 12, 13, 156n7
Carnegie Institute, 4
Carnegie Institute of Technology (Carnegie Tech), 3, 10, 38, 76, 157n11
Carnegie Library of Pittsburgh, 6, 32, 80, 162n8
Carnegie Mellon University. *See* Carnegie Institute of Technology
Carnegie Mellon University Architecture Archives, 139
Carnegie Tech. *See* Carnegie Institute of Technology
Carroll Township (Washington County, Pa.), **145**
Carson Pirie Scott department store (Louis Sullivan), 159n11
Central Building, Carnegie Institute of Technology (Henry Hornbostel), 76
Chapin, Paul H., house, 6
Charette, 3–4, 13
Chatham Village (Pgh.), 54, 69
Chicago (Ill.), 158n26
Chicago School, 6, 24
Christiansen house (Joseph Maria Olbrich), 31–32, *32*
Churchill (Pa.), 123, **130**

Cluhey, Robert E., house, **71**
Coleman, James H., and Mary M. Coleman, 45; apartment building, 42, *42–43*, 45–46, 52–53, 80, 82, 159n9, **38**
Colonial apartment building, 8
Colonial Revival, 18
Comes, John T., 7
Commercial buildings, 22–24, 46–51, 125–28; unidentified, 126, *126*, **31, 91, 143**. *See also* by project name
Competitions, architectural, 22, **3, 23, 95**
Conneaut Lake (Pa.), **111**
Coonley house (Frank Lloyd Wright), 81
Craven Hills (Pa.), **145**
Crawford, James S., houses, **21**

D. L. Dillinger Properties, 70
Daily Notes (Canonsburg, Pa.), 127
Daily Republican Model Home, 13, 128–30, *129*, 133, 165n11, **142**
Daily Republican (Monongahela, Pa.), 126, 128–29
D'Ambrosio, Joseph, house, **73**
Darmstadt (Germany), 31, 38, 83, 158n13
Das Englische Haus (Hermann Muthesius), 6
De Bobula, Titus, 7–8, 22, 55, 155nn11–13, 158n26, 161n1; works of, 7, 8, 22, 55, *55*
Dean, Ellsworth, 22
Deiters house (Joseph Maria Olbrich), 159n3
Dekorative Kunst, 45
Democrat Messenger (Waynesburg, Pa.), 127
Democrat Messenger Building, 126–28, *127*, 165n10, **139**
Dempster, Sam, 158n24; cottage addition to Old Heidelberg apartment building, 36, *36–37*, **49**
Deniston School, interior alterations to, **28**
Der Architekt, 38
Dillinger, Daniel L., 39, 64, 70, 82, 125, 159n2, 160n13; alterations to house, **148**; Aurelia Street row houses, 57–60, *58*, 60; double house, 64, *65*, 160n13, **89**; houses, **34**; Linwood apartment building, 39–42, *41*, 53, **36**; Penn store and office building, 125, 164n6, **121**; row houses, 66. *See also* Highland Towers apartment building
Donehoo, Thomas M., house, **10**
Doran, Mary, group cottages. *See* Meado'cots group cottages
Dorfman, Harry, house, **128**
Douglass, A. R., **104**
Dunlap, W. K., alterations to Ament house, 162n10, **79**
Duplexes, 117

169

East End (Pgh.), 4, 10, 25, 83
East Liberty (Pgh.), 12
Ebberts, William M., houses, 83, 84, 85, 51, **61, 63, 64**
Edgewood Acres (Forest Hills, Pa.), 96
Edgewood (Pa.), 6, **42**, 51, 61, 62, **63, 64**
Eicholz, Theodore, 161n2
Elmwood Cottages (M. H. Baillie Scott), 162n20
Embury, Aymer, II, 111
Exhibition houses, 128
Eyre, Wilson, 134–35, 158n22

Fair Oaks (Pa.), **123**
Federal Housing Administration, 165n11
First National Bank of Monongahela City, 127, **133**; apartment building, 127, **133**
Floreale, 6, 155n11
Foerster, Emil, 10
Forest Hills (Pa.), 96, **94**, 96
Forssen, Emma C., house, 13
Fort Couch Tower (Arthur Lubetz), 160n4
Foster, Dwight B., houses, 80
Francis apartment building (Frank Lloyd Wright), 81
Frank Avenue row houses (Titus de Bobula), **55**, 55
Frease, Jennie D., house, 123–24, **124**, 130
Frederick, Louis T., house, 96
Frederick Scheibler vs. M. H. Nolan and Fannie B. Nolan, 104, 163n30
Friendship (Pgh.), **78**
Furness, Frank, 157n11

Gage Building facade (Louis Sullivan), 24, **24**
Gamble, William K., house, 161n2, **32**
Gamble house (Greene and Greene), 163n8
Ganss house (Joseph Maria Olbrich), 157n11
Garden City Movement, 54–55, 60, 63, 83
Garden suburbs, 54
Garth, The (M. H. Baillie Scott), 157n10
Gesamkunst, 158n11
Gibsonia (Pa.), **146**
Gill, Irving, 45, 67, 69, 134–35, 160n17, 164n25; works of, 67, **68**, 160n17
Glasgow School of Art (Charles Rennie Mackintosh), 74; exhibition booth for, 159n16
Glasgow Secession, 6, 31, 42
Glenshaw (Pa.), 13
Glückert house (Joseph Maria Olbrich), 159n17
Gothic style, 103, 122–23
Greene and Greene, 109, 163n8
Greenfield School (Kiehnel and Elliott), 165n8
Greensburg (Pa.), **5, 148**
Greentree (Pa.), 123, **129**
Gropius, Walter, 122
Group cottages, 54–69, 82, 119–21, 125; unidentified, **77**. *See also* by project name

Half-timbering, 85, 161n2, 161n3
Hamilton Avenue row houses, **65**
Hamilton Cottages, 55, 58–60, **60–61**, 63, 68, 160nn8–9, **70**
Hamilton Realty Company, 25, 58, 82, 157n9; Bennett Street row houses, 56–57, 57, **52**; Singer Place row houses, 55, **88**. *See also* Robinson and Bruckman; Robinson, Bruckman and McClelland, Inc.; Hamilton Cottages
Hamnett, William E., 23, 93; Rockledge, 23, 93–94, **94–95**, 162n15, **69**; store and apartment building, **12**; store buildings, 23, **23**, **15**, **43**
Hampton Township (Allegheny County, Pa.), **134**
Harrington, James, house, **22**
Harter, Frank K., and Eva R. Harter, 12, 17, 105, 109–10, 114, 119, 121, 156n13, 157n21, 163nn10–11; apartment building, **151**; double house, **124**; houses: (Conneaut Lake, Pa.), 109, 164n18, **111**; (Margate City, N.J.), 109, **126**; (Pittsburgh), 17, 109–11, **110–13**, 113–14, 116, 163nn11–12, 164nn17–18, **114**; (Ventnor City, N.J.), 109, **110**, **132**; (Switzerland), 109, **152**. *See also* Woodlands, The
Harter, Jacob A., house, 163n10, **116**
Hasson, Harry D., 39, 70, 82, 160n13; garage, 160n13, **113**; Whitehall apartment building, 39–42, **40**, 53, **37**
Haus Eines Kunstfreundes competition, 159n7
Hawkins School, 22, **22**, 30, 51–52, 159n15, **23**
Heidelberg, Old. *See* Old Heidelberg apartment building
Hellmund, Rudolph E., 100, 156n18; house, 96, 98–100, **98–99**, 163n24, 163n26, 164n4, **99**. *See also* Hellmund and Borgman house
Hellmund and Borgman house, 163n26, **112**
Henius house (Kiehnel and Elliott), **152**, 163n14
Hetzel, George, 9
Highland Park (Pgh.), 13, 106, **38, 92, 103, 104, 105, 106, 109, 110, 119**
Highland Towers apartment building, 14, 17, 39, 70, **70–73**, 74–82, **75**, **77–79**, 105, 130, 134, 161n4, **84**; advertising brochure for, 70, **71–73**; exterior of, **74–76**; interior of, **76–79**; sources for, 79–81; recognition of, 4, 161n15
Hill house (Charles Rennie Mackintosh), 159n13
Hoffman, William C., house, 36, **36–37**, 162n4, **54**
Homes of Tomorrow, 128, **130**
Homewood (Pgh.), 25, 55, **18, 19, 41, 52, 53, 65, 82**
Hornbostel, Henry, 4, 76, 157n11, 164n2
House and garden in Switzerland (M. H. Baillie Scott), 88, **89–90**
House and studio for A. Sutro (C.F.A. Voysey), 98, **99**, 162n22
House at Crowborough (M. H. Baillie Scott), 35
Houses, 18–21, 83–117, 122–25, 128–30; unidentified, **15, 87, 98**, 162n23, **93, 98, 117**. *See also* by project name
Houses and Gardens (M. H. Baillie Scott), 87

I-beams, 8, **8**, 27, 57, 64, 125, 133, 135, 157n11

Inglenook Place, 159n5
Inglenook Place row houses: (1907), 55–56, 56, **41**; (1909), 56, **53**
International Style, xi, 3, 96. *See also* Modern Movement

Janssen, Benno, 4, 164n18
Japonism, 5, 79, 81
Jarvis, A. Wickham, 35
Johns, Benjamin S., apartment building, 11
Johnston, Frank, apartment building, 17
Johnston, W. Hugh, row houses, 85
Johnston, William D., and Clara E. Johnston, 106, 114; house, 106–07, **106–08**, 109, 113–14, 163n7, 163n9, **109, 110**
Jones, Dr. Enoch L., house, **101**
Jones, Dr. Wesley W., 96; house, 96, **97**, 162n20, **94**
Jugendstil, 6

Kaiser, John G., house, **55**
Kane, John, 155n4
Kappel, Howard B., house, **42**
Kato, Kantero, 17, 79, 157n27
Katselas, Tasso, 160n20
Katselas house (Tasso Katselas), 160n20
Kaufmann, Edgar J., 164n18
Kiehnel and Elliott, 83, 161n1, 163n14, 165n8; works of, 83, **83**, 163n14, 165n8
Kinter, George L., and Jessie M. Kinter, house, 123–24, **129**
Kismet apartment building, 25–26, **26–27**, 39, 41, **19**
Kitzmiller, Edward A., 18; house, 18, **19**, 157n2, 162n4, **2**
Klages, Allen M., and Elizabeth Klages, 114, 116; house, 114, **115–16**, 116–17, **117**, 159n3, 164n20, **119**
Knorr, George A., **20**
Kreider, O. H., house, **150**
Kreuer, William V., and Albert A. Kreuer, row houses, 160n16, **87**
Kropff, Henry, 156n4
Kuntze house (Joseph Maria Olbrich), 33, **34**

Lang Avenue apartment building, 159n1, **35**
Larimer (Pgh.), **73**
Larkin Building (Frank Lloyd Wright), 45, 80–81, **80**
Larkin Company workmen's houses (Frank Lloyd Wright), 58, **59**
Lawrenceville (Pgh.), **33**
Le Corbusier, 67, 122, 160n20
Leet Township (Allegheny County, Pa.), **123**
Lemington (Pgh.), **87**
Letzkus, Lawrence C., house, **105**
Lewin, Dr. Adolph L., store and apartment building, **33**
Lewis Courts (Irving Gill), 67, **68**, 160n17
Lincoln Highway marker and street sign post, **95**
Link Wienzeile 38 (Otto Wagner), 47, **47**
Linwood apartment building, 39–42, **41**, 53, **36**
Little and Pfeil houses, **24**, 25
Logue, Eleanor Mae, house, 87, **90**
Longfellow, Alden and Harlow, 9–10, 19. *See also* Alden and Harlow

Longfellow School, 21–22, *3*. *See also* Deniston School
Loos, Adolph, 45, 122; works of, 45, *45*
Louisiana Purchase International Exposition (St. Louis, 1904), 12, 32, 34, 80
Lubetz, Arthur, 160n4
Lutyens, Sir Edwin, 163n5
Lyongrun, Arnold, 35, 159n3

MacDonald, Frances, 42, 159n5
MacDonald, Margaret, 42, 159n5
Mackenzie, H. Jordan, 158n26
Mackintosh, Charles Rennie, 42, 79, 85, 96, 131, 135, 159n5; works of, 35, 44, 45, 49, 74, 76, 94, *94*, 159nn9–10, 159nn12–13, 159n16, 162n14; influence on Scheibler of, 35, 42, 45, 49, 51–52, 74, 76, 94, 102, 159nn9–10, 12–13, 16, 164nn6, *16*
Maher, George W., 100, 103, 106–07, 134–35; works of, 100, *101*, *103*, *107*
Maisons Jaoul (Le Corbusier), 67, 160n20
Margate City (New Jersey), 126
Marshall, Elder W., house, *74*
Martyr's Public School (Charles Rennie Mackintosh), 159n9
Matthews, Robert L., and Catherine P. Matthews, 18, 22, 98, 157n7, 162n23; house, 18–19, *20*, 157n2, *4*; inn, 98, 162n23, *58*; store building, 22–24, *23*, 157n7, *14*
Maybeck, Bernard, 103, 134–35
McArthur apartment building (Frank Lloyd Wright), 80–81, *81*
McCafferty, Fred C., 156n16, 164n5; row houses, 125, 156n16, 164n5, *135*
McDowell, Robert P., row houses, 67, *76*, *83*
McKeesport (Pa.), 9
McKelvy School, *29*
McKim, Mead and White, 10, 19, 157n4
McLaughlin, Thomas, house, 100, *101*, *102*, *97*
McNair, Herbert, 42, 159n5
McNall, Dr. James M., house, 8, 83, *57*
Meado'cots group cottages, 60, 62, 63–64, *63*, 68, 100, 160n12, *82*
Mercer, Henry, 16, 157n21
Miller, Ralph E., house, 83, *84*, 85, 162n4, 163n26, *30*
Milligan and Miller, 22, 157n5
Milligan School. *See* Hawkins School
Minnetonka Building, 46–47, *46*, *48*, *49*, 50–51, *51*, 74, 156n10, 163n10, *47*
Mission Style, 135
Model home. *See* Daily Republican model home
Modern Architecture: International Exhibition (1932), 3
Modern Movement, xi, 3, 6, 96, 122, 134
Modesto (California), *115*
Monongahela Clay Manufacturing Company, *129*
Monongahela (Pa.), 126, 128, *133*, *142*
Monongahela Publishing Company, 126
Monongahela Valley (Pa.), 13, 128
Moravian Pottery and Tile Works, 16, 156n21, 164nn17, *23*
Moreland, Thomas B., house, *149*
Morningside (Pgh.), *34*, *86*

Morris, William, 5, 54, 85
Moser, Henry, 9–10
Museum of Modern Art (New York), 3
Muthesius, Hermann, 6, 42
Myers, John C., house, *103*

Neamann, Harry I., store building, *18*
Nelda apartment building, 25–26, *26–27*, 41, *19*
Neoclassicism, 10, 18–24, 26, 30, 87, 92, 107, 156n6. *See also* Renaissance Revival
Neutra, Richard, 164n18
New Brutalism, 67
New Traditionalists, 5. *See also* Progressive movements
New York World's Fair (1939), 128, *130*
Niagara Square townhouses (Tasso Katselas), 160n20
Nolan, Mark H., and Fannie B. Nolan, 104, 163n30; house and double duplexes, 100, 102–04, *102*, 163n30, *106*
North Side (Pgh.), 4, *14*, *50*
Notes Publishing and Printing Company, 127, *138*
Notes Publishing and Printing Company building, *127*, *138*

Oakland (Pgh.), *91*; South Oakland, 9, 8, 11
Oakmont (Pa.), 87, *32*, *44*, *74*, *77*, *79*, *144*
Observatory Hill (Pgh.), *50*
Olbrich, Joseph Maria, 5–7, 31–32, 35, 45, 80, 85, 122, 158nn11, 13, 26; works of, 6–7, *7*, 31–34, *32–34*, 80, 89–90, *89*, 157n11, 158n26, 159nn3, *17*; influence on Scheibler of, 31–36, 38–39, 53, 83, 89–90, 157n11, 159n3, *17*, 163n6, 164n25
Olbrich house (Joseph Maria Olbrich), 158n13
Old Heidelberg apartment building, 12, 16, 28–36, *28–29*, *34–37*, *38–42*, 47, 53, 63, 70, 79, 82, 119, 158nn5, 24, 26; description of, 29–31; sources for, 31–36; cottage additions to, 36, *36–37*, *38*, 158n24, *46*, *49*; recognition of, 38, 158n27
Orchard, The (C.F.A. Voysey), 96, *97*, 162n20
Osterling, Frederick J., 4

Park Mansions apartment building. *See* Wherrett interior design for apartment
Park Place (Pgh.), 25, *28–29*, *16*, *20*, *21*, *26*, *37*, *46*, *48*, *49*, *54*, *69*, *85*, *102*, *131*
Parker, Barry, 68. *See also* Parker and Unwin
Parker and Unwin, 54, 63, 79, 160n20, 162n14, 164n20. *See also* Parker, Barry
Parkstone Dwellings, 17, 117–19, *118–19*, 163n10, 164n23–24, *118*
Paterson, Oscar, 157n12
Penn store and office building, 125, 164n6, *121*
Peoples, U. J. L., 22
Philadelphia (Pa.), 91–92. *See also* Wynnewood (Pa.)
Phillips, Walter O., house, *50*
Pittsburgh: architectural scene, 4, 6, 8, 10–11, 83, 135; Art Commission, *95*. *See also by* name of neighborhood

Pittsburgh Architectural Club, 3, 11–13; exhibitions of, 7, 11, 16, 100, 155n12, 156n10, 158n27, 159n13, 161n10; magazine of, 3–4, 13
Pittsburgh Board of Trade, 11
Pittsburgh Sunday Sun-Telegraph, 3, 13, 128
Pittsburgh Survey, 159n3
Point Breeze (Pgh.), 35, *36*, *55*, *118*
Prairie School, 6, 80, 82, 126, 135, 162n3
Price, William G., Jr., 8
Progressive movements, xi, 5–8, 30–31, 35, 54, 68–69, 122, 131, 134–35; Art Nouveau, 6–7, 31, 53; Arts and Crafts Movement, 6, 10, 16–17, 27, 31, 34–35, 54, 79, 82–83, 91–92, 122, 160n5, 162n21, 164n1; Chicago School, 6, 24; Floreale, 6, 155n11; Garden City Movement, 54–55, 60, 63, 83; Glasgow Secession, 6, 31, 42; Jugendstil, 6; Prairie School, 6, 80, 82, 126, 135, 162n3; Shingle Style, 6, 8, 157n2, 162n9; Viennese Secession, 6–7, 31, 42, 47, 158nn10, *26*
Pyle, Dr. William T., 51; house, 17, 51, *105*, *105*, 163n2, *107*

Queen Anne Style, 18

R. H. Robinson and Associates, 127
Raisig, Louis A., 10. *See also* Raisig and Scheibler
Raisig and Scheibler, 10, 18, 21, *2*, *3*
Red house (Philip Webb), 85
Redd, Penelope, 3, 8
Regent Square (Pgh.), *89*, *113*
Reiss house (M. H. Baillie Scott), 157n10
Renaissance Revival, 10, 122. *See also* Neoclassicism
Richardson, Henry Hobson, 10, 155n3
Rieger and Currier, 22
Robinson, Bruckman and McClelland, Inc., *19*. *See also* Robinson and Bruckman
Robinson, John, *142*. *See also* Robinson, Robert H.
Robinson, Robert H., 126–28, 165n9, *133*, *138*, *139*, *142*
Robinson, William, and Jesse F. Robinson, 25–26, 165n9; cottages, 160n8, *75*; double duplex, *100*; Hamilton Avenue row houses, *65*; Inglenook Place row houses (1907), 55–56, *56*, *41*; Inglenook Place row houses (1909), *56*, *53*; *See also* Robinson and Bruckman
Robinson and Bruckman, 25, 27–29, 36, 54, 58, 82, 158n25, 160n24, *41*, *52*, *53*, *65*, *70*, *75*, *88*; apartment building (East End Avenue), 25, *16*; Arden apartment building, 26–27, *27*, *20*. *See also* Bruckman, Frederick; Hamilton Realty Company; Robinson, Bruckman and McClelland, Inc.; Robinson, William, and Jesse F. Robinson; Old Heidelberg apartment building
Robinson and Wingerson row houses, *56*, *53*
Rockledge (Hamnett house), 23, 93–94, *94–95*, 162n15, *69*
Rookwood Pottery, 16
Ross Township (Allegheny County, Pa.), *58*
Row houses. *See* Group cottages

Rubins, Harry, 119, 125, 164n5; alterations to house, *147*. *See also* Parkstone Dwellings
Rubins, Rose, 119, 124–25, 165n7; houses, 124–25, *125*, 164n3, 131; alterations and additions to store and apartment building: 125–26, *125*, 165n7, *137*
Rudy Brothers Company, 16
Rundbogenstil, 10

St. Louis World's Fair (1904). *See* Louisiana Purchase International Exposition
St. Mary's City (Maryland), *122*
St. Paul's Evangelical Lutheran Church (Wilkinsburg, Pa.), 157n5
Scheibler, Antonia Oehmler (first wife), 10, 12, 18, 52
Scheibler, Blanche Clawson (second wife), 13–14
Scheibler, Eleanor Seidel (mother), 9
Scheibler, Frederick G., Jr. (1872–1958), *ii*, *14*, 155n1; apprenticeship of, 9–10, 156n4; architectural practice of, 4, 10–18 *14–16*, 54, 82, 104, 122, 130–31, 135, 156n9, 156nn18–19; birth and childhood of, 9; decline and death of, 13–14, 131; family life of, 9–13, 131, 156nn14–15; Germanic identification of, 9–10, 29, 100, 135; library of, 6, 32, 96, 153, 162n8, 162n16, 162n20; office locations of, 10–12, *12*, *13*, 156n7, 156n12; personal qualities of, 9, 14–17, 130–31, 156n15; recognition and study of, 3–4, 8, 13, 128, 155n4, 155n15; residences of, 9–10, *11*, *12–13*, *13*, 18, 155n3, 156n13; works misattributed to, 152; works of, 140–52. *See also* by project name
Scheibler, Frederick G., Jr., and Blanche Scheibler, house, 13, *125*; alterations, 13, *134*
Scheibler, Frederick G., Jr., cottage, 10, *11*, 18, 157n2, *1*
Scheibler, Gustavus (grandfather), 9
Scheibler, Will (brother), 9, 13
Scheibler, William Augustus (father), 9
Schlesinger and Mayer department store (Louis Sullivan), 159n11
Schmertz, Robert W., 3
Schmidt, Walter, 164n15; house, 164n15, *115*
Schools, 21–22, 51–53, 159n15; unidentified, 159n16, *140*, *141*. *See also* by project name
Schultz house (George Maher), 100, *101*, *103*, *107*
Scott, Robert J., 91; house, 91–94, *92*, 124, *68*
Secession Building (Joseph Maria Olbrich), 6–7, *7*, 80
Secession Movement. *See* Viennese Secession
Seger, Rose, and Herbert Rose, house, 130, *145*
Sewickley (Pa.), 9, 13
Shadyside (Pgh.), 46, 119, *47*, 60, 84, 120, *124*, *136*
Shear, John Knox, 3
Shingle Style, 6, 18, 157n2, 162n9
Silber house (Joseph Maria Olbrich), 89–90, *89*
Singer Place row houses, 55, *88*

Springcot (M. H. Baillie Scott), 86, 87–88, *88*, 94
Squirrel Hill (Pgh.), 58, 114, 160n9, *59*, *70*, *71*, *75*, *80*, *81*, *90*, *97*, *114*, *116*, *125*, *127*, *128*, *147*
Stade double house (Joseph Maria Olbrich), 33, *33*
Starr, Albert Q., 122; houses: (1912), 162n5, *81*; (1927), 122–23, *123*, 164n2, *125*
Steel, Joseph W., 18; house, 18–19, *19*, *21*, *21*, 87, 96, 98, 157n4, *5*
Steiner house (Adolph Loos), 45, *45*
Stengel house (Kiehnel and Elliott), 83, *83*
Stickley, Gustav, 122
Stile Liberty. *See* Floreale
Store and office building: unidentified, 126, *126*, *143*
Stowell, Kenneth, 3–4
Straub, John N, row houses, *62*
Strong, Carlton, 158n25
Stucco, 30–31
Studio, 6
Studio Flat (Charles Rennie Mackintosh), 35
Styles, architectural, 5, 6, 122
Sullivan, Louis, 24, 76, 82, 159n11, 161n6, 164n24; works of, 24, *24*, 159n11, 161n6
Summit Township (Crawford County, Pa.), 111
Sutro house and studio (C.F.A. Voysey), 98, *99*, 162n22
Sutton, Thomas, 139
Swissvale Borough School District, 21–22, 51, 159n15, *3*, *23*, *28*, *29*, *39*
Swissvale (Pa.), 10–11, *1*, *2*, *3*, 13, 22, 23, 24, 25, 27, 28, 29, 30, 31, 39, 99, 107, 108, 112
Syria, Kismet, and Nelda apartment buildings, 25–26, *26–27*, 41, *19*
Syria apartment building, 25–26, *26–27*, 41, *19*

Talley Cavey (Pa.), *134*
Tapestry brick, 76, 129–30, 161nn5–6, 165n3
Taylor, H.C.A., house (McKim, Mead and White), 157n4
Teach, William C., house, *146*
Tennessee Coal and Iron Company, 13
Tea Salon (Joseph Maria Olbrich), *34*
Thalman, V. Wyse, 9–10, 156n5
Thatch roofs, 110–11, 163n14, 164n15
Thornburg (Pa.), *150*
Thorniley Realty Company, *78*
Tilework, 16, 119, *119*, 133, 164nn23–24, 164n2
Trondle, Florie, house, *123*
Tudor Revival, 161n2
Turtle Creek (Pa.), *135*

U. S. Steel Corporation, 13
United Real Estate and Construction Company, 8
Unity Temple (Frank Lloyd Wright), 45, 80

Van Trump, James D., 4, 139
Vel-V-Tone brick, 129–30
Ventnor City (New Jersey), *132*
Venturi, Robert, 56

Vernacular building, 5, 30–31, 42, 54, 85, 93–94, 96, 110, 158n13
Vienna (Austria), 6, 31, 47
Viennese Secession, 6–7, 31, 42, 47, 158nn10, 26
Vilsack, Leopold, 65
Vilsack Arms apartment building, 130–31, *136*
Vilsack Row, xi, 14, 65–68, *66*, 74, 82, 105, 134, 160nn14–16, *20–21*, 164n20, *86*; recognition of, 3–4
Viollet-le-Duc, 5, 134
Vogeley, Laura E., house, 83, *56*
Voysey, C.F.A., 17, 85, 96, 100, 110, 122, 131, 162n19; works of, 96, 97, 98, 99, 162n14; influence on Scheibler of, 63, 96, *98*

Wach, Stephen, 156n; house, 102–03, *103*, *108*
Wagner, Otto, 31, 47, 155n13; works of, 47, *47*
Wahlstrom, Joseph, apartment building, *27*
Waynesburg (Pa.), 139
Weber, Edward J., 163n14
Wefing, Edward C., 46. *See also* Minnetonka Building
Western Architect, 38
Westinghouse Air Brake Company housing (Wilmerding, Pa.), 160n14
Wetherall, Ella D., apartment building, 159n12, *72*
Wherrett, Harry S., 160n3; interior design for apartment, 160n3, *127*; porch additions to house, 122
Whirriestone (Parker and Unwin), 160n14, 164n20
White, Caroline A., 13, 156n14; remodeling of house, 13, *13*, 156n14, *92*
White house (M. H. Baillie Scott), 162n13
Whitehall apartment building, 39–42, *40*, 53, *37*
Wilkinsburg Natatorium, 53, *53*, *45*
Wilkinsburg Natatorium Company, 53, *45*
Wilkinsburg (Pa.), 10–11, 15, 53, 125, *7*, *10*, *12*, *15*, *17*, *43*, *45*, *56*, *57*, *66*, *67*, *72*, *76*, *83*, *88*, 100, *121*, *137*
Wilkins School, 51–53, *52*, 159n15, *39*
William Morris and Company, 164n22
Willo'mound group cottages, 60, 62, 63–64, 96, *78*
Willow Tea Rooms (Charles Rennie Mackintosh), 76, 159n10
Windyhill (Charles Rennie Mackintosh), 49, 94, *94*, 159n12
Wingerson, Adams, and Robinson row house, *65*
Woodlands, The, 119–21, *120*, *120*
Woods Run (Pa.), *14*
Workmen's houses (M. H. Baillie Scott), *64*
Wright, Frank Lloyd, 3, 45, 58, 79–81, 83, 85, 110, 122, 135, 156nn14, 18, 158n22, 161n6, 164n18; works of, 45, 58, 59, 80–81, *80–81*, 157n4; influence on Scheibler of, 53, 79–82, 99, 161n12
Wright, Joseph, house, 83, *40*
Wynnewood (Pa.), 68

www.ingramcontent.com/pod-product-compliance
Lightning Source LLC
Chambersburg PA
CBHW061118010526
44112CB00024B/2908